Defining literature. In real context.

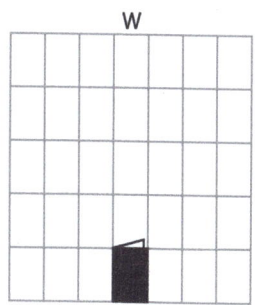

© 2012 by Fifth Wednesday Books, Inc.
Fifth Wednesday Journal (ISSN #1939-733X; ISBN #978-0-9799574-9-9) is published twice annually, in the spring and fall, by Fifth Wednesday Books, Inc., in Lisle, Illinois. All rights reserved. No part of this publication may be reproduced, stored in a retrieval system, or transmitted in any form or by any means, without prior permission in writing of Fifth Wednesday Books, Inc. Permission to reprint individual works remains the decision of the authors. We request *Fifth Wednesday Journal* be credited with initial publication. Refer to www.fifthwednesdayjournal.org for all subscription and submission information.

POSTMASTER:
Send address changes to: Fifth Wednesday Books, Inc., P.O. Box 4033, Lisle, IL 60532-9033

FIFTH WEDNESDAY JOURNAL

Defining literature. In real context.
www.fifthwednesdayjournal.org

SPRING 2012 • ISSUE 10

GUEST POETRY EDITOR
Kevin Stein

GUEST FICTION EDITOR
Donna Seaman

PUBLISHER AND EDITOR	Vern Miller
MANAGING EDITOR	Rachel Hamsmith
ART EDITOR	Jenn Hollmeyer
NONFICTION EDITOR	Monica Berlin
BOOK REVIEWS EDITOR	Daniel Libman
LAYOUT AND DESIGN EDITOR	Kat Sanchez
COPY EDITOR	Sherry Stratton
ADVISORY EDITORS	James Ballowe, Nina Corwin
ASSISTANT EDITORS	Barbara Baldwin, Erin Christian, Peter Clarke, Kelly Davio, Denise Dirks, Gro Flatebo, Maddie Freeman, Nathan Fulkerson, Adam Gallari, Yliana Gonzalez, Katherine Hoerth, Susen James, Angela Just, Christopher Lowe, Sandra Marchetti, Danielle Newton, Meredith Noseworthy, Sherry O'Keefe, Susan Azar Porterfield, Sandra Ramirez, Laura Salamy, Frank Schweihs
CONTRIBUTING EDITORS	Carolyn Alessio, Michael Anania, John Bradley, Susan Hahn, Anna Leahy, Laurence Lieberman, Molly McNett, Edie Meidav, Amy Newman, Lon Otto
WEBMASTER	Barbara Barasa
INTERNS	Mary Egan, Rebecca Sage, Erin Wisti

HONOR ROLL OF DONORS

Fifth Wednesday Journal gratefully acknowledges the support of these individuals and organizations who recognize the importance of literature in sustaining a civil society. Their generosity, especially in a period of declining support for nonprofit organizations, not only sustains the publication of *Fifth Wednesday Journal*, but also nourishes the spirit of all those volunteers who contribute their energy and talent throughout the year. We thank you and we salute you:

Anonymous
Carolyn Cline
Mary Dougherty
Matthew & Lisa Hamsmith
Marie Miller & Alex Navarrete
Amanda Olson
Lisa Ross-Miller
Suzanne Springborn
Nancy Van Leuven

James Ballowe
William & Melpo DeFotis
Barbara Hamsmith
John Curtis Johnson
Danielle Newton
Susan Azar Porterfield
Rebecca Springborn
Kathryn Tecza
Melanie M. Willette

Fifth Wednesday Books, Inc. is a 501(c)(3) organization. Donations are tax deductible to the full extent of the law. A gift in any amount helps to keep *Fifth Wednesday Journal* alive as an independent print literary magazine. Donations may be made at www.fifthwednesdayjournal.org or by check sent to Fifth Wednesday Books, P. O. Box 4033, Lisle, IL 60532-9033.

A PREVIEW OF FALL 2012

Meet Our Guest Editors

Fiction. Eileen Favorite's first novel, *The Heroines* (Scribner, 2008), was named a Best Debut Novel by *The Rocky Mountain News*, and has been translated into Finnish, Italian, Russian, and Korean. The audio version was nominated for best recording by the American Library Association. A writer of both poetry and prose, she's twice received Illinois Arts Council Artist Fellowships (prose, 2001; poetry 2005). Her work has appeared in many publications, including *Triquarterly*, *Folio*, *Chicago Reader*, *Poetry East*, and *Diagram*. She's been nominated for Pushcart Prizes for fiction and nonfiction. She teaches at the School of the Art Institute of Chicago, where she received her MFA in writing, and at the Graham School of Continuing Studies at the University of Chicago. She lives in Chicago with her husband and two daughters. For more about Eileen Favorite, visit www.eileenfavorite.com.

Poetry. Simone Muench was raised in Louisiana and Arkansas and now resides in Chicago. She is the author of four poetry collections: *The Air Lost in Breathing* (Marianne Moore Prize; Helicon Nine, 2000), *Lampblack & Ash* (Kathryn A. Morton Prize; Sarabande, 2005), *Orange Crush* (Sarabande, 2010), and *Disappearing Address*, co-written with Philip Jenks (BlazeVOX, 2010). A former editor of *ACM* (*Another Chicago Magazine*), she is now an editor for *Sharkforum*, a faculty advisor for *Jet Fuel Review*, and an advisory board member for Switchback Books. Her honors include two Illinois Arts Council Fellowships, two Vermont Studio Center Fellowships, a Lewis Faculty Scholar Award, UIC's Frederick Stern Award for Teaching, the PSA's Bright Lights Big Verse Award, and others. She received her PhD from the University of Illinois at Chicago, and currently directs the writing program at Lewis University, where she is an associate professor and teaches creative writing and film studies. Muench is a vegetarian and a lifelong horror film fan. For more about her, visit www.simonemuench.com.

Taking the Fifth: An Interview with Richard Bausch

Richard Bausch was born in Fort Benning, Georgia, and grew up near Washington, DC. He holds a BA from George Mason University and an MFA in creative writing from the University of Iowa. He is the author of eleven novels and eight collections of stories, including *Rebel Powers, Violence, In the Night Season, Hello to the Cannibals, Thanksgiving Night, The Selected Stories of Richard Bausch,* and the recently released *Something Is Out There*.

An acknowledged master of the short story form, Richard Bausch's work has appeared in *The Atlantic Monthly, Esquire, Harper's, The New Yorker, The Best American Short Stories, The PEN/O. Henry Prize Stories,* and *The Pushcart Prize Stories*; and they have been widely anthologized, including in *The Granta Book of the American Short Story* and *The Vintage Book of the Contemporary American Short Stories*. He has received two National Magazine Awards, a Guggenheim Fellowship, a Lila Wallace *Reader's Digest* Writer's Award, the Award of the American Academy of Arts and Letters, and the 2004 PEN/Malamud Award for Excellence in the Short Story. In 1995 he was elected to the Fellowship of Southern Writers. He currently holds the Lillian and Morrie A. Moss Chair of Excellence at the University of Memphis. For more about him, visit www.richardbausch.com.

Meet Our New Book Reviews Editor

Andrea Witzke Slot begins as our Book Reviews Editor with the fall 2012 issue. She has some exciting ideas for FWJ in the area of book reviews, so look for her signature in the coming issues. Her work has appeared in *Borderlands: Texas Poetry Review, Translation Review, Pacific Review, Southern Women's Review,* and *Chiron Review,* among other print and online journals. She teaches at the University of Illinois at Chicago and is also on the editorial board of *Rhino Poetry*. Her first book, *To find a new beauty* (Gold Wake Press, 2012), borrows its title from a line of H.D.'s and has been described by Marge Piercy as being "rich with cool, intelligent and carefully crafted poems that often have a subtext of terror and darkness." For more about her, visit www.andreawitzkeslot.com.

FIFTH WEDNESDAY JOURNAL AT TEN
KEVIN STEIN

Of Ten Fifths and Dog Years

Welcome to issue #10 of *Fifth Wednesday Journal*. Editors love the number ten. It factors easily, rounds nicely, and carries the peculiar larder and heft of a decade even if in this case we're only halfway there in years.

It's a clock's tick-tocking, one's hair thinning, and Letterman's Top Ten list dulling your drifting off. It's a knock on the door but no one's there, the yellow lab Lily's barking at her shadow and then sniffing the locale of her sudden midnight absence.

It's your wallet before you buy your pals a round and your head after you've sprung for it. It's the alabaster plaster of your dental mold and your skewed teeth suddenly standing at attention before the flag of your tongue. It's the iPod shuffle playing when she unzips and "Stardust" circling the LP platter of your brain when he departs without a word or his blown out flip-flops. It's the flag of your tongue.

It's what follows Lennon's incessant white album "Number 9," only that one's titled "Goodbye" not "Hello-Goodbye," which came first by only a year not five. It's the tock ticking its thinning hair but you don't care now that your Manhattan's delivered from tumbler to glass to the flag of your tongue lilting #10, #10, #10.

The life of most literary magazines is like that of a yellow day lily — brief blossom and then the wilt before a fall.

Yellow was the color of my Lily, now gone.

We count them one by one like days, or insults. I might've said kisses but you'd have stopped reading. Where would that get us?

A single issue of any literary magazine burns so much life in its making it's equal to a dog's year.

That's seven not ten but still enough to make one hate the leash hung by the door.

The door means out as well as in, but most mags Exit soon after Enter. Those that last longest learn to slip the leash to run free but smartly sneak home before supper's streetlight serenade. Why's rank stuff the best to roll in? Door scratch, tag wail, and forgiveness. Then the rug beneath thy feet.

If one issue equals seven dog years, then its differential equation goes unlike this:
#1 = 7D x 3.14

Apple 3.14 pie, that is, ice cream and sprinkles for the celebration.

Let the parade begin unleashed. *Fifth Wednesday Journal* is seventy dog-years old.

FIFTH WEDNESDAY JOURNAL AT TEN
DANIEL LIBMAN

You may have heard

Fifth Wednesday Journal turned ten. And don't tell me we are only five. Magazines don't age via time spent; magazines age through publications.

I knew a guy in Baltimore who had been born into a wealthy family, and through pretty good business acumen and deep pockets, made that wealth blossom into bigger wealth. Every year he sent a fat check off to the prep school he still dearly loved. This academy reciprocated with a yearly banquet, at which the moneymen were treated to a program of braggadocio about the genius crop of boys. Sent home with full belly and swelled chest, this sweetheart of a guy had remarked wistfully that the world had changed so much around him. "If I were nine years old today I couldn't even get into that school."

I know the feeling. I got in on the FWJ train early, being offered the job of fiction editor for the inaugural issue over a pint or three with Vern Miller and Jenn Hollmeyer, after their first choice turned them down but recommended me. I fell in love with the vision and the absurdity of it all: forward but retro, new work on the printed page. The only question I had was about the meaning of the magazine's subtitle, "In real context."

For issue one (now a collector's item) we received 152 submissions and published ten of them. And yet here you hold in your hands issue ten, with an accomplished fiction editor at the helm, containing ten stories, whittled down from a staggering 655 submissions, 1.5 percent. Like my friend in Baltimore, I'm not even sure I could get my work accepted at *Fifth Wednesday Journal* anymore, let alone be asked on as the fiction editor. I nevertheless cling to that caboose as tightly as I can, editing book reviews for awhile, now doing the "Taking the Fifth" series, anything to stay on board. You'd have to fling me off like a hobo to get me to leave.

Vern has remained true to the original mission: *Fifth Wednesday Journal* is a place where writers can get their work read and if not published, then at least passed over with dignity. It's the place where the work comes first, even before the writer, and where the images resonate with the writing and the writing with the reader. I still don't exactly know what "In real context" means, but I have no doubt that it'll cause head scratching for many years to come, which is all that matters.

FIFTH WEDNESDAY JOURNAL AT TEN

JENN HOLLMEYER

Ten-Ten

There's a Ten-Ten Road in Raleigh, North Carolina, where I grew up. Of course, when people say the name there, it sounds like *Tintin* — a movie so far on the fringes of my radar that I expected a German shepherd dog to appear onscreen when I finally saw the trailer. As it turns out, you see a lot of dogs along Ten-Ten Road, most of them barking at you from porches.

When we started working on issue ten, I found myself saying the number twice in my head, in rapid, celebratory succession — "Ten! Ten!" — just out of habit. I do the same thing when talking to my dog — "Who's a good boy? Who's a good boy!" — making up for the fact that he can't answer me.

Of course, repetition usually serves to underscore a sentiment, as in, "Hear, hear!" and "All right, *all right*" (eye roll implied). As the press deadline for the tenth issue approached and there was still much work to be done, my exclamations morphed into exasperation. (Ten? *Ten!?!*) The good news is, by the time you read this, we'll all be singing, "Happy, Happy, Joy, Joy" (or the adult equivalent).

The journal itself is made of doubles — left- and right-hand pages that you experience together in pairs. Text, text. Photo, photo. Elements that share a spread inform and enhance each other, whether they belong to the same piece or not. A word in a poem might appear in dialogue on the facing page. A line in one photo might continue in another.

And it doesn't stop there. Many of the words and authors and themes you find in these pages will reappear in other issues, other journals, other books you stack on top of this one. Maybe a character name from one of these short stories will show up in a news article you read later today. Or you'll hear his fictional dog barking from your neighbor's porch. Or the number of this issue will unexpectedly rise from the roadmap of your childhood. That's the fun of defining literature. In everyday context.

Here's to ten great issues, and ten more to come.

FIFTH WEDNESDAY JOURNAL AT TEN

MONICA BERLIN

[More on 5x2, sort of]

At this age you stare out the window at that big dish of a sky thinking, *Soon I'll be six and then I'll be seven, and then eight*. You skip over nine, elide that strange upside-down other figure, but never forget ten, think, *Tententen! When I'm ten I'll be two numbers old!* You ask repeatedly when you'll turn ten. *Turn ten, what a thing!* This is also the year you hear rumors about the discovery of another planet in the solar system. You think, *If they counted Pluto, this would be the tenth planet!* They won't, poor Pluto, and about the new one — turns out they're wrong. Later you'll learn the term *double digit*. You'll learn that if you multiply anything by ten, you only need to add a zero to its end. You'll learn that most of your life will be spent in double digits, and you'll discover you hardly remember the singularly numbered years before — those fleeting ones only nostalgia or synesthesia might return to you.

When you were the age of FWJ you were learning to read. It was physical, that act, coordinating your mouth with your eyes, a whole new seeing, running your finger beneath every word. In your chest, some kind of pressure building, some kind of fear, some kind of thrill for a future you couldn't quite wholly imagine yet, though you had some dreamy ideas of what it'd look like. You probably remember none of this. Your mother can't forget. How she moved her lips along with you, how the sentence — growing longer, growing more complicated — seemed to carry you away from her, even as she helped you turn pages and reminded, *Sound out the words.* You didn't know yet that Mozart, at five, made his first composition, "Andante in C." *A walking pace. A moderately slow tempo*. Literally, in Italian, *going*. Like your small voice, going. Like the years, *andante*.

FWJ's been reading since conception. *Show off,* some would say. *Gifted,* some would say, nodding with approval. Others would recognize FWJ as naturally inclined toward literacy, but really, it's just what FWJ does. *Read on*, you'll say now to FWJ, thinking that if you'd grown up together, you'd have climbed each night into your bunk beds begging for another chapter, another few pages, *OK, just one, just one more page, please*. After lights off, you'd climb down from the top bunk holding the flashlight you keep tucked between pillow and wall, and with FWJ pull up the covers and read until long past reasonable. FWJ never minds a groggy morning if it means a word-filled late night, never minds a cheek-pressed page upon waking.

FIFTH WEDNESDAY JOURNAL AT TEN

DONNA SEAMAN

Something to Count On

Literary types, myself included, often shy away from numbers, admitting ruefully, "I'm no good at math." And yet I find myself enamored of a literary journal with a numerical name, *Fifth Wednesday Journal*, and prompted to confess to a secret love for the numbers five and ten. Because each hand has five fingers, each foot five toes, times two. And so to be invited to serve as guest fiction editor for the tenth issue of *Fifth Wednesday Journal* felt like winning some sort of weird little private lottery.

Ten is a solid, upright number, a sort of yin-yang, and the tenth issue of *Fifth Wednesday Journal* is cause for celebration. With so much of the publishing world in flux, the vitality, stick-to-itiveness, and clear and steady mission of this literary and artistic print magazine is inspiring and reassuring. The journal itself is a harbor and holdfast.

Fiction, too, is something to count on. Stories are always there for us, working their curious alchemy, awakening new perceptions while affirming abiding understandings. Fiction is a wellspring for essential truths about the human condition. Marilynne Robinson writes, "I think fiction may be, whatever else, an exercise in the capacity for imaginative love, or sympathy, or identification."

By some sweet chance, I ended up with ten short stories for the tenth issue of *Fifth Wednesday Journal*, and this elegant symmetry makes me feel that at least in this literary oasis, all is just as it should be.

Thanks to everyone who makes *Fifth Wednesday Journal* possible. May the good numbers keep rising.

FIFTH WEDNESDAY JOURNAL AT TEN
PUBLISHER'S NOTE

Without Bias Toward Ten

Here it is. Our tenth issue. I will not write about it; in the preceding pages the editors of FWJ have expressed the pleasure and satisfaction we feel in bringing our readers the first ten issues. They have also encouraged everyone to look toward the future.

We are ready. We are ready to add ten more issues. Without bias toward the first ten, I ask you, our readers and contributors, to think about continuing our partnership. Create your own riff on the number ten and then multiply by ten. Hang with us and define for yourself the tag line, "In real context." Say to yourself, yes-yes, and help us to reach the double ten-ten; help us accelerate our andante to a lyrical allegretto — we are ready. FWJ is indeed something to count on. Count on it. With your support we can find and share the alchemy of the poets and artists around us. Unto the dog's years of seventy.

With sincere thanks for your backing for the coming ten, here is our tenth issue.

— Vern Miller
PUBLISHER AND EDITOR

TABLE OF CONTENTS

COVER PHOTOGRAPH
          Petra Ford   *Untitled*

Susan Hahn	17	*Yom Kippur Night Dance*
Marc Kelly Smith	18	*Turning Ten*
Allison Joseph	20	*Ode to Areolas*
Ashley Strosnider	21	*The Worst Thing About the South Carolina State Fair*
Keith Ratzlaff	22	*Not a Chariot*
James Carpenter	23	*I Married Her*
Peter Orner	29	*Renters*
Camille T. Dungy	30	*Mother daughter hour*
	31	*Still life with tossed sheets and yogurt cup*
Dean Young	32	*Crying at Weddings*
	33	*Flyers*
Natania Rosenfeld	34	*Gravity*
Kathleen Kirk	38	*Grudge*
	39	*Smorgasbord*
Christine Sneed	40	*Words That Once Shocked Us*
Philip Appleman	56	*Seeing Robert Wadlow*
Joe Meno	58	*The Future*
Kim Addonizio	65	*Divine*
	66	*Thank You*
John Gallaher	68	*In a Landscape: XX*
	69	*In a Landscape: XXI*
Clint McCown	70	*Today's Lessons in the Animal Kingdom*
Melissa Fraterrigo	71	*Crud Face*
Bob Hicok	81	*When swimming is more like flying is still how we think of the soul*
	82	*What the great apes refer to as a philosophy of life*
Janice N. Harrington	84	*White-tail*
Roger Mitchell	86	*Charles*

Jim Elledge	88	*Three Rhymed Secrets*
B. J. Hollars	89	*Surfaces*
Frank Bergon	93	*Tikal*
Victoria Barras Tulacro	108	*Partial Viewing*

IMPRESSIONS PHOTOGRAPHY

Eleanor Leonne Bennett	114	*Handle with Care*
	115	*Battling Winds*
	116	*In Need of Warm Water*
	117	*High Up*
	117	*Self-Portrait*
Petra Ford	118	*street view*
Jenn Hollmeyer	122	*interview*
Petra Ford	128	*my view*

TAKING THE FIFTH FEATURING ANA CASTILLO

Daniel Libman	138	*Ana Castillo Takes the Fifth*
David Hernandez	150	*Ramonita the Avon Lady*
Tony Hoagland	152	*Warning for Shoppers*
	153	*Wrong Question*
J. Allyn Rosser	154	*ABC of the Human Condition*
	155	*Weekend at Trish's*
Mary Quade	156	*Cage*
Achy Obejas	167	*Trial Run*
Richard Jones	172	*My Samovar!*
Jeff Knorr	174	*Taking Leave*
Theodosia Henney	176	*Pit Ponies*
Bayo Ojikutu	177	*The Last Days of Dick and Hank*
James Harms	192	*Other, America*
	193	*The Devil's Eye*
Mike Petrik	194	*Weathering*
Beckian Fritz Goldberg	204	*Refrain*
	205	*Bees on Cocaine*
Mark Halliday	208	*Ducks Not in Row*
	209	*Ferguson High*
Donald Revell	210	*Air and Angels*
	211	*Debris*

Jeff Gundy	212	*Meditation with Wallet, Eyeglasses, and Little Riley Creek*
Betsy Sholl	214	*Atlantic City, Mid Morning*
Dave Schultz	215	*Colt 45*

BOOK REVIEWS

Lea Graham	223	*The Range of Your Amazing Nothing* by Lina ramona Vitkauskas
John Bradley	226	*Seeding the Cosmos: New & Selected Haiku* by John Brandi
Adam Gallari	228	*Aftermath* by Scott Nadelson
Dale Barrigar	230	*Look Down, This Is Where It Must Have Happened* by Hal Niedzviecki
Breja Gunnison	232	*Georgic* by Mariko Nagai

234 CONTRIBUTORS

SUSAN HAHN

Yom Kippur Night Dance

At the end of each prayer, she'd add her own —
to find someone to marry.
In shul, where the men and women were separated
by an aisle, she'd lament and vow
to change the ways she wasn't good, then

break the fast with family and rush
to dress for the Yom Kippur Night Dance.
There, she'd wait with the girls in taffeta and years
later with the women in rayon knit.
Often she took a man

for the night, let him slide into her
because she felt she could hold him
there, pretend her life was like some
romantic song. Beyond the long somber chants,
the half wails of the chorus,

in the dark she'd start to sing
at the high pitch of happiness,
her appetite as huge as Eve's
before she knew she'd have to leave

the bliss, bow her head
and ask again for forgiveness.

MARC KELLY SMITH

Turning Ten

During fifth grade library period, Davy Luper lifted his nose over his book to admire Andy Spur's eyes registering volumes of lines left to right, left to right, down the page, zip zip zip . . . now *there* was a boy who could read. And Davy was fascinated by and envious of Andy's eyes which every now and then would push themselves bulging out of their sockets like William Buckley Jr.'s yawning and stretching wide awake in the red, white, and blue American atmosphere.

Fireline fast those pupils would bull's eye the p's and q's, ingest the ideologies, snap the covers shut, and flip the spines back on the shelves filing down the rows hup hup hup in search of another . . . all before Davy could even figure out what the first word on the third line of the first page of the book he was pretending to read was.

And then strutting proud, as if on post parade, Andy's fingers would march along the Dewey Decimal digits inspecting in the line of labels for a next new title to conquer, revved up like a motorcade MP patrolling foreign soil brashly sending a siren scream into the dead night air calling for "More Words! More Words!"

All this before Davy had time to set his sights upon deciphering the captions under the Marine Corp Action Photos of the picture books he always hid his nose in during third period library session examining and analyzing the photographic deeds done by realistic service daddies on duty in Japan throwing bloated Hiroshima bodies onto the back beds of dump trucks for sacred mass burials.

But, of course, those pictures were not included in the books Davy and Andy were given to read. Their books showed Sergeant John Wayne defending his country, flag, and everybody's smiling mother, not to mention their right to even be there on their soft behinds in stateside schoolhouse libraries reading pages of picture book history.

And while Davy wasted the weeks away day-dreaming of flushing out the fearsome enemy with a flamethrower on a peninsula somewhere in the south seas, Andy Spur's eyes marched double time toward an educated Nam sized 2nd Louie package of grief opened up — surprise! — on a hillside somewhere north of Sector C becoming the gloriously unsung hero Davy had always wished himself to be someday when he was West Point well read as Andy.

And after all those books conspicuously consumed in the fifth grade, Andy Spur came home to his mother wrapped in plastic, pieces of his fast brain popped out of his head like those bulging eyes Davy so much admired.

ALLISON JOSEPH

Ode to Areolas

When I was young, I thought people
called them *orioles*, orange and black
flicker of a bird that could never beat
my Yankees, or Oreos, cookie I craved

every time my mother dragged me,
screaming and whining, heels dragging,
through the supermarket, begging
for the real brand, not Hydrox or generic

cookies in a white wrapper. Now
the whole world stares at them, denies
staring at them, puts black bars on them
so they don't poke from risqué newsstand

covers. Entire country went insane
over a glimpse of Janet's at the Super
Bowl, gasping like witnesses at a public
execution, ready for the collective

fainting couch. But why despise what so many
desire: tip of a mound, slip for the tongue,
site to feed the world? I wake up, look
down, see one, then the other, each

headed in her own direction. Looking
at them, I'm reminded again of sweets —
chocolate chips or Hershey's kisses,
these sweet dollops too fierce for the grocery.

Not fair that you men can strut around,
bare chested, nipples out, but if we women
do so we risk arrest, attack. How potent
you are, little nubbins, sweet tarts,

alive and open every time I pull off
a sweat-soaked bra or T-shirt,
nude vivid trollops always
wanting to bust loose.

ASHLEY STROSNIDER

The Worst Thing About the South Carolina State Fair

Was the New Ferris Wheel Run by a Smiling European
    whose blond hair and bronzed arms gleamed
    under floodlights manufactured in the Midwest,

But Not that it Cost So Much Everyone Had to Chip In,
    to keep Matt from skipping out and sneaking off
    into the Haunted House with the girls he fed cotton candy,

Or that It Wasn't Meant to be a Romantic Affair
    for couples, paired, but instead became a group project
    where riders all piled into a swinging bucket like a hot tub

(Where Wentworth Got Caught with the Wrong Blonde,
    his arms around the shoulders of his just-friends-
    sweetheart decked out in a New-York-City dress),

And that It Didn't Look Down and Out Over the Town,
    schools, houses, and abandoned Lemon Shakeups melting
    in the heat of stolen kisses, but the seats faced inward,

And Lacking an External Reference Point to Spot,
    we dizzied like dancers who blinked too long
    while a partner's strong grasp spun us relentlessly round.

When We Came Back Down from That High,
    we clambered like drunks queasy in the humidity
    of real-time perpendicularity upon walking the midway;

The Sand Rolled Us Forward in Slow-Motion Waves.

KEITH RATZLAFF

Not a Chariot

> *Thunder. My heart trembles.*
> *I lift my head from my pillow.*
> *It is not a chariot.*
>   — *Fu Hsuan (217-278)*

I was snarled awake by the thunder of chainsaws, showering the morning with elm dust. 6:00 a.m., the sun hot even this early on the white side of the house. You were gone already. Or still.

And it wasn't thunder or a chariot or a lover, but a tree with its top green branches now at its feet, then the thudding of chunk after chunk until it wasn't shade anymore, or the storm that started everything last month — the big limb dropped through the pickup's windshield — it was just absence, sunlight on the side of a house.

And at first I misread that poem by a Chinese girl awake at dawn. Her pillow was not a chariot, her head was not a chariot. I wanted it to be about weather but she meant something else — the wheels of desire, their dust and horses. Love, it really was her heart — my heart — making all that ruckus. Not thunder. Not a chariot.

JAMES CARPENTER

I Married Her *Fiction*

I married her, a hasty and violent step. Where others more prudent than we navigate the murky currents of love within the thick-walled safety of wooden sailing ships, meanderingly and with an eye to the compass and the charts, we coursed through them in a cigarette boat, heedless of the swirling waters and the jutting rocks that would have made cautious any love less urgent than ours, our swift passage straight and true and reckless. At full throttle, we sped through courtship's entire cycle in less than a month. Over the last weeks of April and the opening days of May, we clawed through the flirting introduction and its disingenuous dance (her lowered eyes, my awkward smiles), the "accidental" brushing of hands as one or the other of us reached for our host's bread basket; the first tentative meeting alone (a midmorning breakfast of croissants and melon on the veranda of a café overlooking the sea, far enough above the spray not to be dampened by it, but close enough to smell it on the air already pregnant with each other's taste, the patio heater glowing above us, warming us like a second specious sun); the first intimacy in the same hotel where we shared that inaugural breakfast, this time on the side facing the mountains with its balcony view of the snow-capped metaphor for our love, the enduring rock of ages, a love for all seasons, a love that not even a million years of time could erode away; the early passions and disappointments of our callow affair with their earnest professions, the sudden flaring up of petulant words, and forgiveness begged for and given in spite of what had been said, the reconciliations so physical they often crossed the unseen border separating naked communion from depraved debauchery; the cheap rhinestone ring offered melodramatically on bended knee (until a suitably expensive replacement could be acquired), the ring accepted with a single word, an uncharacteristically giggly yet lachrymose *yes*; the purchase of a white lace dress and a sentimental red brooch in the shape of a heart to adorn it; the rushed ceremony before the judge, his assistants our only witnesses, an obese octogenarian filling in as maid of honor and a pimply-faced errand boy standing for me; and finally courtship's tender terminus, the first weeks of the honeymoon in a rented cottage overlooking the sea in Gortaforia, a place neither of us had ever been to but whose name seemed to us hefty with history and redolent of knights and virginal princesses, a place God had no doubt allowed to come to be in the world for the sole purpose of mystical beginnings, a place where our love could flower in spasms of blossom that would shame the spring then greening the Irish coast, whose burst of life, fecund and extravagant as any place on earth, was rendered feeble by comparison to the lush ripeness of our aroused bodies — the same name Gortaforia that has now come to seem more fitting for a horrible, unbearably painful wasting disease than for an erotic retreat.

For a year we traveled, never alighting in any place long enough to become weary of it, each of our invasions in a realm more romantic and bewitching than the last. San Francisco, Gibraltar, Venice, Barcelona, Prague, Paris, Vienna, Monte Carlo, Istanbul, Cannes, Zurich, Bangkok, Maldives, Morocco, Cape Town, Buenos Aires, Kalkata. We dined in sidewalk cafés, strolled beaches of pure white sand, clung to rocky coasts, made love in mountain meadows fragrant with clover and in shaded groves of spruce and magnolias, our dappled bodies striped and scarred with the shadows of their branches as if they had lashed us for daring to love so brazenly. We watched flickering figures flow across the screens of movie houses in art districts all across the world, our eyes on the actors, but our hands inside each other's clothing, not caring at all if anyone noticed and, in truth, actually wishing that they did. In the evenings we drank dark coffees and teas with peregrine flavors in city bistros and country inns, cigarette smoke milling about our heads along with the thoughts of us the other patrons could not help but think in languages we could not understand, but certain that our gazes and electric touches spoke to them the single universal thought, *Don't you wish you were we?* Weeks of naked slippery skin, of long rambling conversations stretching through the night into the sunrise, of poems read aloud in sultry voices, and of shadowy photographs of shared secret places. But every season of passion had interspersed within it days of grim silences and spiteful glances, and for every country we left, we left behind us a sacked and smoldering ruin. We were a rampaging army of two, buckled and armed, with an incipient talent for slaughter and a lust for the brutal blow.

And then home, the year-long holiday ended, her days spent off in the world doing important things, mine consumed with smelting and carving and bringing up from the very stuff of the earth things never before seen or touched. I burnished and buffed and brazed and hammered ever newer, ever more exotic gifts for her, albeit temporary gifts, for they were destined for the world by way of the bazaar, the currency through which I met my share of the fiscal responsibilities implicit in the marriage bed, the fiduciary codicil attached to the rites of coitus. And each evening she brought back to me tales of crusades in her fraught world, mergers acquired or escaped, the bloody remains of a corporation plundered, a politician silenced, commissions earned — the price of her ticket to ride me. I listened in riveted admiration of the things she had the courage to do and the will and the need. And then less raptly so, as she came to give my creations barely a glance as we argued over where we should go for dinner, the ashes of our future darkly, disinterestingly spilling from the flames of her face.

And then the child, that which one romanticizes as the earthly manifestation of a celestial love, but is instead that wide and terrible fissure in the earth that awakens a tectonic shift, its plates up until that moment so deeply buried their threat of ruin never even occurs to any of us, but once aroused shakes the foundation of two intermingled souls with a force neither could have, in a lifetime of childless crises, ever imagined. After an earthquake there is always at least one interviewed observer who claims that the experience was like standing on a bedsheet that God grabs hold of with both his hands and snaps so that the sheet's fabric rolls and pitches as if it will be torn to shreds — and then God does it again and yet again, until it is impossible to stand on the floundering earth let alone cling to one another, and everyone caught up in the chaos simply collapses altogether solitary and isolated in their own pain and fear, with no capacity for empathy with anyone else's pain and fear. And the aftershocks keep coming: The colical, sleepless nights. The unexplained fevers. The juggling of schedules. Friends slipping away. Midnight kisses becoming only memories. Then preschool applications and aptitude tests (should there be an aptitude test for love and a law that forbids love should you fail and a prison term for those of us who ignore the law? — as if the prison of each other isn't censure enough) and first communion and recitals and hurried visits to the hospital. That long night in the ER, the child frantic with pain, our fear (and ashamedly our secret hope) that she had broken a bone. Tenderness resurrected itself beneath the sterile fluorescent of the medical workrooms, as we accompanied her to X-ray, to the treatment room, awaited results. For those hours we were conjoined again, welded briefly back together with the solder of shared compassion for our issue and the hope that her long convalescence would heal not only her, but us. And then the disappointment when the doctor told us it was only a mild sprain and she would be running and skipping and falling down and getting up again in a couple of weeks. And we would not. After that we didn't touch each other for a very long time.

My first Paris show and everything in it, if not for her, was *of* her: the staggering, off-balance bundles of wires; the cantilevered frames flying without any support or fear of falling as we had once heedlessly flown about each other; the rivulets of crimson ink running down the walls like blood, staining sheet after sheet of Lanaquarelle menstrual red and damn the expense. The drunken art student paying me too much attention and impulsively kissing my neck and grinding her thigh between my legs. The wine tossed in the face and the slapping and screaming, the two of them on the floor tearing hair and clothes before the assembled party realized it wasn't part of the show and pulled them apart. Afterward we laughed and forgave one another, though there was nothing to forgive we said, our forgiveness offered to each other a little bit for the memory of love but mostly because the ugly scene made the art pages and the show sold double the pieces we'd expected because of it, and money at the right time is an adequate surrogate for passion, though it lasts not quite as long, which is to say not long at all.

Then the affairs or the perception of affairs or fantasies of affairs. We never found out and it didn't matter, for it isn't betrayal itself that inflicts so much damage, but the brutal accusations of betrayal and quests for proof of betrayal, imagined or real. Denials and rebuttals of denials. And somewhere the truth that infidelity would make not a bit of difference, might in fact be a help, a balm on the wounds of indifference — when the longing for a stranger is really a nostalgic cry to recover the stranger she (or I, I admit) once was, so exotic, so forbidden, so loved. But we let the sliver of light through which kindness might have slithered close. No, that's not how it was. We did not merely concede the loss of that promising light — we slapped it back and bared out teeth, gorgons both, the insults once hurled from bruised feelings now spewing out of new and bottomless vats of hatred, *fucking whore* transposed into *greedy, marauding bitch* and *bastard* into *narcissistic hack*, monsters turning not the other but ourselves to stone, the country of *us* bombed to rubble.

The ever less enthusiastic attempts to reconcile, the first ones from a genuine if misguided hope that love can be re-flamed from its own dead embers, an ethereal phoenix — the planned month-long getaway to the mountains that lasted barely three days, our hope dashed that all we needed was each other, that somehow it was the intervening world that was crushing us and not our own neglect. The pragmatic arrangements, living apart in the same house, because living in different houses was too expensive for either of us, and then because divorcing would have simply been too much work, and finally because we were both too weary to even try to do this one last thing.

And then the giving in, the final surrender. The dividing of property and the dividing of the child (had Solomon been our judge and ordered his subordinates to slice the child in two and render half of her to each of us, we would have shrugged and acquiesced, too spent of spirit to care for anything other than that this be over) and the dividing of memories, our shared earth salted and barren so that nothing of the two of us remained or could ever be re-grown. The only chance for any new alliance would be that if an innocent budding stem somehow found a way to struggle up through the scorched soil of what we once were, we would join forces in unshakeable loyalty to the death of our union and with picks and shovels eradicate its audacious green from the earth forever.

And then I was alone. I retraced our first year's pilgrimage, but more slowly, seeking out not the piazzas and mountain villas and foggy yellow streets but rather the stained tenements and crumbling memorials, the abandoned graveyards and the smoking trash dumps. I did not travel — I wandered. For without her I was no longer a sojourner but a vagabond, a weary sloth toeing my way among the jagged angles of rusting jungles black as midnight that for others flashed with light, but for me were so dark that black sparks chucked from my shuffling arms and legs like electricity's mad, sinister ghost.

Eventually I came home, shrunken and indolent and jaded. In time I picked up my work. But no longer did it fly or long to fly. I wallowed in dregs of waste. I welded chaos, forging it from scavenged clumps of rusted iron and corroded brass and burnt copper. Jars of refuse and ashes. Sulking, blunted shapes slinking along the ground in darkness, hiding from the light. Indeed, mocking the light. And all of it, every bit of it, a simulacrum of decay and corruption. And though not a bit of it mattered, it sold. This despair, the true incarnation of my heart, is also the true oversoul, and the collectors lapped it up at obscene prices just to be a part of it. They just couldn't get enough. If she and I could once again have stood the sight of each other for just a little while, we could have become rich enough to die in leisured peace. But we simply could not, and I worked on without her, my blackened, burning hands singeing to soot the same stuff of the world they had once made radiant.

What was that thing that entered into me the moment I first saw her, alchemizing my blood and bones to honey and silver and then to bitter bile and frozen lead? The elixir that promised eternal life and then festered into poison? How did such a thing as delicate and weightless as a kiss brushing the cheek inflict such ravaging infections that not even time's vast distances can heal them? How did the baptism of semen become an acid bath? How did the sweet language of love debase itself and become Baal's sputtering, guttural incantations invoking the rituals of human sacrifice? And how was it that I couldn't see what was clearly before me: that in its very inception the hunger was already gone, that what I would remember would not be her soft, gentle caress on my cheek but her searing destruction of my heart?

What crushing, irresistible tide made of me a shattered stone on the shingle of her shore?

Yes, my marrying her was a hasty and violent step. But I am with you now — now and forever under all of God's stars. Love me love me love me love me love me.

PETER ORNER

Renters   *Nonfiction*

She was small, with closely cropped hair made to look, maybe, like she'd cut it herself. As if one day she'd seized a hunk of hair and lopped it off. For a couple of weeks that summer I lived across the road. I was trying to finish something I never finished. We were both renting summer places. It was fall. This was in Wisconsin, up north on Little Star Lake. John Dillinger once hid out there. For some reason I thought this fact would help me finish what I couldn't finish. The leaves were beautiful. The owners couldn't really afford these second houses. So they rented them out to people like the two of us who would never have one house let alone two. I have always been more than a little proud of my supposed poverty. I say people like the two of us, but I never actually spoke to her, not once. One morning we nodded to each other, one renter to another, but that was early on. After that, we made eye contact a few times. Once she was unloading groceries from the trunk of her car and I was standing in my side yard, looking at a hole in the clouds. We both pretended not to see each other. No, not that, we both meant to say — by not saying anything — that we had come here to be alone. Except I was lying about this. I never go anywhere to be alone. I kept thinking about why she did that to her hair. I admit that I tried once to spy on her, that one night I crossed the road and peered over the rim of her front window. She wasn't in the living room. She must have been in another part of the house. There was music playing. A book tented on the table.

CAMILLE T. DUNGY

Mother daughter hour

      Callie is reading the book about language,
and I am reading the book about death.

Ball, she says, pointing to an orange.
            I shake my head.

            I read, *Death is the mother of beauty*,
   but she says, *pretty ball*.

I am going to have to put down my book so I can teach her better,
      but first I read her one last sentence
      because I'm struck by all its vowel sounds.

            *That, finally, is all it means
   to be alive: to be able to die.*

            She is listening
and she is not listening.

The afternoon light is brighter here on the couch than any other place in the room.

     With her little thumb and baby fingers, my daughter turns
        her board book's pages.
                       Red, she says,
     pointing to an apple.

Red, I say, and we sit together a little while longer, read some more.

CAMILLE T. DUNGY

Still life with tossed sheets and yogurt cup

Still life with Ensure, vials of fentanyl, oxycodone, water.
Still life with crackers maybe, hopefully, he will keep down.
Still life with *Sports Illustrated* piles in the bathroom, guest room,
on the living room floor, on the dining room table, in recycle bins waiting
near the door. Still life with the younger brother assessing
how to dispose the hoardings of the one man left who shares his face.
Still life with hanging tension and sadness, failed ambition,
medicated dreams. Still life with phlegm and corruption.
With waste, with fanned get well cards, appointment reminders,
hospital garage parking receipts. Still life with the mantel clock,
one birthday's present, still ticking and ticking and ticking away.

DEAN YOUNG

Crying at Weddings

With every new love something must be torn out
because the body is born full. Enough love,
you are empty and permitted to float away.

No more shame beside the generous ocean,
no more infidelities under the hot moon.
The magnets that tugged so hard in the throat

by the lake at the friend's reception
will be powerless, so too the old doo-wop songs.
& that picture hidden in Breton's *Mad Love*

won't cut through you like a scythe through
autumn grains anymore. You'll be floating
over the nests where squirrels settle

after a day chasing each other
and the houses like trapped game-pieces
and the warning lights of control towers

that never go off and the snow's thumbprint
weighing down every wire and branch,
heavy and dense as dark chocolate.

DEAN YOUNG

Flyers

You won't find my name anywhere.
I'm trying to figure out how to be absolutely faithful
to something I can't get near.
I guess whatever part of me wasn't born a pile of ash
and didn't get caught in barbed wire was.
But it's easier holding a match
until it snuffs out against your fingers.
Me and my brother used to do that
staring into each other's eyes
while everyone else was having a childhood.
You know how if you flinch you lose
then the angel goes off to whisper
what she'd like done to her
in the backseat of someone else's car.
I ain't about to let my education go wasted.
I went to this house once with drugs
and they had an honest-to-god tiger on the couch.
It's OK, they said, she's not a year old.
I went from one life to another
stroking that electric fur,
not long but long enough
to see my hand on fire and still be my hand.
These were circus people, trapezists
baby tiger-sitting. I belonged
out on the road somewhere blowing around.
I didn't want to but I did.
The girl, put together tight like a remote-control glider,
kissed me goodbye on each cheek
like I was getting on the Titanic.

NATANIA ROSENFELD

Gravity   *Nonfiction*

Table. Coffin.

I don't trust aerodynamics: every time I fly somewhere, I expect the tail to scrape the ground when the plane lifts off. On the other hand, I'm grateful that airplanes take me to other places. In my forties, I've found myself mired in the flatlands of the great Midwest, and I have to escape, even it's only from time to time. So I've overcome my fear of flying and nowadays feel a kind of exhilaration even as I breathe a sigh of relief that once again, the plane has lifted off successfully.

A few Decembers ago, my husband and I flew to New York City for museums, concerts, plays, ethnic food, and romance. As it happened — emblematically, perhaps — the first show we attended, in the city of high culture, was a performance by Midwestern clowns. We'd never seen them in Chicago, and their antics, we'd been told, combined the absurd and terrible view of life of a Guston or a Beckett with the kind of pratfalls that make children laugh so hard they pee in their pants. A must-see.

I came away from the show with a feeling of mingled delight and dismay. Three mad people — two burly men and a gap-toothed woman — spent most of the hour and a half contending with an intolerably heavy table that consisted of several enormous flaps of wood aligned along metal bars. If that doesn't sound comprehensible, the real thing wasn't, either. Every time one of the characters tried to escape it, or to exert control over it, the piece of furniture came down on his head, or limbs, or torso. The children in the audience laughed and laughed, and so did I. The thing was inexorable, and reminded me of a behemoth I used for a desk in graduate school: my aunt and uncle's first dining-room table, which they bequeathed me in college in a moment of sadism disguised as generosity, and which was made of such heavy wood and such quantities of iron I injured myself whenever I moved it. But I kept taking the thing with me, for years of my life, as if I owed it, or my aunt and uncle, some kind of loyalty.

I felt Neil flinching next to me, and heard him laugh after each time he flinched; we took turns doing this, and it was not unlike those airplane rides in the past where sudden turbulence would send my heart into my mouth and I'd clutch his arm for comfort, then lean my head on his shoulder and breathe relief when the air calmed again, feeling I'd avoided the worst this time. That feeling is exhilarating, perhaps because it makes you believe that having come so close, you're now immune to the plunge and terror of a sudden fall. Of sudden death. *500 Clown* and their dreadful table gave us that feeling — and gave it over and over, as roller coasters do, only roller coasters make me sick, and this didn't.

The table was an animated coffin, an emblem of death made lively. In James Joyce's story "The Dead," the guests assembled for Epiphany Day dinner get to discussing an order of monks who sleep in their own coffins to remember their mortality. As I age, my flesh itself begins to feel coffin-like; no need to sleep in a wood box when the body is quite unpleasant enough, thank you very much. Confirming my increasing stiffness — onset of the final rigor? — I have an increasingly adversarial relationship to objects. They keep falling from my hands, bruising me, cutting me. Then, too, there is this business of seepage, not to be explored; and the business of saggage, of the body parts that need to be schlepped, when formerly, they seemed to convey themselves from place to place quite of their own volition. Then one also has swelling: for instance, what are these lowest extremities that swell and turn red after walking? What's this mound in the abdominal area, inflating every evening, incompletely deflating every morning? What are these asymmetrical thingamajigs thinging around on my ribcage?

Boobs

What they are, I found out the day after the clowns, is "titties," also known as "boobs." Though I like good old English words for genitals, those gawkish terms for breasts never sat right with me. They sound mocking, and unlike cocks and cunts, breasts seem to deserve a dignified nomination, being neither wrinkled nor pinkish-purple but soft, often lovely and the source of all nurturance — worshipable dears. At the Town Shop lingerie store on the Upper West Side, the idea is to help make them as adorable as possible, but the language of the process is no-nonsense, as is the process itself. I had long suspected that I was not wearing the right size bra, and I took myself to the Town Shop for confirmation and a fitting. An ebullient woman with lots of bling and red talon nails, about ten years younger than me but with substantial bulges at waist and hips, took me under her wing in a small fitting room where she had a good look at my "boobies" and informed me that I needed to go a full cup up if I was to do them proud. She bustled off while I waited, returned with about a dozen brassieres of varying laciness, elegance, simplicity, and brazen tartiness, and proceeded to show me the correct way to don them, which was to put the straps over the shoulders, lean forward with the boobs hanging down like eggplants — now these were boobs — push the underwire beneath them, fasten at the back, straighten up, then adjust. Apparently my years-long method, learned from my mother, of buckling the bra at the front, then turning it around and pulling the straps over the shoulders, was all wrong. The way to get a proper fit was through this bending and straightening, followed by a process of pulling and pushing for a proper fit inside the fabric nest.

"Yup, your right one's the bigger one," said Samantha, giving it a push and tug. "Now I'll leave you alone with these, and you call for me if you want my advice."

By that time I was sweating, and unsure where to start. Simultaneously, I felt like a Real Woman for the first time in my life, and was delighted by the confections before me. I had already decided to choose one Practical Bra and one Sexy one; before me hung a few solid examples of the one and several delicious lacy, beribboned, black, pink, purple, and red versions of the other. After some minutes, Samantha popped her head in to see how I was doing and caught me trying on a bra my mother's way. "Uh-uh!" she said, "You gotta bend over and *place* the titties inside the cups." I obeyed, and she went her own way with promises of further help if I needed it.

At length I chose my two brassieres, pleased with the one and in love with the other, and made my way to the counter. Samantha caught me and suggested the matching panty (not "panties," I learned) for the black bra, which was duly beautiful; I grabbed also a little camisole; went to the cashier, and was told a sum that made me reel. I dropped the cami right away, then asked the price of the panty — "$55" — and occasioned much laughter by shrieking, "Take it off, take off the panty right away!" I left the store with a lighter wallet and a full heart, excited about my new look, all lift and pride and forward thrust.

Dancing. Falling.

I wore my sexy secret to the theatre that evening, where I sat with a crowd of New York's literati, glamorini, and designer-bespectacled artsies and watched the magnificent Mikhail Baryshnikov perform the deterioration of the body and the will over and over again in a series of revived short plays by Samuel Beckett. Revived suggests an expired body, or at least one near expiration, and one or two of the works had the feel of something that might have been better left in the grave, but the signature Beckett sense of life's grotesque and funny pointlessness informed them all. And Baryshnikov was a poignant choice for protagonist — the great dancer no longer able to execute the leaps of yore, but still, in his late fifties, a fine figure of lithe, lean, muscled manhood. The dark circles around his eyes were darker than ever, the melancholy face, somewhat vapid in his youth, seemed now a statement on the very process he was enacting. Time and again, his character tried to solve a physical quandary, to leap out of a hole, to run from the scene, only to be mired by gravity. The stage was strewn with sand, and he could not move quickly if he wanted to but walked the way we all walk in sand, sinkingly, listingly, lifting the feet high with the literalism of a child.

Neil and I went to the nearest bar for drinks after the performance. We drank a lot, for the various reasons that one does in this stage of life: excitement, disappointment, the desire to forget responsibility, and because the drinks are better in New York, and it's fun to blow money on them. Unfortunately, inebriation's levity ends in gravity's reassertion. We went back to the apartment we stay in on the Upper West Side, where there are a great many white fluffy pillows on the bed, and by the time we'd removed these one by one and piled them carefully on the floor in balanced towers, collapsed. There was no showing off my uplifted titties that evening.

The next day, however, saw a resurrection, and the proper admiration of my newly trussed beauties. All has not fallen; all is not yet lost — we are only *middle* aged, a dullish thing to be, but relatively painless. We still manage the table every day, though it wants to cave in on us; we bruise ourselves but don't, as yet, bleed profusely. As one of the clowns in the company says, their shows can be thrilling because an audience member leaves and feels, "I saw somebody try something and fail and survive." And go on to try again: which is precisely life's futility, as Beckett saw it. Bravo.

KATHLEEN KIRK

Grudge

I always like to think I'm someone
who doesn't hold a grudge

and then the truncated branch of geranium
broken by the houseguest

in the hanging pot I'd brought indoors
and kept alive all winter

bursts into a tiny clotted bloom
during a heat advisory in its hopeless pot

re-hung from the eaves on the back patio
and I know I'm wrong.

Further evidence: the single furled
blossom of pale pink touch-me-not

on the red stem of twisted, dried-up leaves,
the stem that got a little poison

from next door on a wafting breeze
and not enough water

from me.

KATHLEEN KIRK

Smorgasbord

We're going home from the smorgasbord,
our favorite restaurant, something for everyone,
plus booze,
and my dad's driving too fast, as usual,
coming up too quickly behind the car ahead,
having to break suddenly or swerve,
throwing us around in the back seat.
I'm angry, I'm the oldest, I have to be responsible
if the parents won't be. "You're drunk,"
I say. "Let Mom drive."

But Mom has sudden wet cow eyes,
turning to me over her white shoulder.
"I'm the one who's drunk," she says,
and the air presses down like a pillow
for the rest of our lives, smothering
protest or accusation if we want to keep
eating the sausages and cornbread squares,
rick-racked cheese and carrot sticks,
chicken and cling peaches, limitless
chocolate pudding, a whole corridor
of choices, yes, the whole array.

CHRISTINE SNEED

Words That Once Shocked Us   *Fiction*

At the call center down in the windowless basement of Clean n' Soft's sales and marketing department, with its clicking coffee machine and eerily glowing man-size box that if fed the right coins will disgorge fattening snacks like Snickers bars and Lorna Doone cookies during good weeks, waxen donuts and filling-ruining peanut chews during bad, there are five of us who earn our livelihoods working twenty-five to forty hours per week. The youngest among us is twenty-one, the oldest seventy-two. It is the two people in the middle, Sam and myself, who refuse to reveal our ages, but Kim, who is twenty-one, and Britt, who is seventy-two, happily answer any coworker's question about their ages, love lives, driving records, and weight-loss anxiety. Rachel, who started just two days before I did, is thirty-two. I turned forty a week ago, but even when bribed with cake and Pepsi and a few thoughtful presents — a gift card for movie tickets, an electronic Yahtzee game, and a clover-green scarf that Britt knitted for me after work while watching episodes of *Days of Our Lives* that she Tivos during the day — I refused to tell them that I was turning forty. It seems a strange thing to be — so far removed from childhood and adolescence, some of which is still so vivid in memory, and also past the safest era for bearing children. Forty is more likely than not the midpoint of my life, if I am lucky enough, that is, to live for another four decades.

Employee turnover in the basement of Clean n' Soft is high, considering the not-generous pay and benefits, and the data entry we're required to do when not performing the often thankless task of taking calls from rude or distraught strangers, but Sam has worked in the call center for a whopping five years and Britt is closing in on eighteen months. Rachel and I have been here for almost six months, Britt's birthday scarf possibly begun before I was even hired, but she has said that she plans ahead, stockpiling gifts in her closet for last-minute birthday and hostess gifts. She plays bridge with seven other women she has been meeting on Tuesday mornings for thirty years. She always brings a gift for that week's hostess, though not everyone in the group does, something she knows is reasonable enough, but it is not her way. More than at past jobs, I feel close to my four coworkers at Clean n' Soft, even if we aren't all together eight hours a day. Rachel and I arrive at eight-thirty on weekday mornings and work until five, and Sam comes in at noon and stays until eight-thirty at night, with

Kim and Britt working part-time, their hours different on different days, but usually three of us are here to answer the call center phones and feed regional sales figures — both ours and any competitors' that can be found — into the maw of the company's main frame.

Within our first week of working the WATS line for our soap- and shampoo-company employer, Rachel and I identified four main kinds of callers: the know-it-alls, the neurotics (mostly parents of small children), the kooks, and the lonelyhearts. It is this last category that is sometimes hardest to respond to both affably and professionally, in part because they keep us on the phone for as much time as we will give them. They'll start with a common question, the same kind the neurotics often ask: "Are there any known carcinogens in Quick Clean shampoo?" Or "I got a rash when I used Powerhouse soap the other day and it won't go away. What do you advise?" The answer to the first question is no; the answer to the second is "Please discontinue use for now and call your doctor if the rash persists beyond a few days." Straightforward questions with equally straightforward answers.

But then the lonelyheart will often let out a small, self-conscious laugh and say, "What I really wanted to ask is, how did you get started doing this job? Do you like it? Do you get calls from a lot of wackos? I'd think that you would."

Our training manual has tips for abbreviating calls like the lonelyheart's, which cost Clean n' Soft money because someone has to pay for our toll-free line, but the bigwigs here have managed to cut corners by only paying for calls that come from within the forty-eight contiguous states, and we are told to do what we can to limit calls to five minutes or less (but this can be difficult because, for one, some callers actually have quite a few legitimate questions). Hawaiians and Alaskans have to pay their own way, something that annoys the few people who do call from these far-flung states, but the call center is a courtesy to customers, not a central pillar of the Clean n' Soft business model. It would probably be the first thing to go, along with free soft drinks and fruit juices on Fridays, if we ever fall on harder times. It is relatively expensive to maintain, a fact I don't mention to the Hawaiian and Alaskan grumblers, because I do feel for them. Clean n' Soft is not a free-wheeling company, one that hands out generous annual bonuses to the lesser lights among its staff. And "Customer Comfort Specialists" are indeed among the lesser lights.

Customer comfort. I just love this. Especially when someone calls to say, "Comfort? Who do you think you're fooling? You call this rash comfortable?"

As for the best way to abbreviate a call when we're faced with a lonelyheart's small talk, our training manual prescribes a number of responses. One is that we ask the caller to hold the line for a moment and then leave him in limbo until the blinking red light dedicated to his line goes dim. Another is that we simply hang up on him (while we are in mid-sentence so that it will seem a true accident), and if he calls back, we apologize and tell him that currently we are having technical difficulties and then, mid-sentence, we cut the line again. A third is that we answer his non-product-related questions with a question of our own, repeated until the lonelyheart gets the message: "Do you have any other questions about Powerhouse Soap/Soft n' Clean Laundry Detergent/Quick Clean Shampoo (or Conditioner)/Tub n' Tile Taskforce/Sunshine Dish Liquid . . .?"

There is one other last-ditch tactic in the manual, this one for the chronic repeat offender lonelyheart, "Sir/Madam, I'm sorry, but I now need to speak with another valued customer because there are a number of callers patiently waiting in my queue. But please feel free to call us again if you have a *specific* question about one of our products."

Rachel and I haven't yet found the nerve to use these hardhearted tactics. We are hostages to our sympathetic natures, or else just foolishly patient, rarely cutting off lonelyhearts unless they say something obscene, which, thankfully, does not happen very often. Still, it does happen, and when it does, we laugh over it but sometimes I think about what was said for days afterward.

In the past month and a half, Rachel has acquired an ardent lonelyheart fan, Jack, who says he is in his early fifties and already retired from a career as a stockbroker in Chicago. He also says that he has been a widower for three years and has two grown children. A few days after my birthday, not long before Halloween, Rachel and I are alone in the basement when Jack calls. She gives me a sly smile and puts him on the speakerphone, something she doesn't do too regularly because Sam is often with us, but today he called in sick with food poisoning, an excuse so overused that Rachel and I are sure it's a fib. Jack's voice is deeper than I expect, and there's the hint of an accent I can't place. German maybe, or Italian.

"How are you today, Ms. Rafferty?" he says. "I tried the new Spring Fresh Powerhouse scent like you suggested and it's very nice," he says. "I also want to tell you that my ankle is healing just fine. The doctor says that I can start skateboarding again in a couple of weeks." He laughs and so does Rachel. It looks to me like she's blushing a little, too.

"Do you have a crush on him?" I mouth, raising my eyebrows. Even before now, I had a feeling that she might, but when most of Jack's previous calls came in, I was busy with my own callers or in the bathroom or else loitering in front of the vending machine, trying not to let Flamin' Hot Cheetos win out over the more boring but less fattening Rold Gold Pretzel Twists.

She waves an impatient hand, silencing me.

"I'm glad to hear that," she tells Jack. "I was a little worried that you went waterskiing with your daughter last weekend. But if you're only skateboarding, that's just fine." She laughs again.

"Listen," he says, lowering his voice. "I want to ask you something. But it sounds like you have me on the loud speaker. Is somebody else there with you right now?"

She clicks him back over to the regular line. "You're not on the speakerphone," she says. "The line's just been a little tinny today."

I roll my eyes but she ignores me. He's twenty years older than you, I want to say, feeling vaguely betrayed. The lonelyhearts are the ones we pity, not fall for. Also, she's married.

And only recently — she and her husband, Ben, having signed the marriage license a little over a year ago. Ben is adorable, someone I would have noticed, too, if I'd been lucky enough to meet him at a friend's birthday party like she did. I've seen him a few times when he has come to pick her up, he shyly saying hello and waving when I walk with Rachel out to their red Corolla. They only have one car and sometimes she gets to use it, sometimes not.

"Yes," she says to Jack. "I think I can do that. This Saturday? At the Olive Garden in Coralville? You're sure that's not too far out of your way?"

Right before she hangs up a minute later, my line rings. I answer it, annoyed by the interruption but as always, I use my nice-lady voice. "Yes," I tell the neurotic on the other line. "You can use Quick Clean conditioner with any shampoo. It doesn't have to be Quick Clean shampoo, but we do recommend that you use them together."

To the neurotic's next question, I reply, "It shouldn't give you dandruff if you mix and match shampoos and conditioners, but you'll get the best results if you use Quick Clean hair products together. We recommend Quick Clean conditioning spray, too. It's excellent for getting out tangles."

Rachel is on another call when I finish with the neurotic, someone who might have been a twelve-year-old crank caller rather than a real neurotic; there was a lot of muffled giggling and rustling in the background during our conversation, but I ignored it. I can hardly accuse a caller of cranking me, even when it's clear that's what the person is doing. "Would you recommend using Quick Clean detangler on my pubes?" "What if I stick a bar of Powerhouse Soap up someone's tailpipe? Would their car backfire?" One week not long after I started, there were so many ridiculous questions that I complained to our boss, Mr. Lambert, who sits in an office with four big windows three floors above the basement and looks at sales reports when he's not checking up on us. He gave me a strange look and said, "Well, Marcie, I'm sure you can handle it. That's what we hired you for, after all."

For a number of reasons, it was not a good idea to complain. Sam and Britt were certain that the call center would be shut down if Mr. Lambert or anyone else started to keep track of how many pranksters and how many legitimate callers we have each week. There really aren't too many crank calls, but we do have outbreaks from time to time, as if the whole graduating class at Coralville's high school is pulling a senior stunt before they go on to college or jobs at the mall.

It's several minutes before both Rachel and I are off the phone and I can grill her about what happened with Jack. "Is he coming to see you?" I ask.

For a long second, she doesn't look at me, but when she finally does, I can see that she's embarrassed. "Yes, he is. He's coming to visit his son who's a professor at the university and he asked if I wanted to meet for lunch."

I feel sort of strange when I hear this. I'm worried for her, but also, I suppose, a little jealous. "Does he know you're married?"

She looks down at the notepad she's scribbling on, one we're supposed to use to record names and addresses when we need to send someone a coupon or a free sample. "It's only lunch," she says. "It's not a date."

"So he doesn't know about your husband."

She shakes her head. "No, but does he need to? I just thought it'd be fun to hang out with him for a little while. Everyone needs a new friend, don't they?"

"Oh Rachel," I say, trying to keep my voice light. "That's how it always starts."

"I've never been unfaithful to Ben."

"I would hope so. You've only been married for a year."

She hesitates. "We almost never have sex anymore."

When I open my mouth, no words come out, only a little croak of surprise.

"We used to do it every day," she says, blushing. "But now it's like twice a week. Maybe three if I'm lucky."

I almost laugh but I can see that she isn't kidding. "That's not so bad," I say, falsely cheerful. "Before Tim and I got divorced, we probably did it once a month. Which I suppose is one reason he started having sex with someone else. If you took a poll, I bet you'd find that a lot of married people would say that twice a week is very good. Even exceptional."

This is the first time in the six months we've known each other that she has spoken so openly about her sex life. Any complaints about Ben have always been more or less G-rated — his mother calls too often and he's afraid to tell her to give it a rest for a while; he won't let Rachel kill flies or spiders — they all have to be taken outside and released behind their apartment building. She also wishes that he made more money as a music teacher at an elementary school here in Iowa City, enough so that they could start thinking about having a baby, because at thirty-two her ovaries probably aren't going to cooperate for much longer. I've told her that she has at least ten more years, maybe even twelve or thirteen, but she doesn't want to use hormone treatments. "I've heard they make you fat and grouchy. No drugs. I want to get knocked up the old-fashioned way."

"When's the last time you had fun with a guy?" she asks.

"What kind of fun?" I say.

"You know." She rolls her eyes suggestively.

"It's been a while."

In fact, it has been a couple of years, since Tim left me, back when I was fifteen pounds lighter and still in my thirties and using my degree in accounting to earn a living. When they closed the tax auditing service I worked for, I couldn't get another accounting job no matter how hard I tried. Every one that I interviewed for had at least fifty applicants, some much more experienced than I was, which is how I ended up in my current circumstances: living on the top floor of my great aunt Judy's creaky old house and talking to kooks and lonelyhearts and neurotics for $11.65 an hour, telling them that they shouldn't gargle Sunshine Dish Liquid when they're out of mouthwash because it will make them sick. "Yes, sick sick," I told the kook who asked me this. "Like you might need your stomach pumped sick." His reply: "Is this stuff actually safe for me to wash my dishes with? Because it sounds dangerous." Not a bad question at all, but I could only give him one answer.

"Maybe Jack has a friend I can introduce you to," says Rachel. "Maybe I should call and ask him to bring him along. Do you like older men?"

"I do, but please don't ask him to bring anyone." I look at her flushed face, her dark eyes still avoiding mine if I try to hold her gaze for more than a second or two. "Are you really thinking of running around on Ben? Wouldn't it just be easier to tell him that you want to have sex more often?"

"I'm not going to sleep with Jack. I just want to flirt a little. That's all."

Rachel, you're heading for divorce, I almost say. Don't you see? If you want to stay with Ben, you shouldn't be courting trouble like this.

What I do say is, "You've never been married to anyone but Ben?"

She gives me a funny look. "No, of course not. You knew that."

A moment later, she says, "I'm not a tramp. You shouldn't think that about me."

"I don't."

She regards me. "But you don't approve of me meeting Jack."

"It's none of my business. You should do whatever you'd like. But I do think you're inviting trouble into your life. What if this Jack guy is dangerous?"

"He's not. I googled him. He has a web site. He uses it mostly to write about his beagles, Georgia and Otis." She laughs self-consciously. "He takes them to dog shows. Since he left the Board of Trade, he's been traveling all over with them."

"Lucky dogs, I guess," I say. "What does his son teach?"

"Environmental science. I googled him, too. He's there, like Jack said. His name is Mace Taggart."

"That sounds like a fake name."

"It does, but I guess it's real. He got his PhD from the University of Colorado, which is where I wanted to go, but I had to settle for Iowa because it was a lot cheaper than Boulder. Maybe I'll get to meet him at some point. Maybe you'll get to meet him and he'll be the perfect man for you."

"He's probably married. Or else he's gay."

"No, he's probably divorced."

I look at her and we both laugh. "Probably," I say.

A couple of things happen on Saturday, the day Rachel is meeting Jack. Kim reports to Mr. Lambert that she has contracted mono and can't work her Saturday morning shift and probably none of her other hours for the next couple of weeks. Even though I'm supposed to take my aunt to play bingo at the Elks (her favorite thing in the world, along with George Clooney movies), I agree to cover the shift because Rachel won't be able to do it, Britt is already scheduled, and Sam isn't answering his phone, being smart enough, unlike me, to know better. Mr. Lambert, in the rare emergency, will cover a few hours, but he is probably off playing golf or visiting his mistress or buying silk socks in Chicago. I have to call and beg seven different friends, some mine, some my aunt's, before one of them agrees to take her to bingo in my stead, and then when I show up at the call center, the coffee pot is filthy, crumbs are scattered all over our work area from either Sam or Kim who both regularly eat Twinkies and Cheetos from the vending machine like they are the purest health food, and Britt is also sick, but she tells me that she only has a cold and didn't think that it warranted calling in sick. I try not to touch my eyes and nose, and also try to apply hand sanitizer every half-hour without her noticing, but eventually she smiles at me and says, "I'm sure you won't catch my cold. You're hearty as a horse, Marcie. Didn't you once tell me that you take that, what's it called? Euronasia?"

"Echinacea. I do, yes, when I remember to."

"You'll be just fine," she says, reaching across the table to pat my hand, which I just put hand sanitizer on. She laughs a little, seeing my face. "Sorry," she murmurs, trying to suppress her smile. She is a pretty older woman, often in good spirits, and frets needlessly about her figure. She's more fit than I am from frequent two-stepping with her long-time boyfriend, Wayne, a man she says she doesn't plan to marry, mostly because they both have houses, ones they've paid off, and the fuss of selling and moving is just too exhausting to consider. There are also his three children, a boy and two girls who don't like her and think she's a gold-digger, which she isn't, but some day she says that she might marry Wayne just to spite his greedy kids.

The second thing that happens on Saturday is Rachel calls around five-thirty, a few hours after I get home from work, and tells me that Jack stood her up and she ate too many garlic breadsticks and got drunk on white Zinfandel at the Olive Garden. Ben had to come pick her up, too, which wasn't so easy to do because she had their car.

"What did Ben say about you being drunk at the Olive Garden by yourself on a Saturday afternoon?" I ask. "Did you even tell him you were going there?"

"I told him I was doing some shopping and that I might have lunch afterwards. So, no, he wasn't surprised when I called from there but he didn't like that I was kind of drunk. I still feel a little tipsy."

"Where are you?"

"At home. Ben's out jogging. He wants to run a marathon in the spring."

She wants to fool around on this gorgeous, athletic man? I really don't understand her.

"Has Jack called you?" I ask.

"No, but I was wondering if he called work. I thought maybe he'd lost my cell number."

"Or else he's just too damn cheap to call you on a regular line," I say, irritated. "No, he didn't call."

"I wonder if he's all right."

"I'm sure he is."

"I almost called his son. His email address and office phone are on his department's web site."

"I think it's good that you didn't."

"I was so sad that he stood me up. That's never happened before. Has it ever happened to you?"

"Yes. Once."

"Were you crushed?"

"I suppose I was."

"What happened?"

"It was Tim. I should have known then that he'd be the wrong man to marry. It was our second date. He told me the day after that he'd called and left a message on my machine the night before saying that we'd have to reschedule, but there was no message. He stood me up to go to a Bulls game with some buddies who called at the last minute and said that they had an extra ticket."

"What an asshole."

"I know, but at the time, I refused to believe it."

"Do you want to come over and have dinner with us tonight? It might help put Ben in a better mood. He thinks you're cute."

How nice she is to say this, whether or not it's true. "I don't know," I say. "Wouldn't another night be better?"

"Oh come on. Ben's fine. He's not mad at me anymore. I'll make hamburgers and cook up some hash browns. The way I make them, they're pretty amazing."

My aunt is already ensconced in her easy chair in front of the TV watching some old movie with white guys in face paint playing the Indians; she's eating pickled herring from a jar and carrot sticks for dinner. I was planning to read and watch a movie, too, or maybe go out to one by myself. Most of my friends in town are married, with kids, or else they travel on weekends to other cities to see their lovers (or else host them here). I'm from suburban Chicago, not Iowa City, but I went to college here and eventually met Tim here, and I haven't left, not even for a little while, despite the divorce and faltering job market. I want to go to Rachel and Ben's place, but I also know that it's unlikely Ben will be in the right mood to entertain me or anyone else.

Even so, my boredom or loneliness, or maybe it's fear of becoming a woman much like my solitary aunt (who is kindhearted but sits home most days and watches too much television and has never traveled beyond the Midwest except for two trips to San Francisco with a man who didn't end up proposing in 1965), wins out over reason. "I'm on a diet," I tell Rachel, "but all right, I'll come over. I can only eat salad though. I'll bring it."

"OK," she says. "If you insist. This'll be fun, Marcie. I promise."

They live about two miles from me, in a brick apartment complex with a dozen units, theirs on the second floor, and when Marcie buzzes me in, the first thing I notice in the stairwell is the overwhelming smell of buttered popcorn. My stomach leaps, always hopeful, and I know then, salad or no, that I'm going to eat everything they put in front of me, and seconds, too. I feel more defiance than dread, even as I notice my thighs chafing against the seams of my jeans. Still, I could probably run a marathon, too. I could be like Ben and start training and burn down the fat cells my body doggedly persists in carrying from one day to the next. And maybe I will. Maybe if I change my routines and the way I look, my life will be better. I will find a new job and a nicer man than Tim, one who will not stop for pizza on his way home from work when he knows that I'm making us something special for dinner, one who will not sleep with his much younger coworker and leave me for her before leaving her for one of her even more dimwitted friends. Maybe I will run and run and it will clear my mind of all the self-doubt and angry grudges and petty fears, and l will become a better judge of character and also find the guts to tell the crank callers just where to stick it when they ask if I've ever tried soaping my "boobs and beaver" with Sunshine Dish Liquid. Maybe I will become so healthy and cute that a promoter for an energy bar formulated specifically for middle-aged women will see me at a race and ask if I want to be their new spokesmodel.

These things happen. Apparently they do.

Ben answers the door in khaki shorts and a Cubs T-shirt, his dark blond hair falling in his eyes. He is so good-looking that I feel nervous and sweaty-palmed the second I see him. He smiles and leans in close, but I pull back until I realize that he's trying to kiss my cheek, both of us laughing a little. He smells wonderfully of shaving cream; it has been so long since I've gotten close enough to a man to smell his freshly shaven face that I have to stop myself from asking him to stay where he is for a few seconds longer. "Thanks for coming, Marcie," he says after he manages to kiss my cheek. "I hope you're not allergic to cats. Did Rachel tell you that we have two?"

"I'm not allergic at all. I love cats."

"Good, because they're not like most cats. They're actually friendly and will demand that you pet them."

"What are their names?"

"June and Mimi."

"That's so cute," I say.

"They're my grandmothers' names. I think the lazy beasts are on the couch in the living room. You can go in and join them if you don't mind. Rachel's finishing up in the kitchen."

"Does she need any help?"

He shakes his head. "No, we're almost ready."

I give him the salad I've brought, and with a dimpled smile, he takes it and disappears into the kitchen. The cats are both curled up on a forest green couch that dominates the living room, right where Ben said they would be. The living room also appears to be the dining room; a card table has been set up a few feet from the couch, plates and forks already arranged on it. I stand for a moment and look at June and Mimi, both of them peering back at me impassively. They are pretty cats with thick, healthy-looking fur, one gray-striped, the other solid black. The black one yawns and squeaks adorably as she does, then closes her eyes, having decided that I don't need further monitoring.

"Marcie," Rachel calls from the kitchen. "What do you want to drink? We have Rolling Rock and Coke."

"Coke," I say. "Diet if you have it."

"There's only regular."

"That's fine."

She brings the Coke half a minute later and whispers, "He called. He said one of his dogs was sick and he had to take her to the vet. He wants us to meet tomorrow instead."

"He does? Do you believe his excuse?"

"I don't know if I do, but I told him that I thought I'd be able to meet him."

"Do you really want to give him another chance to stand you up?" I set the Coke on the table. "I don't know why you want to risk losing Ben for some stranger who called to ask if he could use Powerhouse soap to spot-clean his sofa."

"Are the hash browns done?" Ben calls from the kitchen. "They look like they're starting to burn."

"Take them off the stove," Rachel yells. "They're done." She looks at me and whispers, "I'm not sure if I'm going yet. Ben wants to drive up to Cedar Rapids for a concert at Coe College tomorrow afternoon. I told him last week that I'd go."

"You should. Jack can stick it."

"Ben will need the car, but I could take the bus or ride my bike to meet him."

"That's hardly the issue."

"I know. I'm still thinking it over."

Ben comes in with a platter of hash browns and my salad bowl and sets them on the table next to my Coke. Both of the cats jump down from the sofa and run over to him, the black one leaping up to paw his leg. "This isn't for you, Junie," he says. "You little glutton. You already ate." June meows and Mimi stands mutely, tail swishing, staring up at him with her glowing green eyes. My aunt had a cat for a while but he was a foul-tempered codger named Dragonfly who hissed if you got within ten feet of him. When she had to put him down last spring, I felt bad for her, but not so much for him.

"Stop it, you two," Rachel says, shooing the cats back to the sofa. They actually listen, but while we eat, I can feel them staring at us, an occasional pitiful meow escaping their furry throats.

Rachel chatters about a night class in basic photography that she's thinking of taking at the high school, and Ben tells us about his attempts to get second-graders to play the recorder without one of them hitting an ear-splitting note for an entire round of "Mary Had a Little Lamb." The age difference between us is only eight years, but I feel a lot older and much more tired than they seem to. I don't know if either of them has any idea of the disappointments coming their way — ones they will suffer as a couple, as aspiring artists, and maybe as parents, if they make it that far. I look at Rachel, at her animated, pretty face, no wrinkles yet that I can see. I look at Ben, too, his surfer beauty so rare for our small Midwestern city, and before I can stop myself, I glance at Rachel again and say, "Don't go tomorrow. Just don't."

She stares at me, alarmed. Her eyes widen in a silent plea.

Ben is bewildered. "Don't go where? To Coe College? Did Rachel tell you we were planning to see a concert up there?"

My face burns fiercely. "No," I croak. "I mean, don't go in to work if Mr. Lambert calls and asks you to fill in for Kim like I did today."

Rachel is still staring at me mutely but Ben laughs and says, "No, she won't go in if he calls. I won't let her."

"We could use the money," she says, recovering herself. "If he calls, I should go in."

I realize then that I have just inadvertently given her an alibi — she can tell Ben that she is going to work to cover for Kim and even have him drop her off before he goes to his concert in Cedar Rapids, and then she can have Jack the lonelyheart beagle lover pick her up and take her to the Olive Garden or the Motel 6 or wherever it is he plans to take her.

"I thought we'd already made up our minds to go to Cedar Rapids and have dinner up there too," says Ben.

"We'll see, OK? If Mr. Lambert calls, I'll probably have to say yes."

"Don't answer the phone," he says.

Rachel regards him. "I'll see. Maybe he won't call."

"But maybe he will," he says, distraught.

The hamburger I'm chewing tastes ashy now, and it's all I can do to get it down. Rachel's appetite doesn't seem to have suffered, though, and Ben is managing to eat a second heap of hash browns. He glances up from his plate and says, "When Rachel first started at the call center, I loved hearing what kinds of calls she'd get each day. We have this list called 'Words That Once Shocked Us,' and we can only put words on it that we've heard at work. I don't hear too many at the school because I'm not a recess monitor, but I do hear some. What about you, Marcie? Are there any words you can think of for our list?"

"Don't bother her with that, Ben. It's boring," says Rachel.

"It is not boring," he says. "It's awesome."

"What words are on your list?" I ask, very curious.

"Pussy," says Rachel, drinking from her Rolling Rock.

"That word still kind of shocks me," I say. "It's so, well, it's so vivid." I laugh. "I mean, it just sounds nasty."

"I like it," she says. "Always have."

"Me too," says Ben.

"A lot of people probably do," I say. "What are some of the others?"

"Faggot," says Ben. "Dildo. Those are both from my school. I heard a third-grader using them on a second-grader in the hall outside my classroom. She got a two-day after-school detention and the principal called her parents."

"Jesus H," I say. "Rough crowd."

He laughs a little. "I know. A few of them are pretty hardcore."

"Someone asked me about my beaver the other day," I say, blushing for what feels like the hundredth time in the past hour.

"Really?" Rachel gasps. "You didn't tell me that."

"You were on break when it happened, and Sam was there, so I didn't want to say anything when you got back."

"Beaver's such a strange-sounding word," says Ben. "I like it though. It's kind of charming."

"For months after Tim told me he wanted a divorce, the word adultery shocked me," I say.

"Adultery is shocking," Ben agrees. "But if you didn't hear it at work, it doesn't really qualify for our list."

Rachel looks toward the couch, staring at the staring cats, but I can see that her face is pinker now than it was a moment ago.

"No, I guess it doesn't," I say.

"Fuckwad," says Rachel. "That's another one."

"That's also from my school," says Ben. "I guess I've heard more shocking words there than I thought."

"Time to get out the bar of soap," I say. "Tell the potty mouths to line up."

"Ha! Yes," says Ben. "I wish we could get away with it. Some of those kids could definitely use it."

"Let me get dessert," Rachel says abruptly, standing up. "We've got chocolate chip cookies and vanilla ice cream. You'll have some, won't you, Marcie?"

We don't exactly linger over dessert. Rachel eats hers fast and takes her bowl back into the kitchen before Ben and I are halfway done with ours. When she returns, there is no offer of coffee or tea, and it's clear that she's ready for me to be on my way, whereas Ben seems in no rush to bring the evening to a close. It's not yet nine o'clock but she yawns and says how tired she is, though I can hardly blame her. I have done her no favors tonight, except for the accidental alibi, which makes me a little sick to my stomach to think about. She will use it, I'm sure, if she decides that she really does want to meet this Jack character with the college-professor son and the show-dog beagles.

"Do you want to play Scattegories?" Ben asks after we've finished dessert, ignoring his wife's fake fatigue. "I love that game, but it's not as much fun when it's only the two of us."

I don't plan to stay, but I look at my friend to see her reaction. She shakes her head. "No," she says. "Count me out. I'm going to bed, and maybe I'll be the one to get up to go running at six-thirty while you sleep in."

"I'm getting up then too," says Ben.

"I should probably go home," I say. "I like to check on my aunt before ten to see if she needs anything before she goes to bed."

"That's so nice of you," he says.

"I don't know," I say, abashed. "She lets me rent the top floor of her house for half of what she could charge."

"I'll walk you out," says Rachel.

"Where's the fire?" says Ben. "Relax, baby. You don't need to go to bed this second, do you?"

"It's fine," I say. "I should head home. Thanks so much for dinner. It was delicious."

"Do you like to run too, Marcie?" he asks. "You could go with us sometime if you do."

"Thanks. Maybe I will."

He gets up from the table to hug me goodbye, but I feel awkward because Rachel is watching us and I know she's mad at me.

"Thanks for coming over," he calls after us. "It was fun."

The hallway still smells like popcorn, and I can see that Rachel is

Fifth Wednesday Journal • 53

furious. "What were you trying to do?" she hisses as soon as we're in the stairwell that leads down to ground level. "I haven't even cheated on Ben and you're acting like I made a deal with the devil or something. You're my friend, remember? Not my husband's. Ben has his own friends."

Before I realize what's happening, I've started to cry. Rachel stares at me, confused and annoyed, before worry softens her face. She puts a hand tentatively on my shoulder. "I'm sorry, Marcie. I didn't mean to yell at you."

"I'm sorry," I say, wiping roughly at my cheeks. "Just ignore me. I'd better go." I turn away, but she tightens her grip on my shoulder.

"Just tell me what you were thinking earlier when you made that comment about adultery," she says. "Do you have a crush on Ben? Do you want him to divorce me?"

I shake my head. "No, of course not. I just want you both to be happy. I wish you'd never given that Jack guy the time of day. I'm sure he's a creep."

She sighs. "I understand your concern, but it's really none of your business."

"You're right," I say. "It isn't."

"Don't take this the wrong way," she says, "but you shouldn't take your unhappiness out on other people. I know your husband cheated on you and he's an asshole, but I'm not like him, and Ben's not you."

I look at her but say nothing. Of course he's not, I could say. But despite what you think, you are like my husband. He had excuses, too. He didn't think he was doing anything wrong until he had done so many things wrong that no one with half an ounce of sanity would have said that he was blameless. There are always excuses. We will never suffer a shortage.

"Thanks for dinner," I say. "I'll let you get to bed."

"You're welcome," she says, uncertain now. "Don't be mad at me. I'm just tired and I only want to have a little fun. That's all."

"You should do whatever you want. I won't say anything about it anymore. Goodnight."

"Goodnight, Marcie." She hugs me and then I go down the stairs and out to my car with its ailing muffler. On the drive home, I notice a lot of students walking in groups of three or four, many of them in red and white, the university's colors. I haven't been a student in eighteen years, but I'm still here. I have been married and divorced here. I have become an adult here, whatever that really means. A wave of exhaustion rolls over me as I drive slowly back to my rented rooms and elderly aunt, to the clothes that don't fit me so well anymore, to the hairbrush on the dresser with all of its fine graying hairs. I will use it before bed. There are routines that bring me comfort. There are people I have loved without them knowing it. So many more than seems sane or worthwhile. What do you do with so much heartfelt but unessential affection, I wonder. Because I doubt there is a remedy.

PHILIP APPLEMAN

Seeing Robert Wadlow

Imagine those seasons of mist:

Amos n Andy   Romeo n Juliet

Lum n Abner   Pride n Prejudice . . .

And then, on a day as quiet as a quilt,

as flat as felt, as dreary as dirt — on a day

when nothing at all could possibly happen,

right there in the hazy streets

of South Bend, Indiana —

he loomed up . . .

We'd had all those second-hand thrills:

Charles Atlas's leopard-skin pecs,

The Lone Ranger's bone-chilling call, etcetera —

but this — this was something completely

different — not just *here* and not just "big,"

but World-Class, World-Record BIG:

you could jump in his shoes, grab the oars,

and row away from the dock,

you could snitch his shirt, prop your posts,

and pitch a tent for the family,

you could — oh, anything,

anything at all was possible, once

your very own eyes had seen

the tallest man in all the world,

in all of history, not

some pop-eyed desert nomad's wild

exaggeration, but a real-for-sure Goliath,

eight-feet-eleven

in his two bare feet, no guesswork here,

but reality, measured with yardsticks

and tapes . . .

And afterward — what then? Well,

Back to the fuzzy radio, back to the books,

Fibber n Molly   Antony n Cleopatra,

Benny n Hope   Keats n Shelley —

and to read, one drizzly day,

that foghorn, Dr. Johnson, saying,

"A man who has seen the Great Wall of China

is superior to all other men" — and realizing,

after all those years, that Robert Wadlow

was our own Great Wall of China,

come into our soggy lives

to leave behind him mountain peaks, pleasure-

domes, and gardens in the mist.

JOE MENO

The Future *Fiction*

At the Annual Association of Progressive Psychoanalysts Mid-Winter Meeting, a minor catastrophe is taking place. Everyone in the Association of Progressive Psychoanalysts is present for the conference dinner, all but the guest speaker, Dr. Toshiro, whose plane, having originally departed from Tokyo, is still circling the pink snow above the midwestern municipality where the convention is now underway. In the airplane several thousand feet above, Dr. Toshiro flips through his note cards, rehearsing his speech; some of the cards are blue, some pink. He does his best not to get upset, but when he finds his foot shaking nervously, tapping at the back of the seat in front of him, he takes one of the note cards from the stack and begins folding it, following the ancient, sequential art of origami. His breath slows. The sound of the airplane becomes the sound of his own thoughts: Do not fear the future. All is not over, all is not lost.

But things have begun to go badly in the middle of the burnished banquet hall back on the earth below. At Table One, Dr. Bernhard, the eldest of the conventioneers, has been served soup before everyone else and is now eating; the soup is a murky split pea, and stains the corners of the formidable white beard he wears, giving his otherwise somber expression an entirely fraudulent look. Everyone takes notice, staring at Dr. Bernhard out of the corners of their eyes, marking down an illegible note to themselves in the various notepads they have placed in their laps, because, everyone present knows, it is a great offense to begin eating before the formal recitation of the Oath of Psychoanalytic Health. Dr. Bernhard, aged ninety-two, then smears the soup from the side of his mouth with a cloth napkin and accidentally spills several drops onto the pristine sleeve of Dr. Edel, who is sitting beside him. Poor Dr. Edel. Dr. Edel, tall, somber, narrow-faced behind her rigid, oblong glasses, practices the controversial Rejavik method of analysis, and only ever wears white. Her office is floor to ceiling white, and her prescription for her patients is to adopt the same color palette while they are in "transition," white clothing, white food, white furniture, an aesthetic means to purify their thoughts and feelings. Dr. Edel stares down at the green splotch, looking aghast. Immediately her white cheeks go crimson. She departs from the table staring at the stain as if she has been mortally wounded.

At table Two, the Jungian table, Dr. Wiseman tastes the soup and finds it is full of black pepper. The roof of his mouth seems to be seizing and convulsing. He lifts his eyebrows and raises an accusatory finger to Table Three, where the Post-Jungians all watch his displeasure and laugh haughtily to themselves.

At Table Four, the Consortium of Silent Therapists — analysts who all believe a therapist's best advice is not to speak at all — look at the goings-on of their colleagues with a quiet displeasure. When an analyst from Table One comes and steals their dinner rolls, none of them are able to complain.

At Table Five, a psycho-linguist named Dr. Dipthar speaks unceasingly in a language of his own invention, one without the common, depression-inducing connotations of English, or, say, Russian. Dr. Dipthar has hazy, uncommonly-bad breath, which is certain to affect the mental health of his tablemates. When he asks for someone to pass him the salt, no one can understand a word he is saying.

At Table Six a Future-Modernist records his tablemates' conversation on a tape recorder, and examines it for future study.

At Table Seven the dream analysts all remark how the tomatoes in the salad make them think of a breastfeeding mother. Or death. Possibly everything — even their odd reflections in the silverware — reminds them of death.

At Table Eight the Israeli Confederation of Psychiatrists learns there is ham in the split pea soup. Dirty looks pile up like dinnerware, dirty looks upon dirty looks.

At Table Nine two Primitive-Animalists are eating with their hands, nodding at each other from behind their animal-shaped masks.

At Table Ten, three psycho-somatists, who have ingested large quantities of prescription sleep aids, as is their method of practice, believing sleep is the most curative of all therapies, snooze soundly throughout the entire dinner service.

Everyone in the Association of Progressive Psychoanalysts is present, all but Dr. Toshiro, whose plane is still circling above the pink snow. Up in the airplane, Dr. Toshiro continues to fold his pink note-card, and when he is done, the card has become a thin, origami deer. The deer has antlers and a tail. Origami is a meditation practice which Dr. Toshiro recommends to all of his patients: at least one hour of origami each day. Dr. Toshiro considers the deer but feels his nerves are no calmer. Why is Dr. Toshiro so upset? Though he has a relatively minimal fear of flying — as much as any rational person when confronted with the truth of human flight — which is, let us be fair, a completely irrational, unpredictable endeavor, though he is, at the moment, late for the conference, and missing his speech, Dr. Toshiro's face is a steely knot of nerves and obvious distraction for another reason. Dr. Toshiro has traveled the greatest distance to attend the convention, over four thousand miles, first, from the nearly uninhabited Pacific Island of Got, where he has been studying the sexual customs of a tribe of somewhat cannibal pygmies for the last twelve years, back home to Nagasaki, to celebrate his great-grandmother's birthday — his great-grandmother whose shadow was forever separated from her during the atomic firestorm of 1945 — then after a slice of plum cake with his great-grandmother, back to the island of Got to take part in the fertility ritual, in which the people of Got bury themselves up to the neck in mud, then back to Tokyo to deliver a paper at the Institute on Sexual Relations entitled "The Penis Gods of Got," and then back into the air once again, convention ticket in hand, circling round and round the midwestern American city where, a few thousand feet below, his few colleagues are now all finishing their meal. Why has Dr. Toshiro traveled from so very far way?

If we look inside his briefcase, we can see a large framed photo from last year's meeting of the Annual Association of Progressive Psychoanalysts. Third row, fourth from the left, there is Dr. Toshiro, looking esteemed in his wool coat and well-trimmed black beard. Beside him is Dr. Duras of Paris, who is a pale impression of a woman, with tightly combed hair, large, liquid blue eyes, and a smile that would rather not identify itself as such. Dr. Duras's chin almost rests on Dr. Toshiro's shoulder in the photo. In fact, if one were to look closely, they might see Dr. Duras's bare elbow brushing against the back of Dr. Toshiro's hand. Days later, Dr. Duras emailed her colleague and said that this was no mistake. No mistake. She been a great follower of his work for some time, particularly the paper he had written about his avant-garde origami treatment, and then, at the end of this otherwise professional email, she wrote, "I have been finding myself wondering what it would mean if we were to touch." Beneath the photograph of the entire consortium of smiling and unsmiling psychoanalysts, rests this selfsame email. Dr. Toshiro retrieves the single piece of paper, rereads it for the one thousand, five hundred and thirty-fifth time, and then grins, his beard bristling with excitement. He takes a deep breath and begins to fold the page into a delicate white doe, and places it beside the paper stag. The plane continues to circle around and around through the tufts of pink snow, awaiting permission to land.

But what do we see here, back in the confines of the convention room?

Alone, at Table Eleven, the dinner service is ending and Dr. Duras is still waiting. She stirs her fizzy tonic water around and around, trying to imagine what might be keeping Dr. Toshiro. She sneaks her iPhone into her lap and carefully pages through the email which Dr. Toshiro sent to her only a week ago.

"I hope we can, during the time allotted during this year's convention, become better acquainted, and to see if there is indeed a possibility you might feel the way I feel."

Dr. Duras looks around at the other banquet tables, sees her colleagues carrying on, joking, having fun, feels a pang of anxiety echo within her stomach, and searches for something, anything to fold into a neutral origami shape. There is a roll, an uneaten bowl of soup, an untouched plate of a salad, a cloth napkin, and her glass of tonic water, none of which are suitable mediums for the restorative art of origami. She sighs and looks again at the tables around her, wondering what could be keeping Dr. Toshiro. Waiters and waitresses dart in between the tables, serving the last course, a bowl of pink ice cream. Dr. Duras leaves her ice cream untouched. She wanders out of the banquet hall, out of the hotel entirely, finding herself standing on a remote expanse of snow-covered lawn. It is a golf course. Placing her arms in front of her chest, stomping through the cold, she startles a mother deer and two fawns, their breath trailing behind them like fog.

Back inside the banquet hall, utter chaos has erupted. At the lectern at the head of the banquet hall, Dr. Polvis asks, "Dr. Toshiro? Dr. Toshiro? Does anyone know what has become of Dr. Toshiro? Dr. Toshiro? Dr. Toshiro?"

A Tragic Realist stands and declares, "Disappointment is the only truth we can count on. We can always safely assume the worst. I believe Dr. Toshiro may be dead."

An Irrational Optimist stands and announces, "We have no reason to hope and yet hope we must. We must believe Dr. Toshiro will join us soon. Let's all close our eyes and picture him walking safely through those doors. Please. Let's all try."

Just then a Spontaneous-Ontologicalist falls to her stockinged knees in prayer, imploring others to do the same. "All we can do now is put our faith in the Lord above. Only he can show us the error of our ways. Who would like to join me in a prayer of apology?"

Moments later, an Eastern European schematicist declares "Dr. Toshiro is a myth we have created to placate ourselves. Like our ideal selves, he does not exist. We must stop waiting for Dr. Toshiro and begin living our lives now."

Moments after that, a blind Anti-Empiricist declares, "How do we know Dr. Toshiro is not here among us? Because we do not see him with our eyes? Because we do not hear his voice in our ears? Because we do not feel his breath upon our lips? What fools we are. All of us, yes, all of us, are Dr. Toshiro."

Moments later, a leery Hypnotist stands and swings a large gold watch back and forth, muttering, "Try to remain calm. You are all getting sleepy. Very sleepy."

Finally, a member of the Professional Society of Psychoanalytic Reenactors, dressed in the garb of Sigmund Freud, lights a large pipe, arranges his beard, and declares the hotel bar is now open. Several other analysts, who — as part of their professional practice — dress as Sigmund Freud, all light their pipes and begin to applaud.

The meeting is ended thusly.

After several hours, Dr. Toshiro's airplane is finally given permission to land. He arrives at the hotel around one a.m., though, by then, most of the evening's proceedings have come to a close. All that are left are a few drunk psychoanalysts commingling with even drunker psychoanalysts at the unnamed hotel bar. Brief, ill-planned arguments break out and then are just as soon forgotten. Former rivals lean in close to divulge their patients' most contestable secrets. Light flees the tiny hotel bar, and without light, even stranger things begin to occur. Awkward hairy hands make their way beneath even more awkward gray-knit sweaters. Stiff white beards brush up against stiff red beards. Two interns kiss, and then, almost immediately, begin to analyze their feelings in regard to the kiss, free-associating in a shameful sort of rhyming love poetry. Dr. Toshiro looks around the small hotel bar, feeling a deep, abiding, professional shame. He snatches his laminated name-tag from his suit-coat lapel and walks off in a rush.

Along the way he passes a group of Neo-Freudian Feminists who, even at this late hour, are protesting this year's theme for the convention "The Future of Mental Health," as they do not approve of the prefix "men" in the word "mental." Beside the Feminists are the Nudists, a small concern of analysts from California who believe acceptance of one's physical imperfections is tantamount to achieving inner peace. There are only two or three of these nudists, it is hard to tell exactly as Dr. Toshiro does not look at them head-on, all of them old, their withered genitalia looking like meek townspeople stranded beneath avalanches of white hair and rounded bellies. Dr. Toshiro hurries on, giving them all a vague nod.

Back in the marbled lobby, Dr. Toshiro unfolds Dr. Duras's email and quickly scans it, looking for the number of her hotel room. Room 453. He nods to himself and then rushes into the elevators. The golden doors quickly close on his heels. Inside the elevator, Dr. Dunkin Pierce, experimental psychoanalyst from London, is lying on the floor, his tie fixed about his head like a Native American. Dr. Toshiro tries to ignore the debauched, ruddy look on his colleague's face. On the fourth floor, the elevator dings, Dr. Pierce opens his eyes and says, "I believe our hour is up," just before Dr. Toshiro, still embarrassed nods, and hurries out.

Dr. Toshiro's heart, his human heart, is pumping hard. Though he knows this is a physiological response, not a mental one, it's hard in the moment to think of himself as anything but a boy, a teenager again. His palms grow sweaty and he stumbles down the hallway, searching for Room 453. Some of the doors to other hotel rooms have been left open: inside are strange scenes of professional analysts analyzing each other, using the most bizarre, avant-garde methods. In Room 450, Dr. Umwet is dressed up as a polar bear, using animalism to cure a colleague's smoking habit. In Room 451, Dr. Droo has a fellow analyst hooked up to a portable electroshock device. The sounds of his colleague's displeasure reach a near symphonic level. In Room 452, Dr. Amblin is using a doll to try to heal the psychic wounds of one of her associates. "Where did your parents first break you? Point to the spot on this doll and the healing will begin," she announces a little too loudly.

After he passes these open doors, open rooms, Dr. Toshiro suddenly thinks: *What can be so very wrong with us that we need such unconventional methods in order to make ourselves feel any better? When all we really need is. . . .*

Here he does not finish his thought, as he finds himself standing before Room 453. He looks both ways down the hall and then takes a step closer. He coughs once, to check his breath, and then gives a solid knock. He thinks about knocking again but does not. Only then does it occur to him to check his watch: it is 1:45 a.m. This realization nearly undoes him. Who does he think he is, that such a woman as Dr. Gwen Duras would be sitting in her room, flipping through cable channel after cable channel, simply waiting? He begins to knock again and then stops himself. Of course she has gone to bed hours ago. Of course, she is lying in there, refusing to acknowledge the sound at her door. Dr. Toshiro lowers his hand and nods to himself. He picks up his suitcase, turns to face the empty hallway, and begins walking down the hall. Before he makes it a single step, there is the sound of a lock being turned, then the tumult of the heavy hotel door being opened.

There is Dr. Duras in a rumpled cocktail dress, her hair flattened on one side.

"You came," she says. "You came."

Dr. Toshiro nods. He does not smile at first as he realizes how odd it is that the two of them should be standing here, at this moment, only inches apart. A day before, even an hour before, they were so very far apart, and the thought that two people such as they should ever meet, ever think to meet, how funny, how unpredictable it all is. That life, even in this modern world, hinges so much upon chance, that one plane should land and another doesn't, that one taxicab should stop for him while another wouldn't, that one year before, by mere happenstance, Dr. Duras happened to be photographed beside Dr. Toshiro, that their elbows happened to touch, hers against his: but here, here they are, here they now.

Dr. Toshiro feels a little overcome.

Dr. Duras seems to notice and smiles, then says, "Hold on. I want to show you something." She leans inside her hotel room and grabs her coat, a gray parka with a fur-lined hood.

Outside it is still snowing. In the floodlights of the hotel's adjoining golf course, Dr. Duras takes her colleague's hand, and together they make their way past the empty outdoor pool, past a few frozen golf carts, past a tennis court sheeny with ice. About fifty yards up the snow-covered golf course, Dr. Duras stops, leans over, and points.

"Here," she says. Dr. Toshiro looks at the woman's face, her soft cheeks having gone pink, looks back at the bright lights of the hotel, and then down at where Dr. Duras is pointing. Dr. Toshio leans down and there, there in the snow, are a number of hoof prints, deer prints, if he is not mistaken, a series of upside down hearts, gone silver, trailing off toward the woods.

"I saw them and thought of you," Dr. Duras says, as a means of explanation. Dr. Toshiro looks up from the staggered aisle of hoof prints and smiles, an old smile, a smile he hasn't used since he was a boy, and then, hand in bare hand, they make their way forward to see where everything leads.

KIM ADDONIZIO

Divine

Oh hell, here's that dark wood again.
You thought you'd gotten through it —
middle of your life, the ogre turned into a mouse
and heart-stopped, the old hag almost done,
monsters hammered down
into their caves, werewolves outrun.
You'd come out of all that, into a field.
There was one man standing in it.
He held out his arms.
Ping went your iHeart
so you took off all your clothes.
Now there were two of you,
or maybe one, mashed back together
like sandwich halves,
oozing mayonnaise.
You lived on grapes and antidepressants
and the occasional small marinated mammal.
You watched the DVDs that dropped
from the DVD tree. Nothing
was forbidden you, so no worries there.
It rained a lot.
You planted some tomatoes.
Something bad had to happen
because no trouble, no story, so
Fuck you, fine, whatever,
here come more black trees
hung with sleeping bats
like ugly Christmas ornaments.
Don't you hate the holidays?
All that giving. All those wind-up
crèches, those fake silver icicles.
If you had a real one you could stab
your undead love through its big
cursed heart. Instead you have a silver noodle
with which you must flay yourself.
Denial of pleasure,
death before death,
alone in the woods with a few bats
unfolding their creaky wings.

KIM ADDONIZIO

Thank You

for the heavy glass skull
with which I could crush the actual skull
of an intruder, if ever my home were invaded.

Or it may come in handy
for a production of Hamlet
in the event that, late in life,

I take up acting and am chosen for the lead
and find myself by an imagined graveside
pretending to mourn a clown

and philosophizing about Death.
Death hosting the most successful party
because everyone comes,

most people because they have to
but some of them showing up early,
shoving through the door

to gobble all the hors d'oeuvres,
dressed up in nooses and plastic bags,
festooned with blood and razors.

It really is a lovely gift, especially
in the morning when it refracts the light
and seems to burn from within

the way the brain burns in the body,
inventing things both dumb and profound.
The hole carefully trepanned in its center

is meant for a candle, I think,
but I prefer to fill it
with sugar water and set it outside

to see if a hummingbird

will come out of the redwoods,
thinking it is some kind of shiny flower.

But back to Death. Maybe Death
would rather be imagined
as a hummingbird drinking from a skull.

Maybe I should stop thinking about Death.
But you have given me a skull.
But thank you. I am grateful.
Now every hummingbird reminds me of you.

JOHN GALLAHER

In a Landscape: XX

The prompt is that you're supposed to imagine
your favorite food, and then make it a
person, starting at its death, and then pass it
to the person on your left, so I chose you.
Now I'm deep in thought
but not about anything. Maybe the question
is between, "Is the world something you need
to get past?" Or, "Is the world something
you need to accommodate yourself with?" Or maybe
the question is to find out if there's a difference.

Richard just stopped by. He's off to lunch,
where he's going to have his last "solid" before
the procedure tomorrow, so he's going to miss the
office thing tonight. We talked a little about
research. He likes it. I'm ambivalent. I wish
I had more to share at times like this, something
concrete. Like, "Hell, yes!" Or "Damn fine!" But
I just noticed awhile ago walking with Robin
that the little red wax string that used to help one
open a Life-Savers pack seems to no longer
be there. When did that happen?

I just thought to say that I was dragged into a large vacant lot
once, Orange County, California. It would've been
first grade, the year the toddler next door drowned in their
swimming pool, coffin the size of a large suitcase. I don't
remember anything more about it other than I was
dragged into a plywood fort by some other kids. I've often
felt since that I'm being dragged someplace,
and I'm never sure if it's against my will or not.
And how we keep saying things like,
"I left them where I thought they'd be safe."
We went to Disneyland thirty-five times while living there,
and one time I got stuck for forty-five minutes on the Pirates
of the Caribbean ride, right at the "Yo-ho, Yo-ho, a pirate's life
for me" bit. There are many levels to negative experiences,
some really aren't all that bad at all, and you remember the ones
you think about. No one's sure where the rest go.

JOHN GALLAHER

In a Landscape: XXI

In heaven, according to Kurt Vonnegut's
play, *Happy Birthday, Wanda June*, you are
whatever age you were your happiest. Maybe it
wasn't in that play, now that I'm thinking
about it. Well, it was in one of his (or Kilgore Trout's) plays
or books. And I wondered what age I would be there. We all
give ourselves a story to base the narrative of our lives
upon. Let's say we tried to draw circles when we were ten
and our circles were terrible. And then it's one long series
of wobbly completeness. Where to go next?
Let's hope it's a romantic comedy.

Brenda was saying last night that she still has a long list of things
she wants to do and she now realizes, as she's close to 50,
she'll not do them all. Is it more a problem of the past,
or a problem of the future, how perhaps one makes
impractical lists of what one wants to do with one's life
or one travels along without proper attention
to what one is meaning to be doing. "Meaning," and
"to be doing" have always been problems for me. Let's say
for a minute you're 50. Where are you going to live
and what are you going to look like? Let's say now
that you're 10. Same thing. You never know.
And then here we are at a blackboard, everyone watching
and we're attempting our first big circle.

And then there's the flip side, all those other things one does
that don't seem to matter much in Vonnegut's heaven. Both
of my brothers-in-law have spent time in jail, and now
Ben, the oldest, a year or so younger than I am, is in a clinic
of some sort after blowing out the bank account on drugs,
leaving his wife and young daughter destitute, the house in foreclosure,
a little pile of bad checks. Addiction is stronger than love,
some say. Who knows? I'm thinking about his daughter. Her name
is Celeste, meaning "heavenly," from the Latin, and the name of
Babar the elephant's wife. *There's no place to go but up*,
hopeful people say at times like this, but really
there are many directions things can go at any time.

CLINT McCOWN

Today's Lessons in the Animal Kingdom

The horses need more room to run
so I'm pulling fence posts
that divide the larger field.

It's late July, heat shimmering
from the yellow dirt,
and I pace myself, digging a while,
sorting old boards, digging again.

I guess correctly as I turn
the knotted planks, expecting
black widows before finding them.
We're infested here.

I step with purpose on the largest one,
though when I lift my boot she's gone.
I pick my shovel up again.

The job takes longer
than I thought it would,
as most jobs do.
Each inch is earned,
so tight and sure
the stone-like grip of earth.

The horses watch my progress
from a farther field,
flinching against deerflies,
patient in the sun.

The dog watches from the porch,
too wise to leave the shade.

MELISSA FRATERRIGO

Crud Face *Fiction*

The face was disfigured so impressively that others rarely made eye contact with Sidney, and if they accidentally glanced at him, you could see them suck air and look away. Sidney had been that way since the accident, and could have remained at his parents' house beside a grove of trees in the unincorporated section of Elsevier. Instead, he hunched in the front window of the coffee shop on Main Street beneath flags advertising the end-of-summer sales and sipped his coffee, dared them to look his way.

It was his half-day off from Buster's; he didn't have to be at the restaurant until three p.m. From where he sat he could see the triple loop of the Hurricane, the most popular coaster at Glory Days. Just beyond the perimeter of the park the brown water of Lake Erie frothed against the muddy shore. It was noon, but the lights on the coaster and above the tram that traveled from one end of the park to the other were already lit. All day and night the lights winked like some Morse code that Sidney couldn't crack.

He hadn't forgotten boarding the Hurricane that last day in October nearly a year ago, the cool metal bar clamping down on his and Amanda's laps, the rows of pink and yellow lights flashing in a wave, a recording telling them to keep arms and hands inside the ride at all times, their bodies suddenly thrust forward, then hurled up a steep incline, wind picking up as they rose, hair from Amanda's ponytail unleashed, slapping against her cheek and into her open mouth — she was already laughing, that sound like water trickling over stones. Wind skirted over Sidney's sunken cheekbone, the side of his face that hung down, skin shiny but mottled and stretched like taffy that's near ready to snap. The left side of his mouth permanently twisted up like he was trying to spit out a cherry pit.

"Are you ready?" Amanda squealed as they reached the top, squeezing his knee before fastening her hands on the bar.

It was one of the few times she had touched him and he hadn't been able to respond, a lump in his throat barricading any sound. She could do that to him.

How stupid he had been to think she would want to be with him, Crud Face. Amanda Percy and Crud Face?

He blamed his mother. It was easy to do. She had been the one to kiss the top of his head after the accident his eighth grade year, tell him he was loved, that he was no different from anyone else.

You just go and work on your studies. Make something of yourself. Stay in school. You're smart, Sid. In first grade your teacher took me aside, said she'd never met a child with such a wild imagination.

Sidney's mother and dad had only completed the ninth and tenth grades, and they never let him forget it. They spent evenings scrubbing the toilets at the high school, waxing floors, and emptying waste cans. They wore blue shirts with their names in red cursive above the pockets. But then after the accident there were doctor bills and follow-up visits to specialists in Rockford. His mother started doing laundry for rich people, the sight of her standing over a wash basin in the basement, bleaching the yellow pits of some stranger's undershirts, the skin on her hands reddened, tiny cuts etched around her fingernails. No matter how much lotion she applied, the skin grew white and peeled in large, irregular patches.

Because of him. Sidney.

And then she got a cold. Only the runny nose, the wheezing never disappeared until it settled in her lungs and she couldn't walk more than a few steps without stopping to rest. She quit doing laundry, filed papers for disability, and took up residence on the couch beneath a quilt, slept for hours on end, her chest rising and falling like a little animal.

Bad things happen, she is fond of saying. *And you make them a part of your life.*

What then do you do with the guilt? The forever pangs of regret?

For a while, when Amanda Percy was coming up to Sidney's locker and saying "hi!" or waiting for him to pull the paper sack lunch from his locker and then follow him to the cafeteria, sit alongside him as she nibbled on nachos, carrots the size of toes, he had begun to think maybe his mother was right, maybe he could still do something with his life.

What do you want to be after high school? Amanda had once asked, then without waiting for his response had leaned forward, said she wanted to be an executive, wear suits and heels, drive a convertible and live in an apartment in New York City — a really tiny one — said that's how you know you've made it. When you only have space for essentials. *Not like out here*, and she'd waved her hand and he knew she was gesturing at the rows of chicken houses and corn on 200 South, the Super Saver on County Line Road that was three times the size of the Elsevier High School football field; the houses where she and most of their classmates lived were grouped in small treeless subdivisions — then the amusement park appeared out of nowhere, drew RVs and minivans from across the state.

She winked at him conspiratorially as she said it, and inside he'd jumped, but outside he forced his eyes to meet hers, to say: That sounds cool. You'll be good at whatever you do.

Felt her presence the rest of the day. Sidney wanted to take her hand and clutch it to him; he imagined yanking her with such force that her arm popped off and his chest opened up and swallowed her arm, and then she would be disfigured as well, the two of them a perfect pair. And then she'd never leave him. Which was stupid to think of considering he'd never had her in the first place.

It would have been easier if he'd died, which is exactly what he'd been hoping for in the four years since the accident until that first time Amanda Percy looped her arms through his in gym class, said she'd be his partner during badminton and he'd asked her to repeat herself, wasn't certain of what she'd said. *I'll play with you*, she said. *Let's be partners*. Later that week she'd beckoned to him from beneath the gym bleachers, said she saw him looking at her, stepped real close to him, closer than anyone had since the accident, pushed back her shoulders until he couldn't keep from noticing the generous swell of her chest beneath her green phys ed shirt; she smelled sweet and minty, eyelids shaded with two colors of purple, which made the blue of her eyes pop even more. And then she took his trembling hands and placed them over her breasts.

I know you want to. Go ahead.

Frozen. His hands cupping her breasts, the faint tapping of her heart beneath his fingers. How he'd steeled his nerves. Gulped. Then turned and ran, nearly tripped over a metal rail. His breath raspy and shallow, face sweaty.

The night of the accident, he had done exactly what he'd been told. Sidney had finished his English homework and had made himself a grilled cheese with bacon and was planning to spend the rest of the evening watching pro-wrestling on TV. His mom usually called to check on him during their lunch break. He scrubbed and rinsed the pan he used, wiped off the counters and sticky prints on the refrigerator. The commercials ended and music for the start of the match keyed up.

He was hurrying when it happened.

As soon as he heaved the cast iron pan in the cabinet beneath the stovetop, he knew he'd done something wrong. Could hear the insipid hissing, stuck his head further inside the cabinet, was searching for the leak, the flexible tubing he'd punctured, when it blew.

Most of his memories from that night picked up in the hospital in Rockford. He remembered the white sheets and gown, the curtains folded over the windows, the heat glowering from his face like a great oozing eye. There was a nurse in teddy bear scrubs that patted the mattress beside his hip when he woke, gauzy bandage disguising much of his face. *You're all right. Just had a bad accident.* She showed him how to turn the dial on his IV, administer the pain meds. *Nobody needs to be a tough guy around here.*

And the way she'd said it made him believe the injury wasn't too bad, that she'd seen much worse.

Maybe he'd just been hopeful.

But then one week turned into another and not one of his doctors even mentioned his release. His mother made the two-hour drive north alone, always bringing something from home — a handful of comic books, the derby car he made with his dad in third grade, the rock collection his grandfather had given him. She came after her shift at the high school had ended, the pits beneath her eyes dark. She'd stand beside his bed and play with the strap of her purse, absently touching the sheet that covered his leg. She talked about the new stove they ordered and showed him pictures of the cabinets and floor that were being installed in their kitchen. When Sidney's eyes began to tear, his mother shushed him with a quick chop of her hand. *That's why we have insurance*, she said. Then a few moments later she asked if he wanted a pet when he returned home. A bird? A guinea pig? As a boy his mother had always said animals were filthy, that they weren't meant to live alongside humans. How many Christmases had he printed puppy at the top of his list? But nothing she said mattered much. The TV played nonstop in his hospital room, the blue and gray images looping past.

Where was his dad?

Can't trust anyone but your family, his dad always said. But where was he now?

Six and one-half weeks later, his dad entered Sidney's room at the hospital. They were discharging him that day, sending him home with a boxful of ointments, salves, pills, and bandages. His dad took five steps into the room and stopped, Sidney standing there in a new navy sweat suit, tags still dangling from the sleeve. They locked eyes and the ground suddenly felt as if it was spinning, and when it stopped, Sidney sensed a great chasm between them.

He'd never seen his dad cry, the choked sound similar to a horse giving birth, the agony of a body coming undone.

His dad darted out of the room. As the door slowly wheezed shut Sidney heard the rubber-soled shoes of the nurses, gurney wheels on the waxed floors, multiple telephones ringing somewhere in the distance.

Sidney's dad picked up an extra job cleaning office buildings. When they sat down to a meal together, which was now an even greater rarity, his dad kept his eyes on his food. If Sidney said something that begged a response, his dad would look at the outer rim of Sid's ear. Sidney could feel his gaze like a heat lamp illuminating the only normal- looking part of his face.

He liked it best when his parents were at work and he only had to attend to the innocent yapping of the puppy his mother had thrust into his arms after he had been released from the hospital. The nightmares were constant then, and he would be screaming, thrashing inside flames; only he wasn't the one being burned. Here he stood helpless as the stove erupted and his grandfather, mother, and dad were eaten by fire. He stood beside them but was unable to reach out and save them; nightly he was forced to watch them experience the accident he'd survived. Sidney always woke screaming, his mother's cool hand tapping his chest, telling him to wake up. But what he craved was a crushing hug. He wanted her to surround his body with hers, rock him back and forth on the tiny bed just as she'd done when he was a boy. Instead she scooped up the puppy, placed it in his arms. Watched it wiggle in Sid's grasp. *That is one cute pup!* she'd say, rubbing its wet nose with her thumb.

He felt utterly empty. Like he had swallowed some of the flames that had ravaged his face and they had eviscerated his insides as well.

Then after their meeting beneath the bleachers Amanda Percy started dawdling outside his locker, waited for him to gather his books at the end of the school day. Told him she was hungry. *Let's go get something to eat*, tugging his elbow, that flimsy bone buzzing with her heat. They could go to Mighty Gas. They had snacks and drinks there. He had money. *Wanna go to Mighty's?* he asked, kept his chin low.

Everyone will be at Obermeyer's. I've got to have one of their shakes or I'll die. She said things like that: everything was life or death. There was no in between, just a constant glimmering exclamation, every day Christmas morning with its brightly wrapped gifts and expectations.

I can't go there. He said it quietly. He'd never eaten at Obermeyer's after school when everyone was likely to be there. *I can drop you off.*

Puhleez, she said, grabbing onto his sweatshirt. *You look like you could use a monster burger with double cheese.*

And so they went, heart ramming away in his chest, face shiny. He held the door open for her. All the tables filled with kids from their school slurping sodas, eating handfuls of onion rings, laughter and high-fives. A couple embraced in a corner booth. Two guys swatted a paper ball back and forth with their fists. He might have seen more if he'd lifted his eyes from Amanda's leopard-print flats. He did hear a sigh, a subtle pause at the sight of the two of them: beauty and the beast.

He placed their order, paid. Watched the guy behind the counter heap food onto a tray, knew he had more right to be serving fast food than buying it for Amanda Percy.

Sidney watched him place the drinks and straws on the tray, then the paper-wrapped burgers. He felt the color in his face rise. Where had she disappeared? He turned around and saw a sea of normal-looking faces. Didn't trust his arms to carry the tray, his feet to direct them both. He fingered the rim of the tray, baskets of fries still sizzling. He couldn't stay. He would just go back the way they came in, he was thinking, when she came up behind him, *There you are!* Like he'd been hiding all along.

She guided him to a booth behind a fake potted plant a little ways off from everyone else. *Now we can really get to know each other*, she said, popping a fry in her little mouth and winking. *Ya know what I mean?*

He likes the dreams best. In them, the divot in his cheek has been filled, the drooping eye centered. His skin is supple the way it should be, stubble at his chin and along the lower section of his face just like any other eighteen-year-old, and he's out in some public place and no one's looking at him, he's just casually chatting with friends, his arm slung across Amanda's shoulders or tucked in the back pocket of her jeans, the ones so tight they look drawn on. Or maybe he's back in school and raises his hand in geometry or American history — all the answers he knew and had kept to himself. Only when Sidney speaks in his dreams he knows they think he is smart and witty and good-looking. He's gotta be good looking for Amanda Percy to choose him.

Her face cupped in his hands, kissing her, kissing her ever so lightly at first, then clenching her face, his grip so tight, the popping beneath his fingers, smashing the bones of her perfect face. Stop it! Please stop it! She'd plead. But he wouldn't. Stop. Sometimes the dreams were like this, as well.

Sidney has come to like his job at Buster's, where he is a short-order cook. He makes burgers, drops baskets of frozen mozzarella sticks and fries into vats of bubbling oil, marvels over the way hot fat transforms them, making them crispy outside, soft and juicy inside.

It is good for him to see heat in this way.

Sidney wore a blue button-down shirt and a paper cap while he worked. Still, he'd learned how to keep an eye on the front counter. Once someone from his class did venture inside Buster's, and when Sidney noticed him placing his order his hands began to shake with rage so great that he had to run into the john and splash his face with water. In the process he left a basket of French fries suspended over the oil, and the shift manager had written him up, said if it happened again they'd have to let him go. He was a nice man with a generous belly. Sidney didn't hold it against him. *They're safety regulations for a reason, son.*

And he looked him right in the eye as he said it.

Could have hugged the man for doing so.

Sidney has an apartment above the town's two-room maritime museum. He has his own entrance and three windows: one looks out over the parking lot, the other two face north, a perfect view of Glory Days, the soft lap of Lake Erie just beyond that. Earlier that summer there had been a string of storms, and he'd stood at the windows and watched the sky flash with tentacles of light followed by a torrential downpour. He knew that afterward the water would rush down the curb and into the park drains. Then the men in gray jumpsuits — the ones who afterward had helped him — would rush out with their brooms and push empty paper cups and wrappers, cigarette butts, into dustpans. The railings used to keep visitors in line would bead with water, tracks of the rides glistening like melted butter; the slow rise of steam from the pavement, everything wiped clean, new.

How he wished it could be so for him, as well. A fresh start. Nothing before this moment. Nothing at all.

There were rules, and Amanda made them clear from the start. He had to do as he was told and when. They would be eating their lunches casually, and then she would poke his wrist and say *come on*, and he would follow her up the gymnasium stairs to the cool darkness of the rafters where the wrestling team practiced, dust motes traveling along a stream of sun from an overhead window as Amanda fitted herself against the cement wall between two towers of mats, pulling her arms out of her shirt, unclasping her bra and telling him to put his hands on her, then: *kiss them*, she'd say. *Your tongue! Pretend they are lollipops!* Little brown cones of nipples, the soft flesh in his hands, the taste of peanut butter still in his mouth as he licked her, his breath rocketing from his chest, head dizzy, short of air, this power she had over him, and sometimes it did seem that she liked it, right?

No, she didn't touch him. Wouldn't let him kiss her mouth. But he didn't fixate on that. Hadn't spent much time analyzing it at all, much too grateful for the brief moments they had, and then as if a button had been pressed, she'd push him away, turn her back to him and dress. She'd stomp forward, chin held high and lead the way back to their lockers, the bell signaling the start of the next class. If he asked her something she wouldn't respond; it was like afterward he didn't exist at all.

Still, he was OK with that. His mouth tasted of peanut butter and that same sticky residue now coated Amanda's white flesh.

Sometimes Sid would see her standing real close to another guy, books clutched in front of her chest, giggling, and Sid's stomach would flip. Was this it? He wondered. Once he'd even seen her place her small manicured hand on Rob B.'s cheek and kiss him on the lips. But she was right: it wasn't easy to hang out with Crud Face. *I've got to make it look a certain way for both our sakes*, she had explained early on, and he'd agreed. Said he understood. But did he?

As time went on the dreams became more frequent and in them Amanda was his girlfriend. A real one. They'd walk the halls of school with their arms around each other, and he'd cup his hand beneath the curtain of her hair and lift her face to his, pause to kiss her against the lockers. When they messed around they would both be naked and she'd touch him freely, run her hands along his body, a ripple of muscles at his midsection, and then he'd place her gently on her back and he'd tenderly push himself inside her, kiss her softly on the mouth, but then the thrusts would intensify — something he could not control, and then she'd be crying and still he would push on until she gave one final scream and broke in two, her insides red and slick, steaming on the ground before him.

All he wanted was for someone to ask what it was like. In all those years since, not a single person had asked how it felt. He wanted to explain how his eyelashes, the hair on his eyebrows and above his forehead had singed, disappeared in a flash, the odor not unlike dust; flames stretched from his face so that from his perspective it looked as if he were trapped in a burning tunnel — the gold ball extending from his arm a fiery scepter, the rank stench of him — Sidney — burning. He'd grabbed a damp dishtowel and slapped it at his head and hand, liquid heat already searing his face, the top of his hand. Flames ratcheted over the stove and out the cabinet drawers, up along the wall and onto the ceiling. He ran out the back door and stood in the yard, snow mid-knee, watched the flames burn so brilliantly that it looked as if a star had landed on their house. He cowered there in the cold, hand and face already puffy and red, the overwhelming pain of it, how he shook with fear and blubbered like a baby.

Did you even try and stop it? His dad had asked months after the accident when the bills were piling up.

Sidney *had* meant to do something to halt the flames, only it had been in his mind — that is where he yanked the extinguisher from beneath the washtub, sprayed the stove and cabinet with the white foam until everything smoldered.

To his dad, he shrugged.

That's it, huh? Ten thousand dollars in damage and that's all you've got to say for yourself?

He shrugged again.

Fright Night, over Halloween weekend, the last evening Glory Days would be open for the season. Sidney had been thinking about asking Amanda to winter formal. He had dressed carefully in new jeans and his Nike high-tops, a black fleece over a green T-shirt, a color Amanda had said looked nice on him. The park was decked out in spooky theatricals — a school bus with busted out windows and a skeleton driver at the wheel, animal heads lolling about in a cemetery bubbling with blood. The people taking tickets were dressed in costumes and masks, and creepy music echoed from the park speakers. Sidney had never enjoyed Halloween. He could buy candy bars in the stores, why beg for them from strangers? But as he and Amanda started the ascent of the Hurricane's first dip, he wasn't thinking about Halloween or the fact they'd likely run into lots of Amanda's friends. He simply enjoyed sitting close enough beside her to breathe her perfume.

They neared the top of the coaster and she lifted her arms overhead and yelled: "Let's do the haunted house next!" and then they flew into the sky, spun up and down in rapid succession, bodies pummeled in a corkscrew, turning faster and faster on their sides then jerked upright; they sped through a tunnel of flashing lights, a series of smaller dips that made his neck snap, and then the ride slowed abruptly. Stopped. Please remember to take all personal belongings with you and have a glory day!

"That was great! Didn't you love that?" she said, smoothing her hair. "My legs are like, totally wobbly," and she steadied herself by grabbing the arm of his fleece.

The haunted house was an elaborate cut-out of a Victorian mansion, and it seemed like half of their high school class was in line with them. People were waving at Amanda, and Sidney could feel them looking at him, the two of them still a novelty as they leaned against the railings with a group of her friends in front and behind them.

Just outside the haunted house there was a path of upright coffins surrounded by fog, and every few minutes the coffins popped open and the ghouls jumped out and started chasing pedestrians. They were watching this mass scramble and were next in line to get into one of the narrow two-seat cars when Amanda brushed a hand over the front of his pants, a gesture so innocent it could be accidental. But it couldn't have been. He looked at her laughing with her friends, the queerest smile on her face. He wanted to ask her if she was feeling OK, but then their cart pulled up and a mummy told them to hop in.

Amanda rubbed the inside of his leg the whole ride even though she had never so much as fingered a hair on his head. It struck him as odd. A black-robed faceless creature with green glowing eyes ran beside their cart. Doors opened and shut suddenly. Headless creatures screamed and cradled wounds made by axes and power saws; hands reached out to grab them. It wasn't scary, but Amanda clung to him, hugging him, her perfume suddenly struck him as overly sweet. When the ride took a slow turn, she grabbed his hand and stood, told him to follow. He was not used to being touched by her and was surprised by the coldness of her hand in his. It wasn't right. He thought of the whispers while they were in line, a few people even pointed at him. It was over. He felt it now. Whatever game she had been playing with him had ended. They had been moving toward this all along.

She pulled on his hand and he followed her out of the cart. He wanted to ask where they were going but didn't. She directed him away from the curving track, the carts clicking past. She pushed him into a little alcove and squashed herself against him. They must not have been far from the end of the ride because he could see the faint outline of light around the corner, the distant sound of friends reunited.

"Let's do it," she whispered, pressing him against the blackened wall, her hands fumbling with his belt. The laughter, her laughter is what he heard first, and he would never understand how she'd gotten so far away from him so quickly. "Showtime!" a guy's voice said and then there were the lights raining down on him, garish fluorescent things, light so bright it burned.

BOB HICOK

When swimming is more like flying is still how we think of the soul

Today I sent a check to help dolphins remain
out of our mouths and wondered how many
not killings one hundred dollars is, not stabbings
with long pikes from small boats in lovely coves, one,
likely none, did you know dolphins know they exist, I watched
a dolphin watch itself upside down in a mirror, according
to the guy who trained Flipper, who was not one male
but six female dolphins called "boy" on the show,
they're self-conscious though not about their weight
or clothes, which are shimmering and I've read dolphins
rape each other so they're not perfect, as ducks
rape ducks, not dolphins, as nature
tears the shit out of whatever it wants
when we're not trying to pet it
into our zoos and aquaria, I've gone to aquaria
in Baltimore, Charleston, Chicago, and in Monterey, wanted
to be one of the seals on its back eating abalone
in the bay among the kelp because I'm unhappy
with my illiquid body and saw dolphins
arcing beyond the reach of a boy
with no hair and a father with spikes in his eyes
and imagined if my son had cancer, I'd take him to the ocean
and point in front of his palm-sized face where life
was going to take the next breath and never use
the word meat around that child if I could help it

BOB HICOK

What the great apes refer to as a philosophy of life

Looking for someone to mug, asking politely
can I mug you, a kindly grammarian responds, *may I mug you*
and hands me her purse, her child, her mortgage,
I have to feed the child and pay for the house, a small thing
like the smell of piss in the streets
makes me nostalgic for New York in '82, when everyone
was mugging everyone, it was more
like a cultural exchange or a kind of greeting, I'm worried
about the child's standardized test scores,
about how I look carrying a purse, it's not my color
and styles are always changing, just last week
I was looking for someone to kill, the week
before that, someone to scold me
for not being an intravenous drug user, these things,
God does these things like send us half way out
on a rope-bridge before telling us
He's changed His mind about rope,
it shouldn't exist, it's not going to exist
any moment, like we are not going to exist
any moment, and I have never applauded a grape
in an alley, I have never put my hands around the face
of a stranger like a chalice, there's so much to do
if I want to be fully human, not three quarters
or half or sort of human, I have to hoist you
on my shoulders so you can jump over the wall,
I have to build the wall higher, I have to catch you
on the other side, I have to shoot you
for trying to escape, I have to call your mother
and tell her you won't be coming home, I have to set
another place, I have to gather rain
into a body and make love with the rainbody
and teach the rainbody to moan and be taught
by the rainbody how to fall apart
into the most beautiful future reaching of grass
with its billion billion somnolent tongues
into the quiet applause of sunlight, into the pliant embrace
of air, may I mug you, may I kiss you,
may I sit with you on the veranda or build with you

such verandas as we need, such skies
as will hold the verandas in their arms, such martinis
as Plato never went on about or I'd read him
more often, sure the cave, sure the fire, sure the shadow,
sure we're stuck, but a drink now and then
makes philosophy more bearable, in that it's hard
to hold a drink in one hand and a book
in the other hand and a hand
in your other other hand, I choose the drink
and the hand hand over the drink
and the book hand, these are my priorities,
if they suit you, we can may share

JANICE N. HARRINGTON

White-tail

> *By munching on Manx shearwater chicks, the deer are able to get the extra calcium they need*
> — *James Owen,* National Geographic News

In Busey Woods, a herd of six or more,
their hoof prints — the stamps of a divided heart,

pictographs for prayer or mercy — cut
into well-trod paths.

And these others — winter deer, dun-pelted
and starving, stripping the saplings' bark with brutal teeth,

hurdling field fence and drainage ditch,
the semaphore of their tails flashing: the world is feral,

swift to wound; trust has a sour tongue.

Ancients believed that deer were messengers to the Gods.
If so, it is cruel work. They die for it, leaving their rotting hulks

beside the road, maggoted and rank, their broken ribs,
their tongues blue-black on the tarmac. Flies,

crows, hawks, and sun scavenge the remains.
The road sucks each carcass dry.

In a sunlit glade, a buck steps warily through the grass,
nibbling stems and buds, slowing

before a fledgling's broken-winged flutter, walking beside it
(cardinal? red-wing? sparrow?) and then snatching

the bird between soft lips and swallowing beak, wings, feathers,
song, then lowering its head to snag and pluck a tuft of grass.

That the weak earn their deaths?
That we should beware God's emissaries?
That hunger — and not the tooth's sharpness — persuades?

But the deer's message — the deer that ate the bird, the deer
that stands years later before your headlights, before

twisting wheels, the deer's hooves that fracture
your windshield and carve your cheek — the message

you ponder afterward, your head propped against bloody palms,
you never decipher. County roads and highways make you uneasy.

You study shadows, fear to see certain shapes. Some part of you
lies crumpled on a gravel shoulder. You feel an insistent beak.

You feel the sun's teeth. You lie there. (Flies. Ants. Scavengers.)
Your body knows what to do. Nothing will stop it.

ROGER MITCHELL

Charles

I looked in on his room now and then.
Dirty sheets, like mine, a tie across a chair.
We were roommates, first year in college,
and if we talked more than a dozen times,
I can't imagine what it was about,
he already suave at eighteen, at home
in life. I stared up at some craggy peak
for which I had the wrong equipment
and little interest to climb. I was maybe
fourteen. Developmentally, that is.
He tried out for the "lit mag" before I knew
what "lit" was. He and his friends read books,
the same ones so it seemed. I hadn't, as yet,
hadn't a glimmer of what to do or be
except what my parents had in mind,
which I had no way not to say no to.
A cavernous stairway, always dimly lit,
led up five flights to the top. By the door,
a framed list naming all who had roomed there,
year after year, none of whom I recognized.
Ours, I presumed, would be added next year.
I wrote a paper on the origin of God.
Hopelessly earnest, I'm sure; logical.
At least trying to be. My instructor
had me in for a look-see then, possibly
merely amused at a boy, another one,
who'd figured the big one out, or at least
took it on, a lamb caged with a tiger.
Gamov was pushing the Big Bang in those days.
It was a paper I had to write in a course
I can't remember a sentence of, a book,
the prof, the room we sat in, day after day,
but the grunt instructor asking me up
to his office, smiling and leaning back
in his chair, happy, I think, with his work,
as I would be years later explaining
the reasons for things or why reason failed
to explain very much of what we did or were.

You can live a whole year with a ghost,
a phantom much like yourself, marking
his manners and distance and the soiled sheets
and never forget his name and so ask
when you heard it at parties or meetings
if the stranger knew him. It came to be
a game of sorts, a test, until the night
a woman I'd just met said, yes, I do,
he's my husband, we're about to divorce,
and Charles, she called him Charles, has done
important work for us all. I told her
I knew him, really only his aura, his slow
passing in and out of the door. She said, yes,
I know, and looked away. I meant to write her,
meant to explain, but what? So, I didn't.
What could I say to a woman about to divorce
an oddity, to me an oddity, who must have
thought me the same, with twenty or more years
headed all our ways of unreadable
silence before he died, as the paper said,
honored and old, learned and wise,
the day before yesterday.

JIM ELLEDGE

Three Rhymed Secrets

First Secret:
Alone in His Room

A boy screams: his shorts yanked down. They pool. The wind
catches what he yells but tosses it away. The past and all its baggage
arrives unrehearsed but keen. Neighbors don't hear it practice in
Henry's rooms — skits about restraints and bareback — or parrot a
sermon on temptation from the roof. They hear a woman's trill, the
role he fashions, the role his and hers. They hear her —— *him* ——
humming torch songs: part siren song, but mostly accusation.

Second Secret:
All the Spending

Neighbors don't hear it practice in Henry's rooms, among stacks of
newspapers, empty bottles of Pepto-Bismol, broken eye glasses, and
canvas after canvas of little girls with penises — tchotchkes. His
past is embassy and courtroom jury, naïf and hooligan. The future's
a backed-up toilet. The present, a glass eye. By comparison, the
past's a breeze, a snap, even bliss. That's where Henry camps, where
Whillie still breathes, where they visit Riverview each weekend.
Henry still pays for rides then dinner — just like a real honeymoon.

Third Secret:
His Biographer's Confession

1:00 p.m. Lightning strobes each door and window, blanches oil-
speckled walls, then limns the mantle's prayer cards. The kitchen
billows with shadows: stove, fridge, table, chair. Someone stirs in
his sleep. He needs a bath and trim. He sits to sleep, ties bits of twine
into balls, traces paper-doll kids — twins, triplets, quadruplets . . .
and more. (Hand to mouth, his life.) Inside and out, the wind picks
up, gusts, sucks the world in, spits it out topsy-turvy: girls with dicks
or boys with sissy hair. Sirens wail. The sky rumbles and pops.

Outside and in, the storm's blood-shot right eye catches my hunkered
contour: voyeur, spy.

B. J. HOLLARS

Surfaces *Nonfiction*

This is what children look like underwater: fragments of light shifting in the shadow. Sometimes visible but sometimes not, and when you rotate in the water, turn to spot what you could not spot from your place on the dock, you begin questioning if what you thought you saw was just what you thought you saw. *How many times have I been wrong before?* you'll wonder, staring into the deep. *How many ghost children have I tried to swim back to shore?*

I am a lifeguard and this is a summer camp. It is June 2004. But it could be June of the next year, or the year after; the blurring of these years becomes the blurring of the bodies that never needed saving — kids who sank but didn't, kids who bobbed back up. I am nervous, this is my first summer saving lives, and with each splash I envision a new way for a child to die on my watch.

Please do not drown while I'm standing here, I think. *Why not build some sandcastles, instead?* No one ever wants to build sandcastles. Instead, the campers prefer cannonballs and jackknives. Prefer to see who can hold breath the longest.

The camp is on Blackman Lake, where the water is dark but the kids aren't — and as I scan the water, I see a great blurring of white arms and white legs and white bodies. They are an assortment of pale jellyfish, and when they cry out, "Marco!" and "Polo!" we lifeguards sometimes lose count of our number. Rule #1: Lifeguards must never lose count of their number.

Instead, we are to keep track of it and everything — every coordinate, every camper, every moment — this in the hopes that when we blow our Fox 40s, all our counts will add up. It is a strange and imprecise calculus, but the tool we rely upon when guarding bodies in a body of water.

A simple solution: The number that enters the lake must always exit the lake as well. $X=X$.

$X \neq$ anything other than X.

X must always equal X, and if X does not equal X (if you find yourself rounding or estimating) then the number you've reached is the wrong number. And if your number is the wrong number, you will conclude that somebody drowned on your watch.

It is your job to keep this from happening.

Here are some helpful tips for those afraid of drowning: First, a body is more likely to drown in the summer. Do not swim in the summer. Second, a body is more likely to drown on a Saturday or Sunday in the summer. Do not swim then, either. Also, males are three times more likely to drown than females. Do not swim if male (especially if between the ages of five and fourteen).

One study from the Centers for Disease Control and Prevention further narrows the profile of a drowning victim, noting that African-Americans within the five to fourteen age range are most vulnerable of all: 3.1 times more likely to drown than their white counterparts.

While the CDC concluded that African-Americans "reported the most limited swimming ability" of all minorities included in the study, the organization struggled to understand why. They pointed first to the "physical environment" (by which they mean a lack of swimming pools in predominantly African-American neighborhoods), but they noted also the "combination of social and cultural issues." According to the CDC, African-Americans just don't like to swim as much as white people.

Regardless of the "why," all the data points to a clear conclusion: African-American males between the ages of five and fourteen with plans to swim on Saturdays or Sundays in the summer are at risk.

Not everyone fits such precise profiles. On January 23, 1957, a twenty-four year old African-American grocery truck driver named Willie Edwards Jr. drowned while driving his route in Montgomery County, Alabama. He did not drive his truck into a river, but rather, was stopped by four white men who had heard a rumor that Edwards was dating a white woman. They drove him around town, beating him, before arriving at the Tyler-Goodwin Bridge perched one hundred twenty-five feet above the Alabama River. A gun was drawn. Edwards was told he must jump. He did.

He was a husband and a father, and it is unclear what led the white men to believe that he was dating a white woman. Equally unclear is whether Willie Edwards could swim, though certainly few could after plunging from such a height.

Because he was a black man consorting with white men atop a bridge in Alabama in 1957, his body was found four months later — twenty miles downstream, just outside of Montgomery.

A more recent outlier: On Sunday, June 26, 2011, thirty-six year old African-American Marie Joseph drowned in a public pool in Falls Rivers, Massachusetts. Moments after Joseph submerged, a nine-year-old boy informed the lifeguard of her vanishing, though no action was immediately taken. In fact, no action was taken for two days: after swimmers managed to wholly overlook the body at the bottom of the pool, after health inspectors claimed the water was reportedly "cloudy" with a visibility that reached no further than four feet beneath the surface, a group of teenagers snuck into the pool after hours and swam across her.

Nobody had reported her missing. Nobody was keeping count.

Throughout the summer of 2004, when I removed my whistle, I transformed from lifeguard to camp counselor. On Sunday afternoons, upon the campers' arrival, I marched them dutifully to the waterfront, to the deep-end docks, where they were forced to jump in and swim, treading water for a full two minutes before earning their deep-water band. We called it the "deep-water test" — a weeding out mechanism aimed to keep the weaker swimmers from entering the deep end without the proper clearance — though for the campers, the test served primarily as a public display of humiliation.

One Sunday, an African-American camper refused to take the test. It was a rainy afternoon, and the water was cold — freezing, even — but most importantly, the water was water, and it scared him. While the white nine-year-olds thundered across the lake, treading with an ease that came from years of swimming lessons at the neighborhood pool, my African-American camper did not enter the water at all.

Perhaps he had read the studies and knew what it meant to be an African-American male between the ages of five and fourteen on this particular day in this particular season. Perhaps he preferred not to risk transforming himself to a statistic.

He would take other risks that week — climb a tower, pet a snake — but he never allowed his neck to sink beneath the water.

"That water is cold," he told me, shivering on the dock.

It was cold.

But it was also water.

A final example, this one closer to home: On November 21, 2000, fifteen-year-old African-American Lawrence Norwood leapt into the school's swimming pool in Fort Wayne, Indiana, and drowned in twelve feet of water. He was one of eight participating in the swimming unit for physical education, and as fifth period drew to a close and the other seven returned to the locker room, Norwood did not.

"I remember we were jumping off the high board," the gym teacher explained. "I dove all the way to the bottom, and I didn't see anyone down there. No one remembers him actually going underwater and not coming back up."

Gym class ended at 1:35 p.m., though Norwood's body went undetected until approximately 2:16 p.m. that same afternoon. By the time his body was spotted in the water, the gym teacher was already midway through his next class.

As a result of Norwood's death, the school district installed the state-of-the-art Poseidon System — four underwater cameras and sixteen above-water cameras — all of them trained on the lap lanes and diving wells, keeping tabs on every swimmer at every coordinate at every second. Dubbed "the World's First Drowning Detection System," Poseidon could not only recognize drowning motions in the water, but could alert lifeguards as well, drawing attention to those who might otherwise go undetected.

Norwood's race was not made clear until a headshot was published in the newspaper nearly a week later. I never met Lawrence Norwood, though we shared the same water. Since my high school had no pool to call its own, my swim team shared Norwood's pool. For two seasons, I drove to that natatorium in the still-dark hours of winter, and upon reaching the water's edge, every morning I had to convince myself to jump in. Despite all the laps I swam there, not once did I hear mention of Norwood or his fate. Instead, all I saw was what he'd left behind — cameras studying my every stroke, making it all but impossible to lose sight of my very white skin in the water.

A few more rules for lifeguards: Stay vigilant. Act professional. Remember: The difference between life and death is little more than a breath, a ripple, a shadow spotted from the corner of your eye.

As a lifeguard, your job is to keep the kids from drowning. As a *waterfront* lifeguard at a summer camp, the job is a bit more complex, with a unique protocol to be followed in the event that the lifeguard rules are violated.

First, you must survey the scene. Next, you must check the area for immediate danger. After you have completed these steps, you are to lock arms with the other lifeguards, creating a chain that walks in unison for the entire length of the swimming area. You are to perform like synchronized swimmers in a cabaret show, one foot in front of the other, digging toes into the muck and praying — always praying — that your toes aren't the toes to come across the body.

You will not think about the profile of the common drowning victim, Rule #6. Your job is simply to count a number and keep it. To protect that number always. You will not concern yourself with historical implications. You will remember, always, that final rule: any color is better than blue.

FRANK BERGON

Tikal
Fiction

Now that her youngest daughter wanted to go to Tikal over spring break with some college friends, Francine wondered whether these children of the new millennium searched for the illuminations she'd sought as a child of the sixties. Looking back, she scarcely recognized the girl she was so many dizzying years ago, poised like an alien sibyl from a distant star, scanning the cosmos for hidden signs, willing to dive into an abyss on the chance she might drift into a region of light and grace.

That's how she thought of Tikal — a region of light and grace — when the commuter plane dropped through clouds and the salt-white temples floated into view above the jungle canopy. Guidebooks hadn't prepared her for that unfamiliar planet. The twin-prop airplane bucked through turbulent drafts. Her throat clenched. She felt frightened and lonely, despite the man next to her. The dense blanket of green foliage, stretching to the earth's curve, rushed upward with menacing speed.

Morton Peterson — the man she was traveling with — turned from the oval window under the wing and squeezed her hand. He filled the seat with the density of a limestone Maya statue, his broad face fully bearded, and his curly hair knotted at the back in a ribboned chongo. "Don't worry," he cautioned. "These Islanders are designed for these kinds of hops." He explained how the long, wide wing above the fuselage and the non-retractable wheels with double tires allowed the plane to carry heavy loads safely through tropical turbulence along seacoasts and over islands. Francine managed a troubled smile. Morton always had an explanation at hand to dispel her frightening puzzlements. He pointed out the rain-streaked window as the plane banked. "Look. That's the Temple of the Jaguar. We'll be on top of it this afternoon. Magnificent." He leaned back, assuming the tranquil expression of a knowing Maya lord.

The plane issued a loud crack as it thudded onto the dirt runway and wobbled to a halt. The rain forest humidity, thick with spicy, rank smells, enveloped Francine like a swamp. The Guatemalan pilot pulled bags from the cargo hold and tossed them toward the grassed edge of the runway. Morton Peterson, wearing a pith helmet and a tan safari shirt already soaked with sweat, his big chest crisscrossed with photographic equipment, pointed toward the far end of the rutted airstrip where the wreckage of a single-prop plane rusted.

"Oh, my God," Francine said. "I didn't see it when we were coming in."

"That's why I was pointing to the temple," Morton said. His broad mouth smiled within his scruffy beard, but shadows under the pith helmet obscured his eyes in attractive, dangerous mystery.

She was twenty-four, and he — if he was telling the truth — twenty years older. Francine had met him two weeks earlier in Sausalito where his black-and-white photographs of Maya ruins hung in a small gallery. With a plastic cup of warm wine in her hand and the summer sounds of San Francisco Bay coming through the open gallery door, Francine had found herself explaining to this hulking photographer that she wasn't really cross-eyed; green contacts covering her close-together eyes produced that effect.

"Your eyes would be the height of attraction to the Maya," Morton Peterson had told her with characteristic energy. "All the great Maya beauties were cross-eyed."

With her wild, crinkly red hair tied behind her head and a face sprinkled with freckles, Francine believed she looked more like a Dionysian maenad than a Maya princess. She was also too tall and lanky to be a Maya. She'd taken a pre-Columbian art course as an undergraduate at Berkeley but had heard little of what spilled from Morton Peterson's obsessive chatter. "Everyone is interested in the sudden collapse of Maya civilization," Morton said. "I'm interested in the mystery of its sudden appearance. It had to rise out of a profound religious impulse — even a revelation. Catholic missionaries were surprised to find that the Maya had elaborate rituals of purification, fasts from meat and booze, sexual abstinence, ceremonies of baptism and circumcision." He pointed toward a photograph of a wooden Maya cross. "The cross was an important part of their religion before they even saw a Christian crucifix. No people in history have had a more profound and wondrous sense of suffering and death." He swept his hand at the walls of photographs. "You can see it in their buildings and art."

By the end of the week Francine had gone to bed with Morton in her Noe Valley apartment, not far from where she was summer temping as a Kelly Girl. That was the seventies, as she now recalled. Anyone her age who'd lived in San Francisco at the time knew that for the middle class the real libertine sixties fluoresced in the seventies. Even a girl like herself, with a society-conscious mother and a solidly wealthy burgher father installed in conventional comfort down the Peninsula in Menlo Park, could fly off to Guatemala with a man she'd known only two weeks. Men were simple, she concluded by the time she'd graduated from college, they just wanted to sleep with you. In graduate school, where she was studying Medieval and Renaissance

Italian history, her relationships became more complicated when she met a boy who preferred drugs to bed.

Morton Peterson's desire to sleep with her became clear the first night they were together in her apartment, but after they'd listened to some Bob Dylan records and smoked some recreational hash he'd happened to bring along, Francine stretched out in bed beside him and said, "You can stay here if you go to sleep. I don't feel like it tonight." Morton's unprotesting compliance surprised her. He soon produced a window-shaking snore, earning her trust to a degree that allowed her to feel safe enough to fly off to Guatemala with him a week later, after they'd, indeed, coupled more than once. She liked the change an older lover introduced into her life. It was both exciting and comforting to sleep with a man rather than a boy, an older man whose two former wives and romantic liaisons had invested him with a full-bellied laugh and an aura of undemanding ease. It was far more important, she knew, to find a man with some dangerous zest than to marry a daddy clone. She was astonished at how much Morton knew.

"You have to see Tikal," Morton urged with his undiminishable enthusiasm. "It's the most incredible of all the cities — the most massively powerful, the most tremendous. It changed my life. It made me realize that the only thing worth living for is art."

Francine had met enough students whose parents had compensated for their children's lack of artistic talent by buying them expensive cameras to know that Morton was different. He really could take artful, haunting photos of Maya stelae and monuments. More important, he understood the world he photographed. His knowledge was amazing. In college she'd seen a slide of the beautiful jade death mask that had covered the face of Pakal, the great king of Palenque. Morton told her, "The Maya called jade the precious stone of infinite grace." The most valued jade among the Maya, he explained, was translucent green, the color of iridescent quetzal feathers and the symbol of growing corn, of rejuvenating water, of life itself. The green jade mask covering Pakal's face invested his soul with immortality. The glyph for jade was also the day name for rain. The teeth in Pakal's skull, painted red, along with the red pigment in the green mask, linked jade with blood, the source of all life and death. A stela at Yaxchilán showed Lady Xoc pulling a finger-thick cord, lined with agave thorns, through her pierced tongue. Kings like Shield Jaguar and Smoke Shell pierced their penises with sharp stingray spines. Their royal blood flowed onto bark paper and was burned in bowls, rising into clouds of smoke and rain to open visionary passages into the realm of eternal time and cosmic design. Everything gleamed with significance. All meanings in the Maya world were interconnected. A stela displayed smoke from

Lady Xoc's burning blood metamorphosing into the Vision Serpent, its open mouth spewing out an apparitional warrior from the underworld of Xibalba.

Francine remembered how the Maya cosmos contained a clarity that her own disarrayed life lacked at the time. That spring she'd flunked out of grad school. As a straight-A student in the Belmont high school where her parents had sent her to be educated by Notre Dame nuns, and later as an honor student in college, flunking out hadn't been an expected part of her program. A bad break-up with her boyfriend, brilliant but drug-ridden, left her floundering. Now she had to get herself back on track. TV images of the dirty tail end of the Vietnam War and the jowly, baggy-eyed face of a dishonest president offered no standards of distinction or moral direction. Her departure from school and her erratic love life made her parents, in her mother's word, "mortified."

To see for a moment, in Morton's words, a coherent and beautiful expression of meaning buoyed her spirit. It was not the clean, tree-lined, predictable suburban cosmos of Menlo Park. The Maya world flowed with the blood of human sacrifice. Like the vase in the gestalt image that suddenly became two faces, Maya brutality for her came to glow with transformative significance. New meanings emerged, just as they did when she and her friends listened to a tape of the Beatles' "Abbey Road" played backward, or when they came to learn that LSD was encrypted in "Lucy in the Sky with Diamonds," or when it was revealed that Mr. Jones in Bob Dylan's "Ballad of a Thin Man" was an actual *Time* magazine reporter, mocked as a befuddled man, who couldn't understand what was happening right in front of his nose. Francine felt she might be moving from a world of confusion to one of import. Once her former boyfriend had bought a bag of dried hallucinogenic mushrooms from Palenque that caused her to freak out. Morton Peterson said that he would never buy Palenque mushrooms. He always found his own in dewy pastures where they magically appeared with their unmistakable iridescent blue rims. A person, he claimed, would find them if they were meant to be found. That was the difference between the confused life Francine wished to leave and the elegant realm of order she desired to find.

One night, alone in her apartment, with the glint of the distant Bay Bridge in the corner of her window, she listened to a tape of Tzotzil chants, which Morton had given to her, and imagined herself a captive Maya princess with a flattened forehead, a long proud nose, and beautifully crossed eyes, her lovely teeth filed to points and inlaid with sparkling jade. Brilliant tattoos spiraled her arms. Oyster-shell jewelry studded her pierced lips and ears. Warriors with frightening faces, dyed red and black, pulled off her clothes and painted her naked body a glistening blue. Wearing a high-peaked plumed headdress, amid blaring conch-shell trumpets and clattering drums and rattles, she walked blue and naked up the steep limestone steps to the pyramid temple high above the plaza. Thousands of Maya dressed in robes and feathers filled the plaza below her. Four priests sprinkled the altar with blue powder. They stretched her spread-eagle on the blue stone, holding her hands and feet. She stared at the mural on the temple ceiling, while clouds of copal incense swirled over her. A convex stone under her back forced her blue breasts to arch upward. The priest jammed a flint knife high into her taut stomach, cracking open her ribcage, and pushed his fist into the wound. He tore out her heart and held it up, still beautifully beating in the palm of his hand. Francine imagined herself closing her eyes and leaving her red heart and green soul as gifts to the gods. She felt honored.

The clouds over Tikal burst into rain as Francine, hunched under her backpack, ran behind Morton from the airstrip to the hotel. Her short sundress of gossamery India fabric clung to her skin and silhouetted her breasts. Muddy slop streaked her legs and leather sandals.

While waiting for the rain to stop, they ordered lunch at a table in a cavernous concrete room. The dreary place was empty except for a man reading at a table and an older couple drinking beer.

"I guess we didn't need the hammocks," Francine said. Before they'd left San Francisco, he'd explained that there was no way to call ahead for reservations. They would just have to take their chances, and in case the jungle hotels were full, they would bring along light Yucatán hammocks to sleep outside.

"It's the rainy season," Morton explained in the hotel with characteristic assurance. "Things are slow."

A short, chubby young woman with a black eye, the skin so damaged it appeared greenish purple, brought two plates. "I know what you're looking at," she told Francine. She put down the beans, rice, and tortillas. "I got it playing volleyball."

Her name was Roxie, and she looked only partly Hispanic. As usual, Morton knew why. He told Francine that Roxie was the daughter of an American mother and a Guatemalan father apparently killed in mysterious circumstances. Roxie then left college in the States to help her mother run the hotel. Morton pointed out the blond American woman with the red bow in her hair near the kitchen. From the distance the woman appeared to Francine to be in her mid-thirties, although she had to be older, if Roxie, who looked in her mid-twenties, was really her daughter.

"This place creeps me out," Francine said.

Rain crashed on the tin roof and thudded against the enormous leaves of jungle plants pressing against the screened walls of the lunchroom.

Roxie's father had built the hotel two years ago, Morton said, but the government recently halted all further private construction at Tikal, so the place was left unfinished. The government was currently in the process of taking over the tourist business. "They also plan to close the airstrip," Morton said. "They say the vibrations of planes damage the ruins, but the real reason is to stop drug dealers from using the runway." Morton pushed away his plate. "These beans aren't even warm."

"At least they're edible," Francine said.

"Since the government intervened, this place is going to hell. What a crummy country Guatemala is. If it wasn't for the ruins, you couldn't pay me to come to this dump."

Morton's unexpected bitterness frightened Francine, but his spirits picked up when the storm stopped. He led her into Tikal's ceremonial plaza of freshly mowed grass, bright with rain. As she climbed up the Temple of the Jaguar, she remembered her dream. Her wet sandals slipped on the worn limestone steps. To keep from falling, she clutched the heavy chain, placed for tourists up the middle of the steep stairway. At the top of the pyramid she gazed across the plaza at the towering Temple of the Masks, where the wife of King Ah Cacau was supposedly buried. In the Acropolis to her right lay the fifth-century tomb of the Maya king Curl Nose, where she'd read that excavators found the bones of nine sacrificial victims entombed with him. With what brutal splendor the Maya buried their royalty, both men and women! She looked down the steep steps and realized that as a sacrificial captive, with her heart cut out, her body, representative of the setting sun, would've probably been kicked to tumble down these very steps.

Inside the temple at the top of the pyramid, Francine asked, "Isn't this where they cut out captives' hearts?"

Morton's voice was curt. "You've been reading too many historical romances. That didn't happen here, not in the classic age. Here's where the kings and queens did their royal bloodletting. It was mostly ritualistic and symbolic. These people were civilized."

Swollen clouds tumbled ominously overhead. Flashes of blue sky and sunlight came and went amid the ash-colored sky. Francine followed Morton up and down slippery temple steps and into limestone corbel vaults, dark and dank as caves. Bat guano coated the damp floor of a room in the Lost World Pyramid. She climbed through the Acropolis, then the Palace of Windows. An altar carving showed tied-up prisoners ready to be sacrificed. An outside monument, its engraving blurred from acid rain, displayed two priests holding a skull and thigh bones. A sharper image emerged on an altar of a tripod bowl containing a decapitated head. The stela excavated in the tomb of Stormy Sky, Tikal's greatest ruler, displayed the king decked out in traditional Maya regalia. In the crook of his left arm, he carried the head of someone called Sun Jaguar.

"But they did have human sacrifice here, didn't they?" Francine asked Morton.

"Oh, sure," Morton snapped, "but not big time. They lopped off heads, usually of captives. Archaeologists found the bones of only two servants sacrificed in Stormy Sky's tomb. These Maya didn't have massive sacrifices like the bloody Aztecs, or regularly cut out people's hearts like the Toltecs. That came later at places in the Yucatán. If you want to feel creepy, go to Chichén Itzá."

Francine's head began to ache. The up-and-down trudging demands of tourism began to exhaust her. Morton's cold snappishness troubled her. His surly attitude transformed his former charming autodidacticism into the irritant of a know-it-all. She found herself exploring two dark rooms on top of the Temple of the Jaguar Priest. Carved in the sapodilla lintel was a sketch of fat Lord Chitam, his bulging belly — as big as Morton's — wrapped in a jaguar skin, his head plumed with lavish quetzal feathers, and his neck and arms heavily adorned with jadeite and shell jewelry. The grandson of King Ah Cacau, this portly man ruled long after the great kings Jaguar Paw and Stormy Sky. Maybe his showy, dissolute appearance indicated the decline of Tikal glory. Soon after his reign, Tikal was abandoned.

Morton appeared offended every time Francine consulted her guidebook. Friends had recommended it. It contained a rating system of stars *to help readers see at a glance how worthwhile a visit to a particular site would be.*

"Look at the art, not the book," Morton said. "I can tell you what it means."

"You don't know everything," Francine said.

"More than that book."

"I think I need to call it a day," Francine said. "I have a headache. We have two more days to explore,"

"You really need a month," Morton said. "Come on, just one more. It's the highest pyramid of all."

A narrow, dark path through the jungle led to the enormous, partly exposed Pyramid of the Double-Headed Serpent. "OK," she snapped at Morton, "try to keep up." She scrambled ahead of him on a steep dirt slope, more like a trudge up a jungle hillside than onto a pyramid, covered as it was with shrubs and muddy rubble, and only partly excavated. Angry at Morton for pushing her to yet another climb, she grabbed protruding blocks of stone and the old roots of trees in an attempt to leave the huffing and puffing overweight man behind in embarrassment. When she looked down the steep slope, Morton was directly under her.

"Nice view," he said, looking up at her legs.

At the top of the pyramid a rusted iron-rung ladder extended up the side of the temple. Francine's sandals slipped on the wet rungs as she climbed. Ten, twenty, thirty feet, she hurried up the vertical ladder. In the high air, she felt exhilarated, nearly three hundred feet above the jungle. Light-headed, she almost didn't care whether she fell.

"Hold it there," Morton called from below. Beneath her, he clung to the ladder with one arm hooked around a rung while holding a camera to his face, its lens pointed up Francine's sundress.

Francine grabbed the light fabric at her thigh and hiked up the dress, exposing her bare white legs all the way to her hips.

She smiled down at Morton. "OK, shoot."

"Beautiful," Morton responded.

At the base of the temple, a man appeared wearing a straw hat — a guard of some sort — dressed in a khaki shirt and pants. He looked up at Francine and her exposed legs, his dark Maya face impassive. Embarrassed, Francine dropped her dress and hurried the rest of the way up the ladder. She sensed the eyes of the men below her, staring up her skirt.

On the roof of the temple, she told Morton, "You big jerk. You must've known that guy was down there."

"You've got prize-winning legs, babe," he responded. "You gave that poor slob his thrill for the day."

A whistle sounded from below, as the Maya guard waved his straw hat in warning at Morton who was trying to climb higher onto the temple's roof comb, an ornate stone structure thickly carpeted with ferns and mosses.

"He wants you to come down," Francine shouted.

Morton continued to climb. "Got to get this picture."

From the roof of the temple, the jungle spread out below her in a lush green wetness so dark it almost looked black. Cloudy with mist, temples in the distance jutted their white crowns above the foliage. She knew that the temples had once been painted bright red, with their sculptured designs brilliantly colored yellow, green, and blue — a rainbow of stone. More than fifty thousand people had lived here at one time. She felt herself at the heart of the Maya world. Her own heart thumped. Now she was glad that Morton had pushed her to make the climb. No amount of reading could've allowed her to understand what she intuited at that moment. The Maya, she thought, were a people of genius. With knowledge of mathematics more sophisticated than the ancient Greeks and Romans and mastery of astronomy more accurate than the ancient Egyptians, the Maya at Tikal had created a culture that cohered for a thousand years. They lived in a world radiant with significance.

On the sloppy dark path back to the hotel, water dripped overhead from the rain forest canopy blocking out the sky. Francine stumbled and fell in the mud, her sandal lodged in a web of roots crossing the path. Her scraped knee looked like a muddy grid seeping with blood.

Morton helped her up and wiped her knee with his handkerchief. He unzipped his fanny pack. "Here. I've got some ointment."

"It's all right," she said. "It can wait till we get back to the hotel."

Francine saw a man in a straw hat pushing a wheelbarrow through the maze of vines and tree trunks. When she caught his eye, he turned away.

"Follow him," Morton said. "It'll take us on a shortcut."

The path, narrower and more rutted than the one they'd left, passed by shabby stick huts with corrugated tin roofs, the compound of Indian workers, who did the actual excavation for archaeologists. Through an open doorway, Francine saw an old woman in a full skirt and a white blouse with red decorations around the neck. Kneeling on the dirt floor, she rolled corn dough on a metate just like one Francine had seen in her guidebook among drawings of ancient Maya utensils. The woman's thick black hair and long-nosed profile could have served as a model for a portrait on an ancient stela. The similarity astonished Francine.

"That woman could've been a Maya queen," she told Morton.

"Well, they're Maya descendants all right," he said. "But to compare them to Tikal's royalty is like comparing drugged-out ghetto blacks to ancient African kings. These peasants would've been the ones carrying the stones to build the temples."

Morton's racial slur and gruff dismissal of her perception irritated Francine. At the same time she hadn't considered that her vision of a radiant Maya world might exclude so many. No wonder revolution among the forgotten slumbered in this jungle. "You — " she started to say to Morton, but at that moment a rattling noise erupted overhead. A tan-skinned, oval fruit made a splat on the path inches from her feet, splitting open to reveal a rosy interior of pulp and seeds.

Morton laughed through his beard in the hearty, deep-bellied way that had initially attracted her. "Spider monkey," he said. Overhead, a long-armed monkey swung into a dense tangle of vines and out of sight, its crashing departure louder than Francine thought its small body could make. An agitated keel-billed bird, flashing yellow and red feathers, croaked like a frog.

"That monkey was throwing the fruit right at us," she said.

"Absolutely," Morton agreed. "We were the target."

When they reached the thatched-roof, screen-sided bungalow where they'd left their packs, Francine noticed a rank odor. Someone had gone to the bathroom without flushing the toilet. She tried pushing the handle but nothing happened.

"It must've been one of the maids or workers," Morton said. "See what I mean?"

In the main part of the hotel, Roxie, her black eye darker in the fading evening light, turned toward two Indian girls and snapped her fingers while spewing out staccato commands in Spanish that were beyond Francine's comprehension. The girls scurried away with a bucket, plunger, and mop.

"They'll have it cleaned up in a minute," Roxie said. "We've had a little problem. The plumbing's out because one of the workers broke the water line while digging this afternoon. You can wait in here."

Roxie pointed to a small dining room with an imitation sixteenth-century Spanish-style carved table and four chairs. She spit out a command to another girl. In a few minutes, glasses and bottles of beer, the same brand as at lunch, appeared on the table.

"I don't like this place," Francine said to Morton, once they had settled at the table and poured out the warm beers. "She treats these girls like slaves."

"Hey," Morton replied. "These servants have good jobs. Don't go judging by U.S. standards. Without this work, these peasant girls would just be in some hut pregnant, barefoot, and beat-up. Not that they won't soon end up that way."

As darkness pressed against the screened windows of the room, electric generators in the distance kicked on, throbbing in the night, while the light bulb hanging over the table flickered and gathered brightness, until the chugging sounds of the generators cut out and the room fell back into darkness.

Morton laughed, as one of the slave girls came into the room with a candle. "Nothing works in this crummy country," he told Francine. "One of the best reasons for coming here is to see how glad we should be for not having to live here. Do you want a joint?"

"Are you crazy?" she replied. "That's all I need is to end up in a Third World jail." She thought of the look on her father's fleshy face, as he sat at the presidential desk of his insurance company, hearing the U.S. ambassador in Guatemala City report that his daughter was incarcerated in Central America for smoking dope. That would be a fine end to what she had hoped to be a happy, free-spirited adventure.

"Nobody's going to get excited about a couple of joints," Morton said. "You'd need a kilo to get any attention, and even then, the army would just confiscate it and smoke it themselves."

Morton leaned back in the carved, high-backed chair as he sipped his beer. The Spanish-style table and chairs with ornate carvings looked fancy compared to the unfinished concrete floor and bare white walls. The chair creaked as it rocked back on two legs.

"How do you know so much about this?" she asked Morton.

"I told you before that I made a lot of money in the sixties. I was in the export business. I ran a lot of dope into the States. Mostly out of Columbia. That's why I can do what I want now."

Thousands of miles from home, with a man she scarcely knew, Francine wondered how she was going to extricate herself. In the candlelight, the whites of his eyes looked like dried yellow skin. She wanted to go home. "I wish you'd told me this earlier."

Morton raised his hands as though to ward off criticism and rocked back in his chair. "I'm done with all that. That's why I'm here now. I knew when to get out. Everybody too greedy gets caught. The thing about me is I don't care about money. I just made enough to let me do what I care about."

"You mean *art*?" Francine asked, sarcastically raising her voice, although Morton didn't seem bothered.

"Right. Art. Photography. All the rest was just a means to an end. I was the man in the middle. I never had any of the stuff on me, so I was always safe. I just facilitated the transfer of goods between the producer and the consumer. Purely business."

A splintering crash of wood erupted as Morton, rocking too far back, collapsed amid broken pieces of the high-backed chair, his head plunging out of sight as he fell to the floor. When his flushed face reappeared above the tabletop, he was laughing. Francine saw a dark-eyed servant girl flee from the doorway. Morton stood up, rubbing his rear. "No broken bones," he said. His chuckle rolled into a roaring belly laugh. Francine felt an unexpected sense of relief as she surprisingly found herself laughing along with him. "Shall we sue?" he asked.

"What would you collect?" Francine asked, sensing some truth in his cynical response to this country. "The broken chair?"

"How about a couple of these slave girls?"

Roxie and her blond mother appeared in the doorway. A Guatemalan man from the hotel desk began picking up pieces of the broken chair.

"You're going to have to pay for this chair," Roxie's mother told Morton. Up close, in the candlelight, Francine could see fine wrinkles and dark eye pouches in the woman's face. She could've been nearly fifty, although her ballerina-thin body in the full Guatemalan skirt and the red bow in her butter-blond hair made her look girlish. Francine wondered why she should be so serious about Morton's ridiculous pratfall.

"Pay?" Morton blurted out. "You're going to have to pay me. I could've been hurt."

Roxie tried to intervene. "We don't have insurance, you know. This was an expensive set. We can't just replace one chair. We have to buy a whole set."

"It's a piece of trash," Morton said.

Francine didn't know whose face got redder, Roxie's or her mother's. Roxie's mother snapped her fingers at the man picking up the broken chair. "Do you want to go to jail?" she yelled at Morton. "Is that what you want?"

"Don't threaten me," Morton said. "We're leaving right now."

"Yes, you're leaving," Roxie's mother said, "but you're going to pay for this chair first."

"Wait," Francine said. She didn't know what she could say to stop this craziness. With every exchange, the consequences escalated faster than she could believe. Nothing like this could've happened back home. The threat of having to leave the hotel numbed her with fright.

"Come on, Fran." Morton snatched his pith helmet from the floor. "We're out of this dump."

Francine didn't know how it happened so quickly, but three Guatemalan soldiers — none of them older than their early twenties — in combat fatigues, bandoliers, pistols in black leather belts, and what might have been rifles or automatic weapons — Francine didn't know one from the other — surrounded Morton.

"Are you going to pay?" Roxie's mother shouted.

"No," Morton said, his eyes hard and his mouth clamped in thuggish obstinacy. "You all can go to hell."

Roxie's mother waved her hand. A pair of handcuffs appeared in a soldier's hands as the others grabbed Morton by the arms. They were smaller than he was, but they managed to twist his arms behind his back and bend him face down over the table.

"Wait," Francine said. "I'll pay."

"It's too late," Roxie said.

"No," Francine pleaded. "Please, stop this and let me pay. How much do you want?"

Roxie's mother said something in Spanish to the soldiers.

"What's she saying?" Francine asked Roxie.

"That if you pay, your friend doesn't have to go to jail. But he still has to leave the hotel."

"Where can he go?"

"He can sleep in the jungle," Roxie said.

The soldiers pulled Morton toward the door, his handcuffed hands behind his back. His head swiveled toward Francine, his flushed face looking desperate. "What's she saying?" he asked, meaning Roxie's mom.

Francine didn't reply. Angry both with herself and with Morton, she realized that he, like her, scarcely understood Spanish. The obstinate fool could've paid and avoided this fiasco.

"Get the hammocks and our bags," Morton yelled at Francine.

Roxie's mother said something else to the soldiers, and Francine thought the sense of it was that they should get Morton's belongings from the bungalow. They pushed and dragged him through the door. "Come on, Fran," he yelled, his voice urgent. She didn't move. Morton's uncomprehending face grew frightened.

"You don't have to leave," Roxie said to Francine.

"I'm not," Francine said.

Now, so many years later, Francine recalled paying Roxie the equivalent of thirty dollars in Guatemalan quetzals, a stiff price in the seventies before the runaway inflation of the Carter years. Francine remembered Roxie trying to console her, to explain that people had to understand how things worked in a country without insurance. "Before my father was assassinated, he owned a plane that crashed killing twenty-two tourists and he paid out twenty-two million. I'm not happy about what happened, but your friend was wrong."

"He didn't understand," Francine said.

"He should never have laughed," Roxie said.

Francine heard herself asking Roxie, "How did you really get that black eye?"

Roxie's chubby face assumed the stony impassivity Francine had come to identify with Maya stoicism. "I got slugged," Roxie said. "*Mi novio*, my fiancé."

Francine spent the night alone in the bungalow on a damp mattress smelling of mildew. Roxie told her that the afternoon commuter plane from Tikal would be full but a bus left early in the morning for Flores, where she could connect to Guatemala City. That way she could get a flight home in two days. Francine couldn't sleep, surprised that the jungle was so noisy at night. Her scraped knee stung against the coarse sheet. She felt like crying. She wondered where Morton was sleeping. Roxie said he could camp where hippies hung their hammocks. He would be safe there. A loud, frightening roar made Fráncine think a jaguar might be prowling near her bungalow. Her heart beat wildly, afraid now for Morton, despite his stubborn obtuseness, swinging in an exposed hammock in the jungle. She hoped he was all right but wished not to see him again. This entire affair of going somewhere she didn't understand with someone she didn't know had been a wretched mistake. She remembered his distraught expression when she had refused his command to accompany him into the jungle. She saw a confused stranger stunned by his failure to understand her.

Her alarm went off at three-thirty, and by the time she climbed aboard the old Bluebird school bus, the jungle began its clickety, raspy, cawing, hooting, hawking wake-up racket. Sinister-looking Indian workers, their faces muffled in scarves, boarded the dark bus and placed their machetes in the overhead racks. An Indian in a campesino straw hat, his khaki clothes smelling of wood smoke, settled next to her in the hard plank seat. Francine was the only tourist aboard the bus. The Indian driver looked at his watch. It was already past four-thirty, the time the bus was supposed to leave. With a gesture of exasperation, the driver slapped his palms on the steering wheel. He swung from his seat and hurried down the steps and out of the bus.

When he returned, a half-dozen foreigners followed. Mostly in their twenties, dressed in the loose, harlequin-colored garb Francine identified with French hippies, the sleepy-eyed tourists trudged aboard while the driver and his helper tossed their backpacks and rolled hammocks onto the roof of the bus. The hippies must have known that the driver would wake them before leaving. Morton was not with them.

The tired-looking driver walked back to Francine and said something in Spanish. Francine heard the word *novio*. Across the aisle, a French girl smelling of musky patchouli oil translated for her. "He says — the driver — that he not can find you fiancé."

"He's not my fiancé," Francine said. "Let's go."

The driver needed no translation. He settled into his seat, pulled the choke, and rapidly pumped the accelerator while twisting the ignition key. The engine chugged and whined until it caught, blasting the morning air with pistol-loud backfiring pops.

"Did you hear that jaguar last night?" Francine asked the French girl, speculating on the reason for Morton's absence.

The long-haired girl smiled. "Monkey," she said. "How do you say it in English? Howler monkey, I think."

Francine leaned back. The sleeping Indian worker next to her, his nose and mouth covered with a gray scarf, jerked his head after the driver had slammed a boxy eight-track cassette into a jury-rigged audiotape player. Dangling wires ran to a speaker precariously tied with twine in the overhead rack. Even decades later, Francine recalled her astonished disbelief as she heard, in an old school bus filled with Maya Indians in the Guatemalan jungle, the blaring wails and nasal tones of Bob Dylan singing: " . . . *but you don't know what it is, do you, Mr. Jones?*"

Now, in her comfortable Menlo Park home, after marrying an attorney — once an adventurous free-spirited traveler like herself, who evolved from pro bono work into a vice-president in her father's insurance company — her three daughters educated at a nuns' boarding school, she remembered the look on Morton Peterson's face as he emerged from the jungle in his khaki shirt minus the pith helmet, apparently yelling for the bus to wait, his shouts unheard through the dawning jungle clatter and the wails of an electric keyboard and electric guitars as the Bluebird rumbled away. Relieved that he was safe, she felt more grateful to escape, although she still recalled Morton's face glimpsed through the dirty window of the fleeing bus. His anguished look no longer resembled the knowing gaze of an engraved Tikal king. He was no slave, no peasant, no campesino, yet his look of grieving disbelief oddly recalled to her a Maya statue she'd seen of a sacrificial captive, one of the excluded, the forgotten — head scalped, feet mangled, stomach disemboweled, heart still beating, mouth open in a voiceless, incomprehensive howl across the centuries. The rackety Bluebird bus turned up the road heading out of the jungle, and the man's face disappeared.

VICTORIA BARRAS TULACRO

Partial Viewing   *Fiction*

There was probably a better way to handle it rather than sneaking up behind him.

In one scenario, I yelled at him. Hey! Why are you watching me through my bathroom window?

His face might have moved through shades of white, but finally settled on purple, enflaming his red pimples. He might have had braces and his upper lip barely stretched over them. He might have stuttered or cried. Any of those things were a real possibility.

He might have run the fifty yards up the hill to his house. He might have told his plain-Jane mother. (And maybe that's why he liked watching me, because I wore make-up and shaved above my knees.) She might have scolded him and told him to pray. He might never do it again.

In the other scenario, I grab his hand. He is older in this scenario; he can buy cigarettes now, but barely.

It is dark, except for my bathroom window which looks like a movie screen of light. He is startled by me, and he jumps a little because all this time he thought he was watching me through the steam. The flashes of peach between clouds of condensation on my window are buff-colored streamers I have taped to the grate of an oscillating fan. (It's an elaborate plan, but in this scenario it works.)

His hand is surprisingly warm. The night has already sunk its cool teeth in. The crickets click, and the wind shakes through the chaparral. We both hold our breaths when a jackrabbit rustles through a sage bush, pauses, and moves on.

I don't say anything because this, we know, is why we both have come here. *I know*, my body says. *I've been putting on this show every night for you. Here, smell the lavender salts on my skin. Feel the difference in the expensive shampoo. See? No more crunchy hair.* I will my body to say all that, and it does. Expertly.

This is for you, I say, and offer myself to him.

Wait, he says, and pulls out a small package of what I think are condoms and offers me one. No thanks, I say sweetly. You need it more than I. But then, he pulls out a cigarette and nervously tries to light it. His long finger rolls along the metal wheel. Again and again.

I am amused that he is trying to impress that he is calm. That he wants this to happen in a thoughtful way. Men my age don't do that kind of thing. Flick. Flick. The noise is far more desperate than crickets.

It must be empty, he says and hurls the lighter through the darkness towards the yellow glow of his parents' house. We don't hear it land.

It's OK, I try to assure him. I don't want him to feel self-conscious. I don't smoke anyhow, I say, which is true. I have been able to buy them for a decade now, but haven't.

I tug his hands towards the trashcans. But what about, and he nods towards my shower. It's OK. Let it, I say because he doesn't know I have a fifty-dollar credit from the water company. (Again, part of the plan.) I can let it run all night. He allows me to pull him. One step, then another until we are moments away. I am floating. I am a kite string tethered between him and the night.

He lays me down on the driveway; the concrete is still warm from the day. Take me, I say, because that's how I've seen it done on *Lonesome Dove*. Women were always saying things like that as though *they* couldn't do any of the taking.

Here, the kid asks, swallowing hard. He's hovering over me with a peachy upper lip and a boner. A fuzzy upper lip because he doesn't yet like shaving and a boner because, well, that's what happens when tits like these are close by and breathing heavy.

Kiss me, I say, and then I feel bad like I'm supposed to be the responsible one here. I'm supposed to show him how. So I put my hand in front of his advancing face.

Here, I say and grab one of his sweaty hands. There are calluses on the end of his fingers which can only mean one thing: guitar. Will you write a song about me, I ask and press his hand to my left breast. He doesn't know what to do, so I knead my fingers on top of his. Yes, he says, I will learn to sing.

Christian, a voice yells through the dark. My sensor lights on the garage snap on. His mother is wearing a robe and slippers. I hiccup instead of laugh because I have a hard time believing someone made it down the hill between our houses in those flimsy shoes.

Hey Rebecca, I act casual and pull down my shirt over my bra, but it won't go until I undo two buttons. It's an awkward moment, but once my shirt is pulled down, I smile and sit cross-legged on the concrete. The boy has already shuffled three feet away from me, and wrapped his hands around his knees, as though to say, See, Mom, nothing going on here.

Lovely night, isn't it, I ask.

It is, she says and slips into the light so that her face is washed out in a very creepy silent movie kind of way.

Christian, you were supposed to be home an hour ago, she says and before she can fold her arms around her chest, he has scrambled back into the brush like a mythical Bigfoot.

Look, I say. I know this looks bad, but he's just a kid. Cut him some slack. They all do it, I say, even though I know this is a lie.

I am NOT worried about him watching you, she says irritated. I am worried that you were trying to seduce *him*.

Suddenly, I want her husband: a roundish sort of man with a red face and receding hairlines. On occasion he has flirted with me at the mailboxes over the weekly coupons ads. If he were here, he would see that I am a prize for his young son. He would understand what a status symbol it would be for a young man like that to have an *experienced* girlfriend. It's invaluable!

God, she laughs, and I'm thrown out of my head. We all would have been corrupted years ago, watching you shower.

I start to feel small. I understand that everything I've ever done has had a witness. The time I stole a pack of razors from the drug store. The time I masturbated to a Jimmy Stewart movie even though I find him mostly asexual. The time I used someone else's left-behind Irish soap without a washcloth at the gym shower. I pretended it was my boyfriend's; that we were intimate enough to use each other's personal items.

We watch you, she says, smirking and moving further into the light. Her face is a horror movie of white. June bugs and moths swarm around her head. I am hoping she will say they understand that I am a good person, that they know I'm lonely. But she stops cold and asks if I shave my armpits in the upward direction.

But none of that actually happens. I turn on the shower and let it go for a while, let it steam up pretty good before I snap my towel a few times to give color and movement to the audience outside. I charge out into the night, only it's black and it takes a moment to find the side of my house. My eyes aren't adjusting, so I feel my way along the rough stucco, which is unpleasant but necessary.

I can feel him there just beyond the light. My blood is ticking slowly up to my head and rolling like a coaster back down into my feet. I step through the bushes and come up behind him. His head is like an exclamation point of black against the rectangle of light from my window. I am watching him watch me.

Hello, I say in a cheerful way. His head whips around and he asks, who's there, four times before I can respond.

It's me, I say and step closer to him, closer to the light.

Me who?

Her, I point to the window. I come closer to his shadow, but I still can't see who it is. He seems broader than the teenage kid from next door. He looks toward the window, and so do I. The steam rolls against the glass and continues to shield any real view. I blush. It's not even a good view.

Step into the light, he says, and I do. We are standing in the swath of my bathroom light like a picture frame around us.

He is much bigger than me and he is not wearing a letterman jacket. In fact, it is not even the neighbor kid — any neighborhood kid. He's an old man in an aviator jacket, the kind you buy at Wal-Mart, not the real kind with the patches. His nose is bulbous and his face looks pocked with nail heads. Not the kind of stalker I've been dreaming about for weeks.

Clearly, he is unimpressed by me, too. His eyes roll over me in disappointment. Maybe I am one of those women that do look better naked. I tug on my scrunchie and try to run my fingers through my hair like a comb.

He turns to go. The magic of partial viewing has come to an end. I understand how he feels. I feel it to, but if I can't have the neighbor kid pine after me, is it OK to pretend, I ask myself. Would it feel the same if no one were really there?

Wait, I call out before he's reached the end of the driveway. Wait, what if we just go back to the way things were? I'll pretend you're not out there, and you pretend — I pause. I am not sure what he wants from this arrangement. You just pretend to see what you want to see. If you think you see a nipple through the window fog, then by God, it's a nipple, I say.

He smiles and looks at the ground. The hair on his head is mostly gone, just a few threads of white hanging on. OK, he says. I can do that. But no more coming out here.

OK, I agree and quickly run back inside to finish the shower I never started. The bathroom is a hot mist I swim through. I slide down my jean shorts and do a little shimmy to get out of them. I toss my shirt once, twice before I leave it in the sink instead of the laundry basket. I lean against the tile in a distressed kind of way, arm across my brow, but quickly jump when the cold of the ceramic stings my backside. I can put on this show every night. My cheeks ache from smiling.

IMPRESSIONS

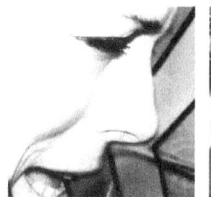

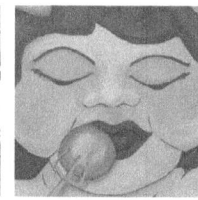

Handle with Care
Eleanor Leonne Bennett

Battling Winds
Eleanor Leonne Bennett

In Need of Warm Water
Eleanor Leonne Bennett

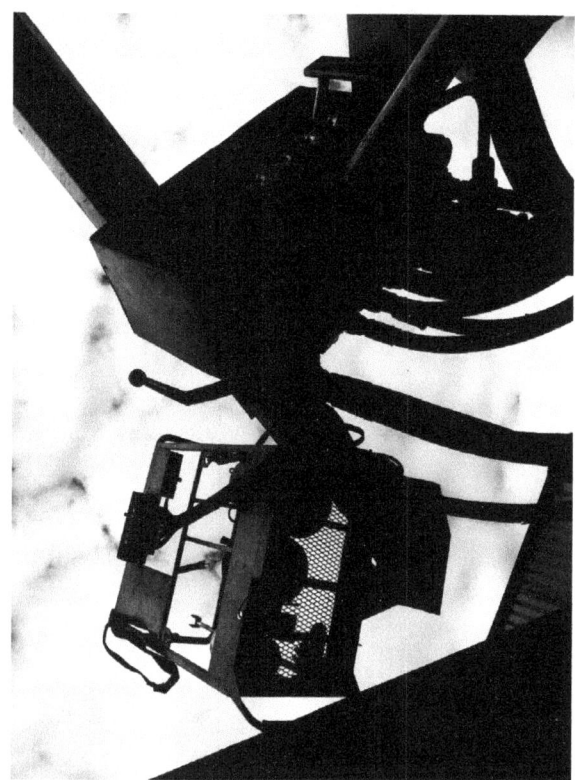

High Up
Eleanor Leonne Bennett

Visit www.fifthwednesdayjournal.org/
selections to read our exclusive interview
with photographer Eleanor Leonne Bennett.

Self-Portrait

Photos on pages 118-137 by Petra Ford and untitled.

street view

a look through the lens with
petra ford

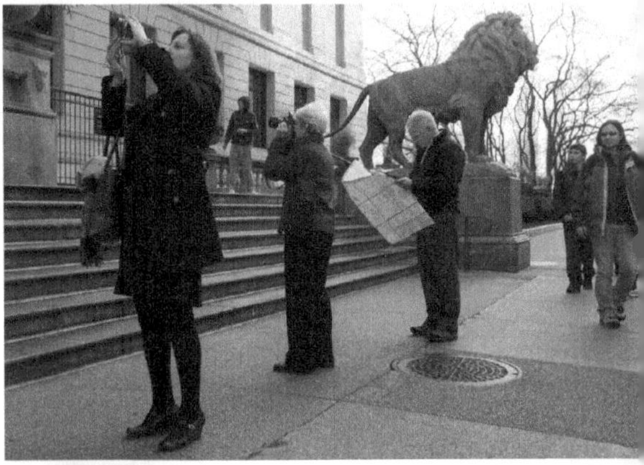

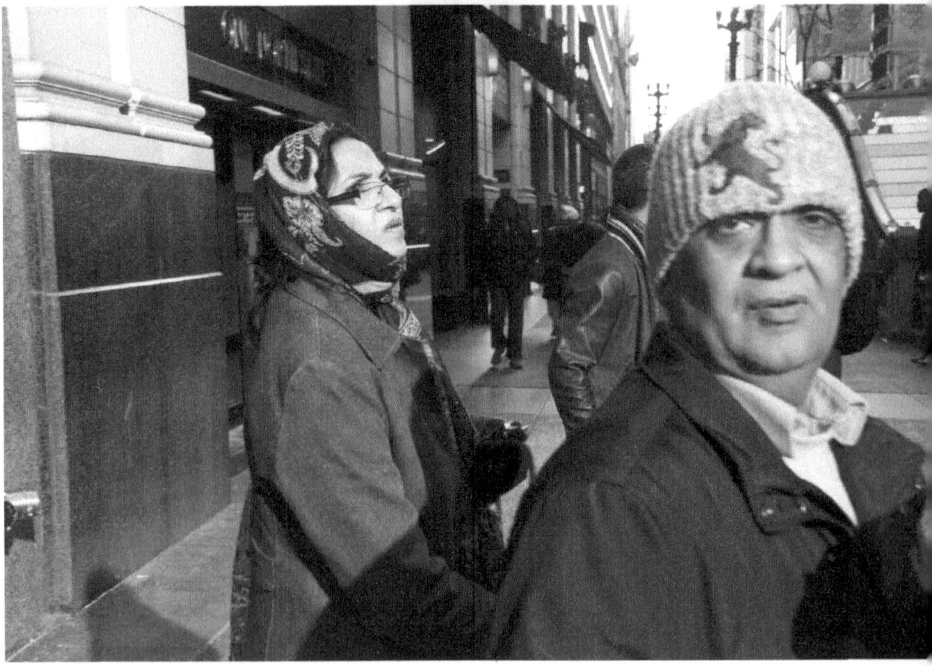

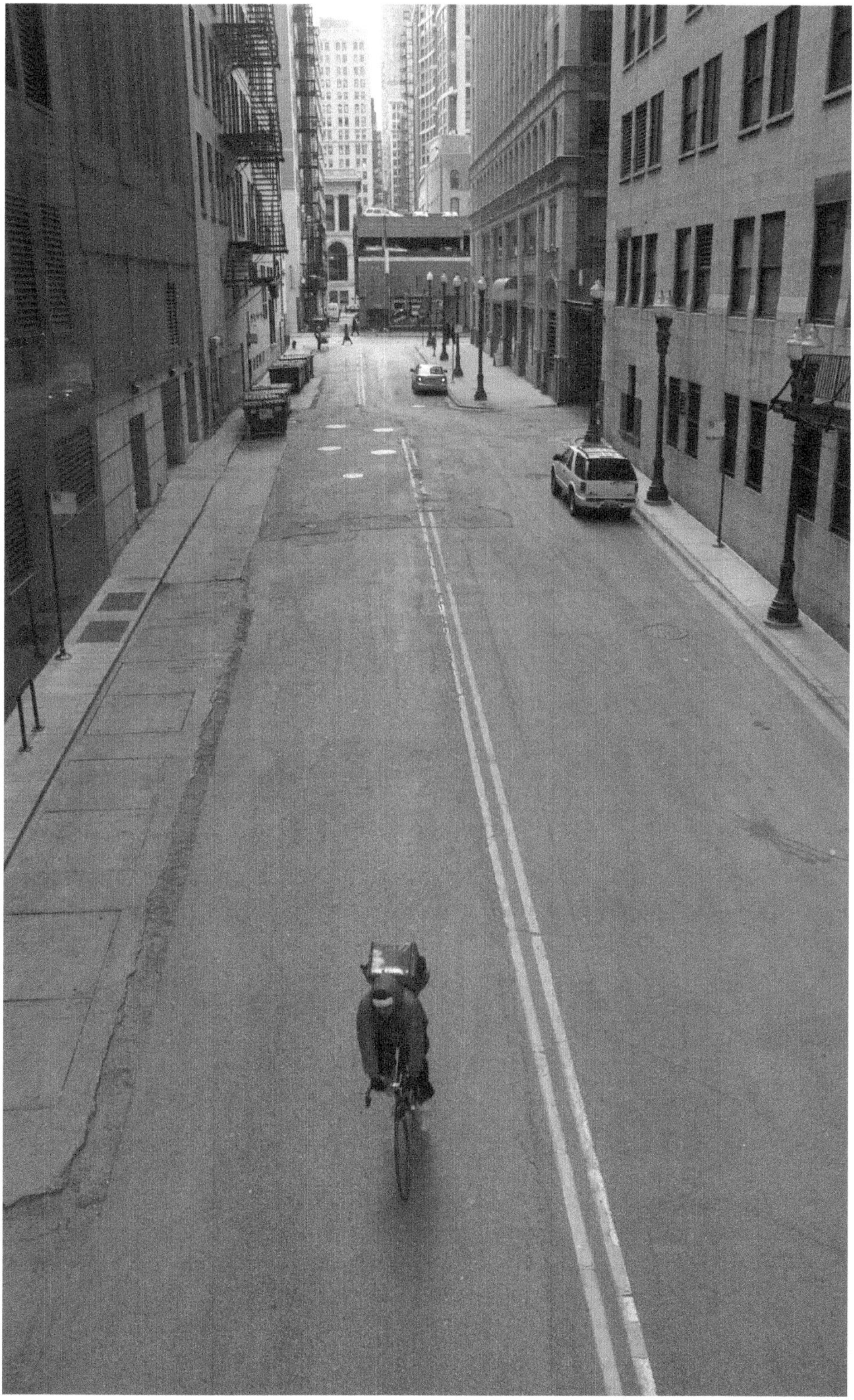

Self-Portrait

jenn hollmeyer
interview

Fifth Wednesday Journal has been publishing Petra Ford's photography since the spring of 2008. This winter she took her Nikon D200 to the street to capture everyday life in Chicago. Then she sat down with us to talk about shooting, posing, and irony.

FWJ: *You're both a photographer and a model. Which came first?*

Petra Ford: I started modeling when I was nineteen, in 1999. I modeled for a couple years with Elite Model Management in Chicago and then took a temporary retirement. I started modeling again in 2008 with Elite, which is now Factor Women, and its sister agency, Stewart Talent. Being immersed in the world of fashion as a model made trying my hand at fashion photography an obvious choice. I bought my first DSLR in 2006 and enrolled in an intro photo class in January 2007. My first solo gallery show was a little over a year later, in May 2008, and then I got into fashion and beauty photography in 2009.

FWJ: *What's your favorite photo shoot you've ever done?*

PF: To date, my favorite shoot was one that I did in September 2010. I used three models — Samantha from Factor Women, Heather from Factor Women (and of *America's Next Top Model* fame), and Josh from Chosen Management. What I loved about the shoot was that the models interacted with each other in a very natural and spontaneous way. My vision was for the photos to look very real, as if a fourth friend had been there with them, taking photos. It was a fun fusion of street photography and fashion.

FWJ: *What are your favorite experiences being on the other side of the camera — as the model?*

PF: I've had some truly incredible and surreal experiences as a model! I've met lots of wonderfully talented people, worn gorgeous couture clothing, had my hair styled in every conceivable manner, and worn every type of makeup from very natural, to very avante garde, to very bloody (including a fake bullet hole in the head!). It's hard to say what my favorite experience has been because there have been so many great ones. Modeling outside in the nude with seventeen other nude women for a fine art project for celebrated photographer Dennis Manarchy was probably my most memorable experience, however! (Disclaimer: it was extremely tasteful and artistic nudity!)

FWJ: *How does your experience as a photographer enhance your modeling skills, and vice versa?*

PF: As a photographer, I have a much better understanding of what may be going through the models' heads during our shoot. I know what questions they may be wondering and explain the way I work so they understand why I ask them to do the things I do. I'm also very aware of the models' comfort level and try to make sure that no one is ever cold, hungry, or otherwise uncomfortable on my set. As a model, my experience as a photographer is helpful because I understand concepts such as lighting, as well as the importance of letting go and trusting the photographer.

FWJ: *What have you learned by watching others photograph you?*

PF: I've learned that every photographer works in a different way and that there is no one right or wrong way to make a photograph. Everyone's style is different and it's very interesting to watch other photographers in action.

FWJ: *What do you think about when you shoot street photography versus fashion photography? How does one style help you with the other?*

PF: When I'm shooting street photography, I like to turn on my iPod and just get in a zone. The zone is one of both total awareness and total instinct. I'm constantly looking, thinking, aware, and ready, and yet I try not to think too much and rely on my instincts to tell me when to raise my camera and shoot — often very quickly! There's also a barrier that I have to break through for the first five or ten minutes of shooting street. Every time I get out there,

there's an initial uneasiness where I feel like everyone is aware of me and my camera. But as soon as I start shooting for a few minutes, I break out of it and start to feel completely invisible. I often compare it to how I feel when I'm jogging — the first few minutes are rough and all I want to do is turn around and go home, but once I've hit my stride I could keep going forever.

When I'm shooting fashion, it's a much more controlled environment. In street photography I welcome the unexpected, but nothing can be left to chance in fashion photography. Everything is carefully planned, from the lighting to the hair and makeup and the model's expression and attitude (and of course the clothing!). My fashion photography definitely takes some cues from my street photography in that I'm always striving for my models to be as natural as possible in terms of movement and expression. I want the story to seem real, even if it's not.

FWJ: *You seem acutely aware of the way commercialism influences daily life — which makes sense, given your background. Your subjects seem to be both engaged with and oblivious to the messages around them. How does our society's relationship with commercialism influence your photography?*

PF: When I shoot outside, the world becomes my backdrop, and advertisements and signage happen to take up a huge portion of our society's backdrop. I'm drawn to the ironies surrounding people, and often these ironic moments stem from an environment filled with ads, signs, and storefronts. Whether we know it or not, we all have a relationship with commercialism, even if it's not directly through the purchase of a particular product. Sometimes these relationships are humorous or ironic and sometimes they simply make our society's commercialism that much more obvious.

FWJ: *Which photographers and styles of photography inspire you?*

PF: My favorite photographer is Helen Levitt. Her photographs have such a quiet humor to them; I never get tired of looking at her art. When it comes to style, street photography really is my true love. Photojournalism in general captivates me like no other form. All photography is based in reality and "real" moments, but photojournalism is the most real and that's what I love about it. I love that all the poignant, funny, sweet, beautiful, horrifying, and captivating moments captured by photojournalists were all once a moment in time, a moment in a real person's life. And I love documentary photography.

For the past three years I've been participating in the annual Easter Seals DuPage and the Fox Valley Region Photography Exhibition. Each year several photographers (current students as well as alumni from the College of DuPage photography department) are assigned a special needs child who participates in the Easter Seals program, and our job is to document milestones and special moments in that child's life. It's really special for me to get to know someone through my lens and to bring them and their families joy through my photography. I plan to participate in the project again this year and hope to be involved with many other documentary projects in the future.

FWJ: *What is the main thing you want people to see in your photographs?*

PF: I want people to be as intrigued and curious about their fellow humans as I am. I want the people who look at my work to see more than just a person in a picture — I want them to see the emotion and expression that lies within all of us. I want people to see that the world is full of irony and beauty in the ordinary and that all you have to do to see it is open your eyes.

petra ford
my view

I've always been drawn to photographs and the art of taking pictures. I had a postcard collection as a young girl, which included photographs of places my friends, relatives, or I had visited. I was also my family's unofficial photographer throughout my childhood. Flipping through my family's photo albums, it's easy to tell which photographs are mine — the square prints produced by my Kodak Instamatic X-15, which I received as a gift from my godmother when I was in kindergarten. Even at that age, I enjoyed documenting and reliving moments and viewing the world through the lens of a camera.

Many people appreciate photography strictly for its aesthetics. However, the reason I came to love photography had little to do with its aesthetic qualities and everything to do with its basis in reality.

The poignant, humorous, ironic, beautiful, and gripping scenes captured by my camera were once actual moments in a real person's life, and this completely fascinates me. Nuances that may have gone unnoticed in real life are now locked in time, making the images that much richer. Wrinkles and laugh lines lead me to imagine stories about who the person is, how they spend their days, and why the lines have appeared on their face. What exactly does that half-smile mean? And the children playing in the background (or the couple holding hands near the edge of the frame) add even more to the original story. Everything and everyone becomes a character through the lens, whether they're a main character or just playing a supporting role. When I'm out with my camera, the whole world turns into a stage and I find my fellow humans to be endlessly intriguing.

I've discovered so much beauty in life through the lens of my camera. I notice color everywhere. Sometimes colors clash and sometimes they complement each other so perfectly, you swear the two strangers walking past each other just *must* have planned it, somehow. I chuckle at the commonalities I see out on the street, while at the same time am blown away by all the different relationships, attitudes, and forms of expression I stumble upon. Seemingly mundane scenes that I would have walked right by before I became a photographer now draw me in. A curiosity inside myself has been awakened, as well as a newfound appreciation for my fellow man. And for that, I'm forever grateful to have discovered photography.

I would like to dedicate the photographs in this issue to Ryan Erikson, who encouraged me to find my inspiration on days when personal stresses could have prevented me from seeing the beauty and life around me. Thank you, Ryan.

DAYGLOW
CD Release
REAL ESTATE
DONALD TRUMP LIVE!
REGISTER NOW!
LearningAnnex.com

NOTHING IS PERMANENT

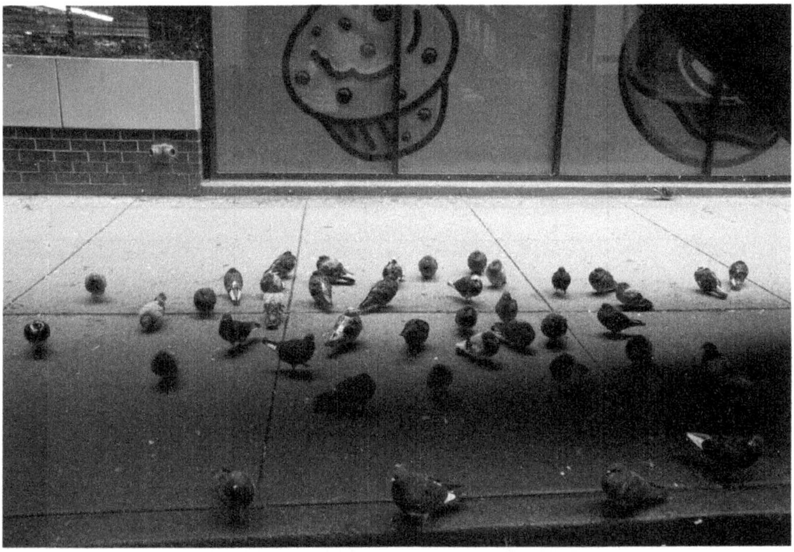

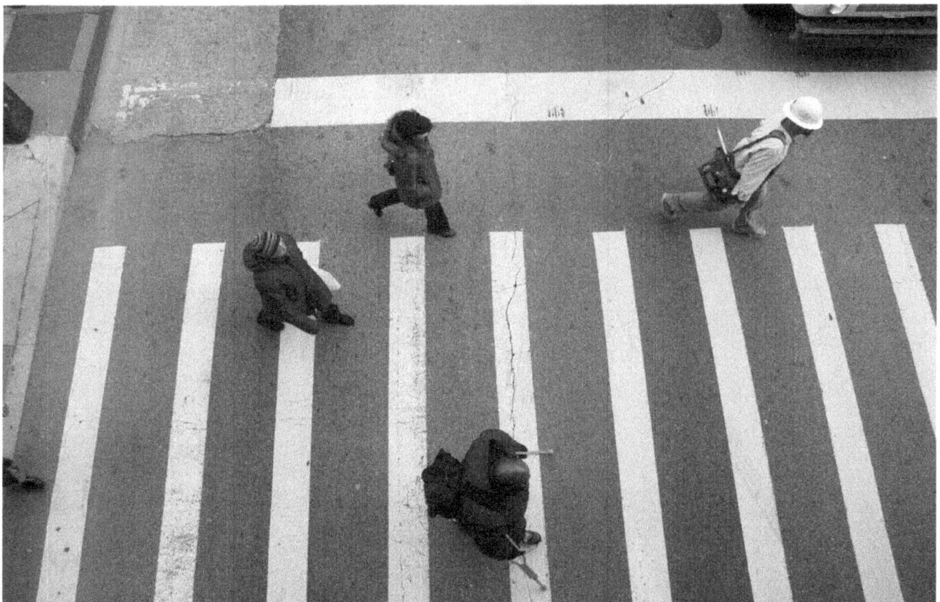

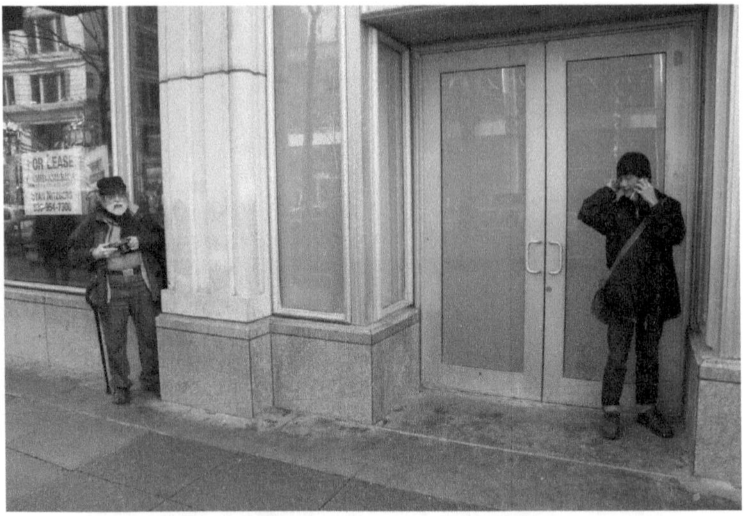
FOR LEASE

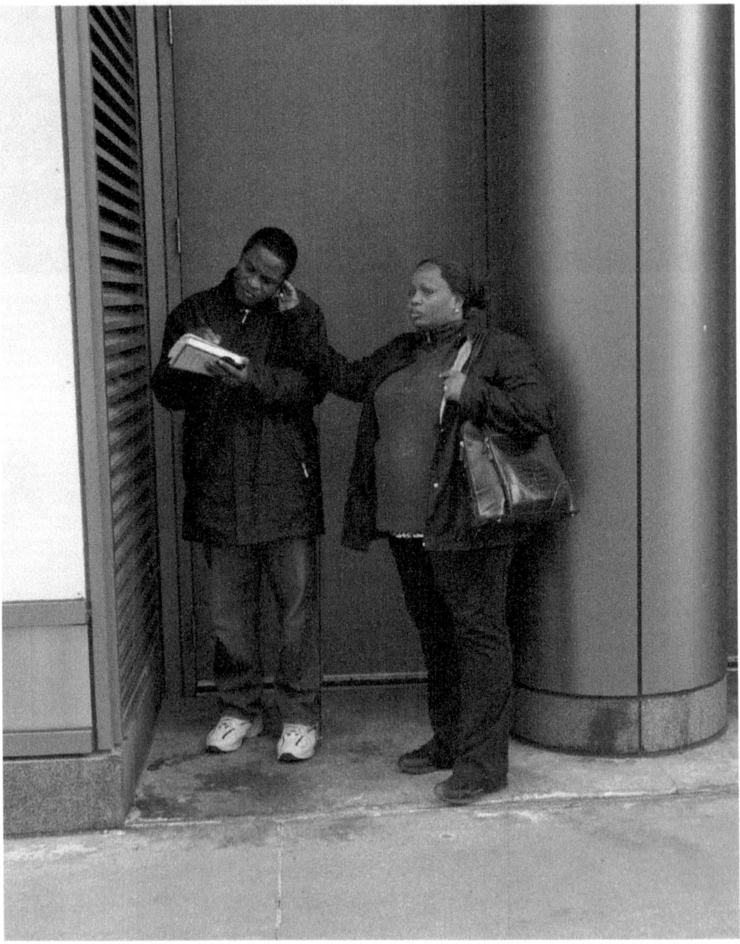

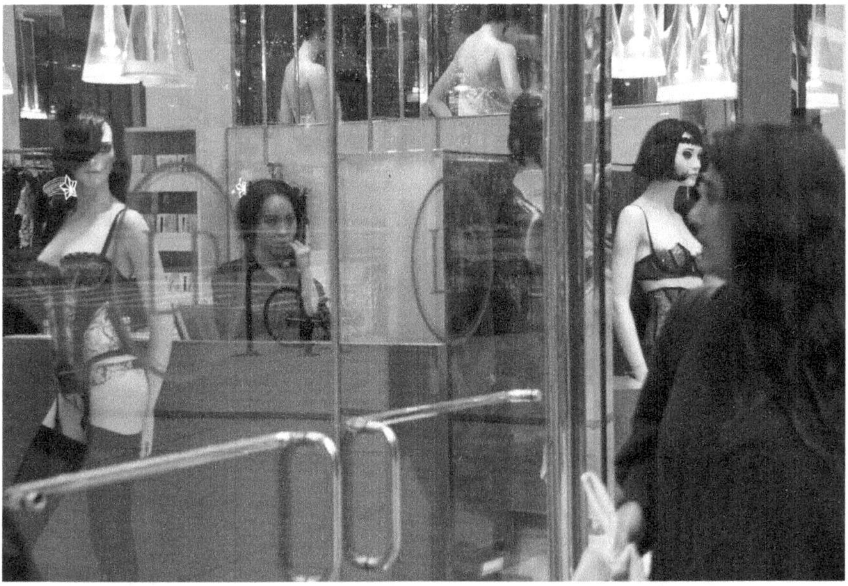

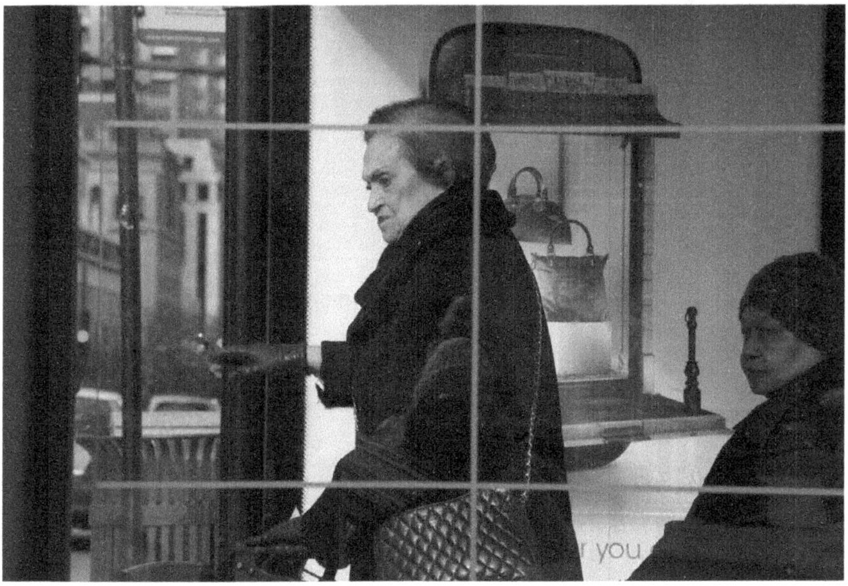

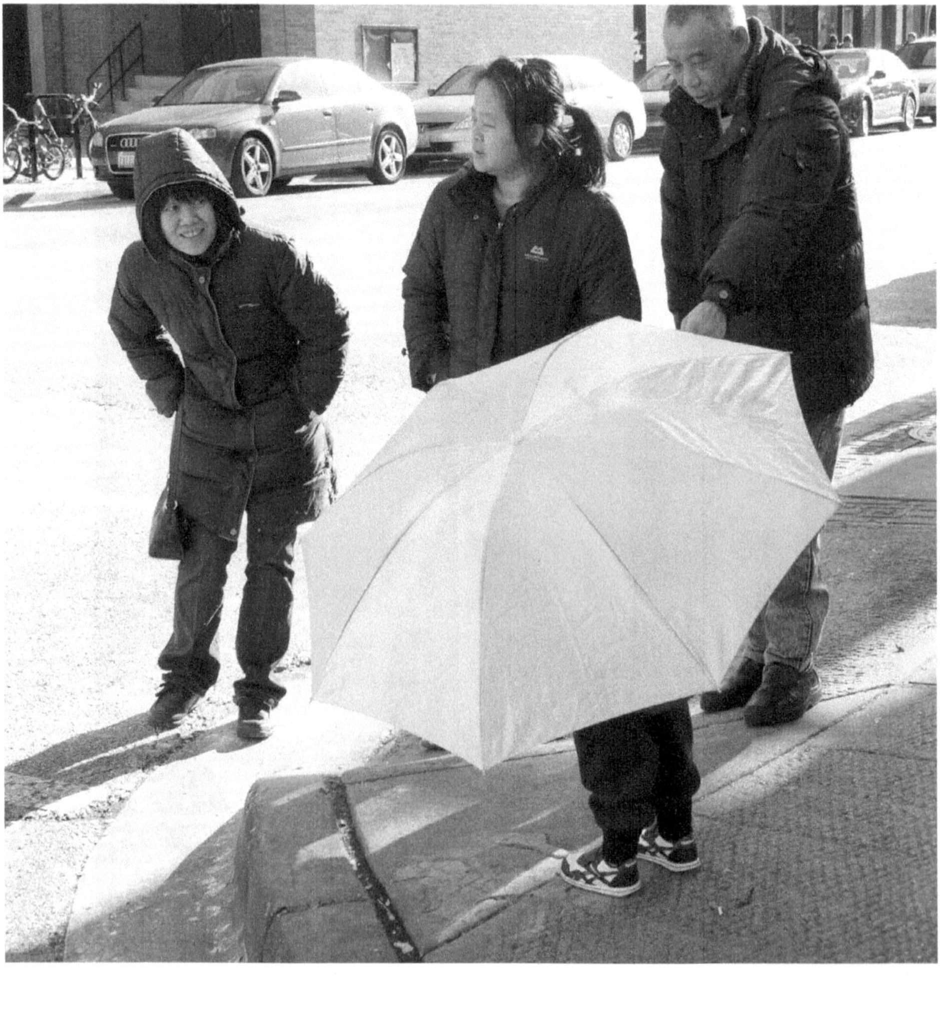

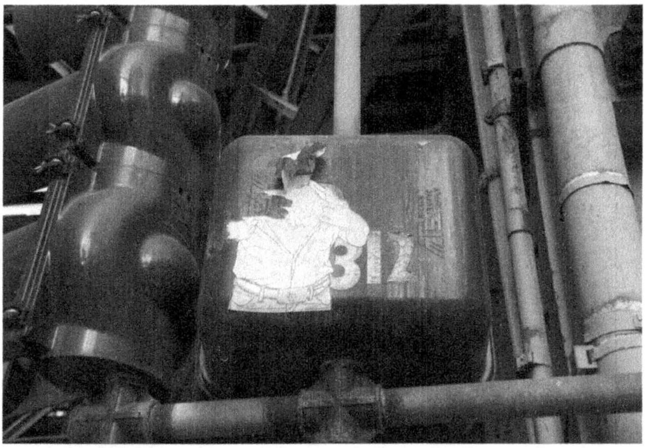
312

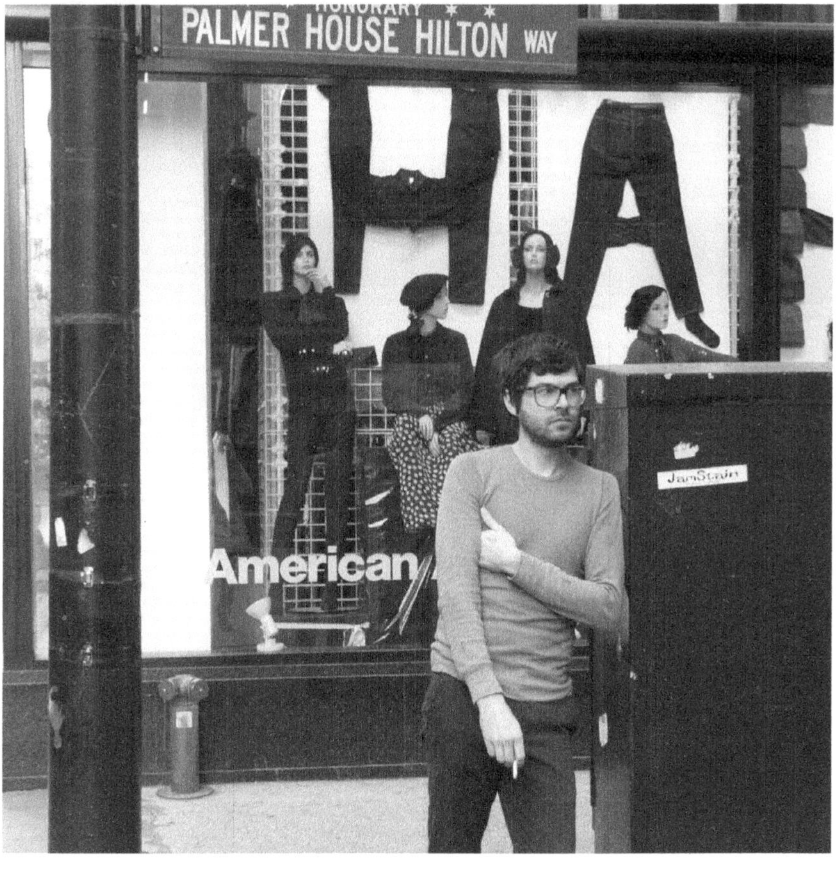
PALMER HOUSE HILTON WAY
American
JamStain

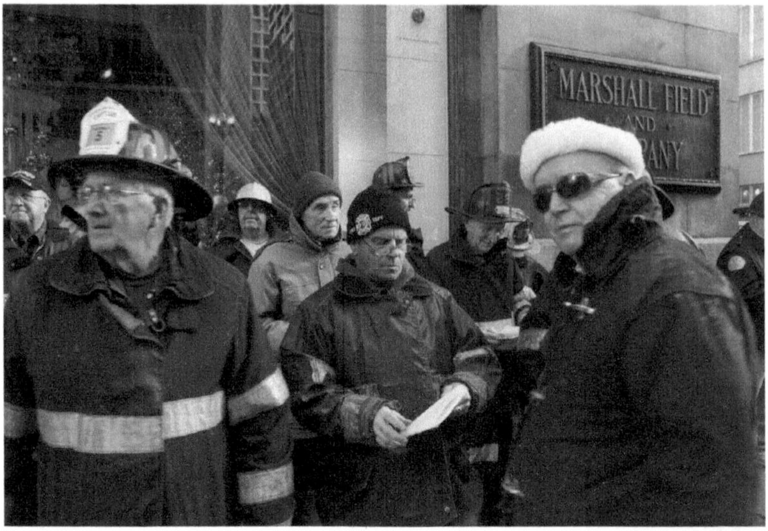
MARSHALL FIELD
AND

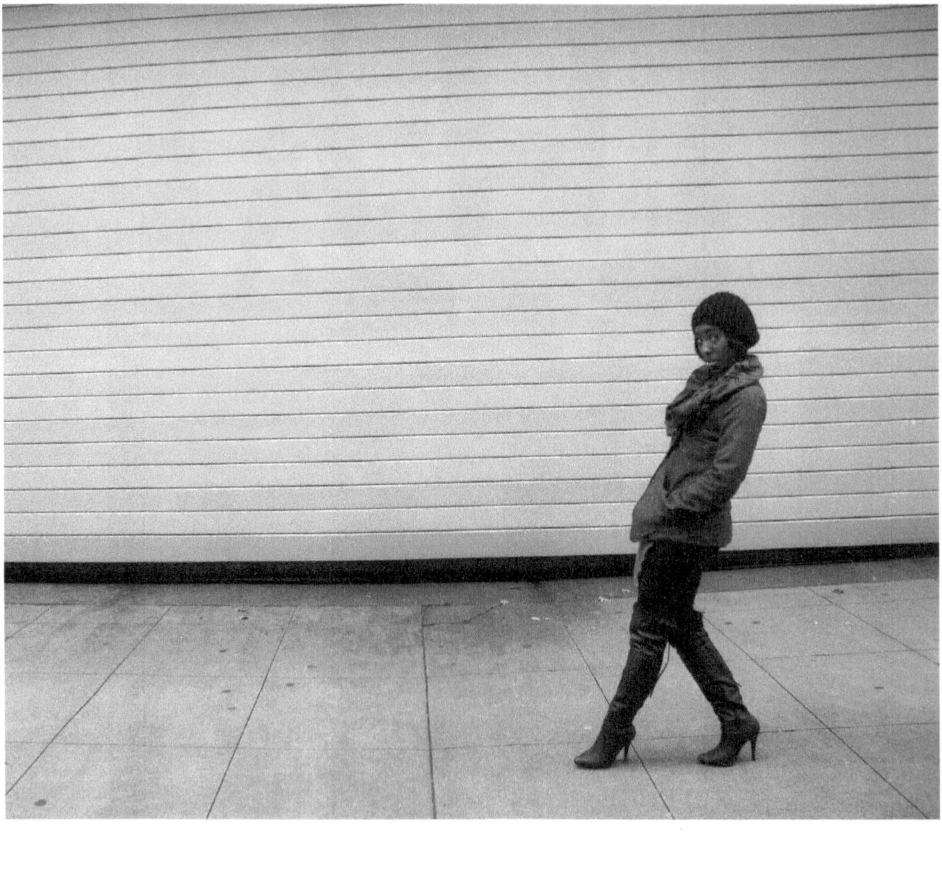

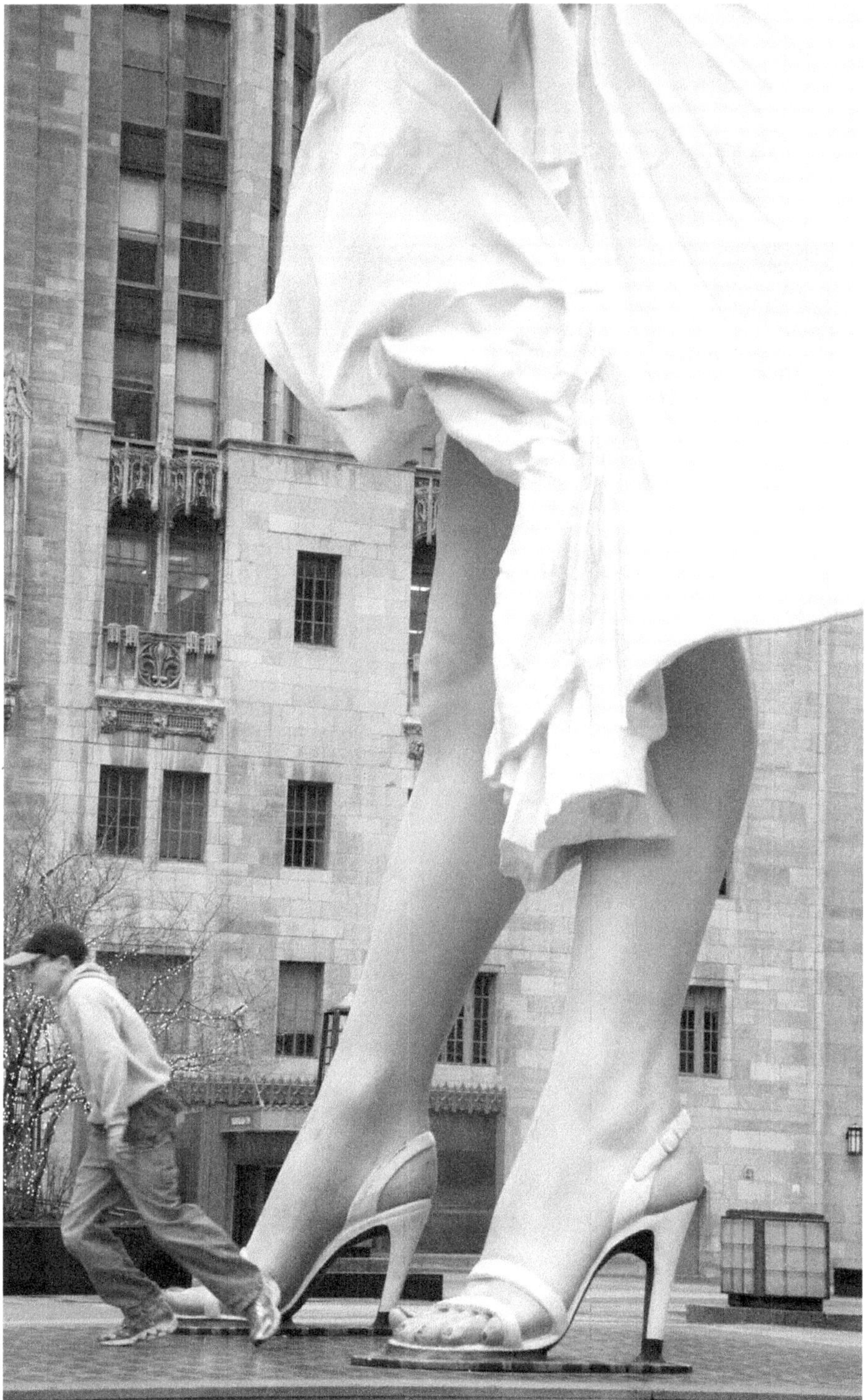

Ana Castillo Takes the Fifth

Photo credit: Daniel Libman

On a warm September afternoon in DeKalb, Illinois, *Fifth Wednesday Journal* got to spend an hour speaking with writer Ana Castillo. We sat on a couch in the Holmes Student Center of Northern Illinois University, surrounded by the buzz of student activity. We talked about Chicago and the southwest, and the amazing genre-defying career she's had, having published poetry, short story collections, essays, memoir, novels, and even theater pieces. We began with the important role place plays in her writing.

FWJ: *You're that rare artist completely associated with a specific region, in your case the American southwest generally, New Mexico specifically. But you're from out here originally.*

Ana Castillo: Chicago born and raised. I actually moved to New Mexico twice, most recently just seven years ago when I got a homestead. The first time I moved was years ago in the nineties; I moved to Albuquerque on my own and I lived there a few years. I wrote *So Far From God*, and I finished my book *Massacre of the Dreamers*. My family was based here in Chicago, and my mother's health was starting to decline. She needed someone to care for her, so I moved back with my son and spent ten years here. I was teaching at DePaul for five years. These winters were getting to me, and I started thinking about New Mexico again.

FWJ: *It's almost Texas where you're at, right?*

AC: I'm right on the border of Land Management. It's almost Texas, but El Paso, Texas, and El Paso almost considers itself part of New Mexico because El Paso has been so disenfranchised by the rest of Texas. But they don't have the regulations that New Mexico does in terms of keeping the adobe atmosphere. I live out in the desert, so it's totally like a free-for-all. It's growing, but it has the New Mexico landscape: old buildings, a lot of stucco, a lot of adobe. I purchased a stucco house that looks adobe-ish, but I actually made the little chapel out of adobe on my property. It was featured in *Real Simple* magazine when I first did it because they thought it was interesting. Some people have an altar in their house and here I go making a fifteen-hundred adobe brick chapel. New Mexico really is a place where people feel — and this sounds hokey or New Age-y to say, but there is a spiritual connection that people have or feel in that landscape. Maybe as a fellow Chicagoan who spends time there you can appreciate it.

FWJ: *Absolutely. New Mexico just feels different from everywhere else.*

AC: Yep. But you have to spend some time there to get it. You have to give it a chance and somehow or other it calls you back. I thought I would never go back, but I started having dreams about a particular place, and it wasn't Albuquerque. It took me awhile, but I figured out it was Mesilla, New Mexico. So I looked there first, but the problem was it was becoming . . . well, it didn't exactly become another Santa Fe, but it was starting to then, and realty was through the roof. So I ended up getting this place out in the desert that nobody wants to go to, but I got that connection again, and got away from the winters, and it's inspiring me again to do what I do.

FWJ: *When you were writing* So Far From God, *were you teaching at the University of New Mexico?*

AC: I never really taught taught at UNM; I did do the graduate creative writing summer workshop with Tony Hillerman. I was doing the poetry part of it and I did that for two years. And I also taught some out of the English department as an adjunct, but I was never officially hired.

FWJ: *Had you not found New Mexico, what do you think you would be writing about? Would the Chicago part of you have been more prominent in your work?*

AC: I had been living in California for many years, maybe ten years in total. And in California you have to find your bearings about what to write because there is so much going on, so many different parts of it. You go to a place like northern New Mexico and at that time you could still find a lot of old families living in original family homes because not much had changed. When I first got there I did have another novel in mind, which would have been part of my own history, my own travels, Chicago. I'm one of those writers who gets affected by place immediately. As a poet and as a fiction writer and even a nonfiction writer, place hits me. In one case, I started a story, and when I had to move and go someplace else my characters had to move too, and go with me. I had to figure out, why did they move? I had to give them a reason because I have to write in that ambiance. This might be changing for me now that I'm older and there is more memory for me than new things. When I first got to Albuquerque I was working on a novel that I intended to have take place in Chicago even though I had been living in California. And I was starting to look at the Chicago that I know, the one I grew up in. But that place, New Mexico, it hits you like a ton of bricks. It only took me about a month to get started, and then I finished the novel in about six months.

FWJ: *And then how long did you spend revising* So Far From God*?*

AC: The novel that you see is the one I wrote with almost no changes. Very little editing. The only thing that came later was the last chapter. I added that after I turned the book in. I ended up doing that because I had written two novels before, but never one that was on contract with a publisher and an editor. Norton had asked me for an outline, and I had never done that, either. So I said, "Yeah, sure, I'll give you an outline." I wrote it, and chapter ten has this very happy ending. And at the time I was going through all this stuff, I didn't get the teaching job I thought I would have, and so everyone died at the end of the novel. My agent called me and said, "You know you promised them a happy ending." So I added that last chapter. And I don't think they even saw that original version without the ending — but what you see there is just basically what I wrote out the first time.

FWJ: *Is that typical of your process, that the first draft is close to the finished product with little revision?*

AC: No. No, it's not. The newest novel that I just completed, which is going to Random House, I started in 2007, and I had many of life's challenges that have just derailed me. It was going to be an entirely different book in every sense of the word. It's evolved into something else. It was going to be a historical novel; it no longer is. It was going to have different characters. There is a little seed of truth, a little tiny kernel that I started out with that's still there. I might have done a million drafts on this one.

FWJ: *It seems like stuff in the real world directly impacts the things that happen to your characters. It doesn't just affect your ability to write, but it literally alters what you're writing about.*

AC: Yes. And I would say that layering and going back and doing that finessing is much more typical of my writing process. I would love to finish the rough draft and send it out and have the publishers say, "Hey, great! We want it." But that doesn't happen, unfortunately. That comes with the territory. I have my own standards, so way before anybody else reads it I've gone through dozens of drafts. This book, for example, that I just turned in, which evolved from something totally different — nobody had read it until it got to that point. I had a two-book contract with Random House, and the second book was whatever. It's going to be a novel, whatever. Well, I had an editor who bought the two books, but with the horrible plunging of our economy and with the reductions of most industries, she unfortunately was let go. She was the original person who bought the books, who I had pitched the ideas to. Now she's gone. About a year and a half ago I submitted the book I had written to a new editor, one I had no relationship with, and she gave me a bunch of notes with a bunch of directions she thought the book could go, which was like basically giving me an overhaul. So I said, OK, and I went off earnestly with those notes.

FWJ: *Do you take those notes seriously?*

AC: Oh, yeah. Yes, I do. When I hear my colleagues whine and complain about the notes they get . . .

FWJ: *I've heard close editing like that doesn't even exist anymore, gone with Max Perkins.*

AC: It definitely still exists. No editor is going to publish a book with her signature on it without her feeling good about it. In fact, I have a friend who is with another well-known publisher, and she came to one of my memoir-writing workshops which I do that are open to the public. And I thought, this is interesting, because she's a published novelist. Why is she coming to my workshop? She must be in trouble. Sure enough, she says, "I just got eight pages of notes from my editor, single-spaced, and I'm just going to throw the whole thing out . . ." On and on. "And now I'm just going to write something else. I'm going to write my story, my memoirs." OK, do what you gotta do, but eventually you're going to have to go back there. And once she said that, I was thinking, well, I got eleven pages from my editor, and I didn't even know my editor. I knew my friend's editor, and I didn't even know my own editor. But still I did take those notes very seriously. I had another conversation with the first editor, the editor of record, and I had yet another conversation with my new agent even though she has nothing to do with that particular book. And so all this is to say that, yes, I do take all those notes seriously, just as I take my career very seriously. I may have started out as a renegade protest poet believing no one was ever going to publish me. But I also fought for people like myself, including all poets, to be published. To be taken seriously. To have our work out there, and maybe even to be able to make a little bit of a living off it. So here I am. And after going through all the notes and I overhauled this whole thing, and then I got a note from the second editor telling me she's leaving the publisher. So now I don't even have an editor, and I've got this manuscript. Sometimes if your editor goes, the publishing house will say, by the way, all your books are gone, too. When this happened they told me I was staying. So my book is still there, but I have no editor. And I just finished the novel, and poor me, I know. No editor. And it was the president of Random House who called to say she was still expecting the novel.

FWJ: *Such problems!*

AC: Yes, right. Such problems to have in my life. So she took it and went off on vacation and I was waiting to hear for some time what's going to be the verdict. But she did come back and place it with a new editor. And who knows? This editor might want me to overhaul it again in a whole new direction.

FWJ: *Does it have a title yet?*

AC: *The Last Goddess Standing*. You know, the title is the thing that I started out with years ago and it's the one part of it that hasn't changed, even when I've wanted to change it. Now it's become symbolic of what's happening with the book so I'm really stuck with it.

FWJ: *You mentioned poetry earlier. It's rare to find someone who is accepted in the literary world as both a poet and a fiction writer. Someone like Ray Carver is really thought of as a fiction writer but his poetry is sort of tolerated. On the other side you've got people like Mark Strand who has been the poet laureate, but he's got some fiction out there which hasn't gotten much attention. You're different in the sense that you're accomplished in both genres.*

AC: I'm happy you say that because I don't think I'm accepted in both genres by the American academy. In my experience, when I've been at poetry festivals and there is one of those guys there, they don't even speak to me. And I think with the success of my books, *So Far From God* in particular, where I was thrown into the view of the mainstream, readers discovered me in that milieu and hadn't heard of any of my other work. I had been working on poetry at that point for eight years without doing anything else, not teaching or trying to make a living. I just wrote poetry, telling myself, if I'm going to make a living on it, this is all I can do. I had some success with my collection *My Father*

Was a Toltec, so when *So Far From God* came out I was really very surprised when people came up to me and asked if I've written poetry. I found that the poetry fell to the sidelines. It already is for a lot of people just a side genre, unfortunately, so the fiction writing was so much more highlighted of what I do.

FWJ: *Sure. Because you've published quite a bit of nonfiction, too.*

AC: And articles. And I have my one official play that I wrote. Two versions of the play I wrote.

FWJ: *Two versions?*

AC: It's called *Psst . . . I Have Something to Tell You, Mi Amor*. And it was based on the story of a torture survivor, which I had originally written as a poem in one of my books. When I was still living in Chicago, a director from the Goodman Theater approached me about dramatizing the story, which had all the elements of a play, the actual story, without changing anything about it. And then I decided to turn it into an actual drama piece, and it had a wonderful premiere there.

FWJ: *You did the actual adaptation?*

AC: I studied a bunch of plays over the summer and then knocked it out.

FWJ: *Can I ask what the plays were that you studied?*

AC: I reread a bunch of plays that I had read before. I can't even tell you the names because I might be making it up. I could say Beckett or somebody, but you know, I had a bunch of plays on my bookshelf. But the most influential thing that happened to me that summer was that I was invited to speak in Germany where I received my PhD; some alumni had discovered me, and they had a conference, and a good friend of mine in Germany had turned into a theater agent by coincidence. A fluke. She'd been teaching but then became this agent looking at plays in English and German. We traveled together to Amsterdam and she had all these plays she had to be reading. I was with her, and I started reading them, too, all these European plays that may or may not have ever been produced, and I got to study all these contemporary styles. There was one that really impressed me. It was done with two characters in tandem and unfortunately I don't even remember who the author was. My intention was to read the stars, you know, read Shakespeare or Garcia Lorca, but it was these I ended up reading that summer traveling around with her, and when I got back I knocked out my play just like that.

FWJ: *That's really serendipitous.*

AC: Yes. And we were talking about sense of place before and that goes back to this idea. Who would have known that my little trip to Germany and Amsterdam with my friend with her little satchel of plays would be so important. So I did the play and it was very successful and it's been produced at various universities and it had a wonderful premier at the Goodman. It was well-reviewed, and I was very happy. It's been done at the University of Chicago and at Cornell. I'm not pushing it anymore because I don't want people to think, "Again, that play?" I have to write another play.

FWJ: *Do you go see it when it's produced? What's that like?*

AC: When they've invited me. I have a very interesting relationship with my writing and my editors or people like the director. I've been told I'm different this way from other writers. I don't get attached to it in the sense that I don't get emotional about it. Once the work is there, the work is there. Once it's in a director's hands, it's the director's vision. When it premiered at the Goodman I had the not very brilliant idea of inviting the person on whom the work is based. The torture survivor, who also published her memoirs, and so forth. And it was packed the first night, so many people, four hundred seats, and I was sitting with her. I had been asked by the director to add a little levity somewhere in the beginning because it gets very intense, very dark. And so I did — new material. So we were watching it and here's this new material and it flows and she's just like, "Mmmm, OK, great." And then the grimness comes in, and she just fell apart in my hands. And when she fell apart, I fell apart. I just started crying and we were weeping and she was clutching me, and so the first night I never even got to see the play because we were both weeping so badly. She basically had a meltdown, and I had a meltdown because she had a meltdown. I never got to see it; I didn't even open my eyes. So the next night I went with some other people in the audience and I finally got to hear it. It was very nice to hear it because now I was so detached from [the narrative] that it was like going to see someone else's writing. Hearing someone else saying words that you've written is a very nice experience.

FWJ: *Were you able to be taken by surprise at all by what was on stage?*

AC: Oh, yes. I was very impressed with myself. You know when you're reading your own work and I'm up on stage I often think, how the hell did the editors let me get away with this crap? And I'm not the only one who thinks like this. I've talked to other writers who say — especially if they're on a book tour — they think, how in the world did they let me publish this? I wish I could go over it one more time. So this was new to me to hear an actor doing it, and it was great.

FWJ: *What's your favorite? Fiction, nonfiction, playwriting?*

AC: I can tell you what I don't like, and that's what I'm doing now. Nonfiction. I just finished the novel and I have a book contract with the Feminist Press for personal essays, and when I turned in that novel last summer, I had to dance around that idea of writing personal essays for a month. Because I know what that's going to take out of me once I start working, the reflection, going back into that place emotionally. The other is the style, the transitional phrase, why am I writing this, why do you want to read this? All of those things come into question when we're talking about writing personal essays or critical essays. You've got to make the personal connection with the universe in a very linear, thought-out, conscious way. No forgiveness there that you can get in *So Far From God*, that you can get in a poem. Readers don't forgive you when they're reading essays. Why am I here? If I'm not connected, I'm not interested.

FWJ: *So is it easier to be honest in fiction?*

AC: Yes! Fiction is total joy for a writer. It's your world. And you only have to hold that reader in the suspension of disbelief. As long as you don't break them out of it, if they get on board in the first few pages or in the first chapter, they're on board with you. You can create any kind of world for them as long as they're a good reader, meaning as long as they don't say, "You can't walk from Albuquerque to Chimayo in a day." I've had those nasty Amazon reviewers who say, "She doesn't know anything about New Mexico." It's fiction. That's why it's not an essay. But when you do nonfiction you have to have the qualifications. You gotta prove it. All that has to come together or your reader is gone.

FWJ: *Where does poetry fit into that spectrum?*

AC: My props go to the poet who really makes a commitment to poetry and isn't writing little stories with broken lines, little anecdotes with broken lines. I think modern poetry has fallen into that camp and is just a lot of that. But if they're actually looking at language, at the craft, which takes a combination of elements of what poetry should be, even if it doesn't end up being in meter, then my hat goes off to her or to him. It takes an incredible amount of discipline to sit down and work on that. It could take ten years to do a book. Easily. It's much more of a blessing from the gods to be able to do poetry, and I would like to do one more collection before I'm gone, but I know that it's a time I have to set aside to do that.

FWJ: *You write your poetry in big batches then, instead of a poem here or a poem there until you've accumulated a book?*

AC: What happened with the last collection is my play went into production, and I must have gone into some state of denial. You know, "I can't be having a play produced in downtown Chicago having never written one before . . ." I was teaching at the time and off for the summer, so I was also supposed to be working on a new novel. I was having a very hard time with the editor I had. She hated everything I showed her. I went home looking for something else, and I had one poem that I had written in the past year, and it was a very dark poem, written in a night of despair. And when I reread it I saw that it was very sad, very suicidal. It was twenty-seven pages long, and I decided to sit down and start cleaning it up. And then sort of cheering it up, too. And as I cheered it up the story grew longer and longer, and there were more stories to tell, all in three-line stanzas. And before I knew it, six weeks went by, and I had three hundred pages. It was several stories about — who knows who the narrator is when you write a poem, but it was about this original narrator. Then I was going into Greek mythology and Aztec mythology and I was telling about the history of Mexicans and I was picking up on all this stuff I might have put in a novel, but instead I was escaping. I had these three hundred pages, and I thought, I really am going to have to stop. I mean, I always wanted to write an epic, but maybe this wasn't the time. So I finished it and turned it in to that editor who never liked anything I wrote, and she said it was very nice, but where was her novel. And I said, "This is a novel. It's a novel in verse." So I turned it over to a small press, God bless them. They published a lot of poetry, a lot of poetry from other countries. This was Curbstone. They just folded up and sold everything to Northwestern. But they published my novel in verse, and it was called *Watercolor Women / Opaque Men*, and it won the Best of the Independent Publishers award in 2005. It was like I got it out in one summer. But now I have to go back and write a novel.

FWJ: *So you stay in one mode as you work?*

AC: Everybody's different, but normally if I'm in prose mode I don't go back and write a poem at night or something like that. I would really like to go back and do a play or two as part of the oeuvre, and I've been thinking about the second play. I don't normally think about it because I don't live in a theater atmosphere. So I'm going to have to just sit down and say, OK, I'm going to write a play now. It's going to be one summer or one winter, and I'll say, now I'm going to write my play.

FWJ: *Are you strict about your work habits?*

AC: When I was young I thought of myself as a nocturnal person, and I used to write at night. My first novels and most of my short stories I would get inspired by the silence of the night when everyone else was asleep and that whole thing. You have your busy day behind you. I have a son who's an adult now, but being a single mom and raising him on my own, I had to start working around his schedule. Also, I taught and had to earn a living, so I had to learn to write whenever I could write. At this point I'm not teaching, but my writing schedule is pretty much something in my twenties I never thought would be the case, which is that I get up, make my coffee, and I go to my computer. And I pretty much can knock out a six-hour day right now. With *The Guardians*, the last time I published, I was doing twelve hours. Nothing else. You don't even want to stop to eat. You just go get something from the kitchen and then bring it back and you eat it. Now I've had a lot of life distractions, so my focus doesn't stay as long as I would like. I would like to rebuild that again.

FWJ: *Do you get anxious if you aren't writing as much as you think you should?*

AC: No, because I'm a very hardworking person, a disciplined person. I know once my days aren't broken up so much that I can make myself go back to it.

FWJ: *How do you see yourself, then, as a fiction writer who also writes poems? A novelist or a short story writer? Are you an essayist who writes plays? If you were to have business cards printed up, what would they say? Ana Castillo . . .*

AC: Writer.

Daniel Libman is a past fiction editor of *Fifth Wednesday Journal*. He is currently the book reviews editor for FWJ. His story collection *Married But Looking* was recently published by Livingston Press.

DAVID HERNANDEZ

Ramonita the Avon Lady

My mother used to order Avon products from the lady who lived on
Newport Street.
She used to visit on Saturday mornings when the house smelled
like fresh coffee and Olde English furniture polish. Her name was
Ramonita. She had gold-speckled eyes set
in a face so sunny that she made me and any 11-year boy blush, sigh,
stutter, splutter, spin around, and run into things. I was in love with her.

The Avon ladies were all beautiful women about my mother's age
in their mid-thirties who knew each other from the neighborhood,
the hair salon, or from the work place at Grant Hospital. My Avon
Lady was married to a guy named Teodoro who looked just like his
name sounded. He was about as exciting as a Wednesday night prayer
meeting, so Ramonita became an Avon Cosmetic Sales Lady to keep
from being bored to death.

I knew that if I was to be her hero, I must free Ramonita my Avon Lady
from the sometimes sadness in her eyes reflecting the restless heart of
a maiden in distress imprisoned in a castle tower. Free her from the
drab clutches of everydayness and fulfill her longing for romance and
adventure. So with my very best adult handwriting, I wrote her a note
that read: "Te amo. Te adoro. Vente conmigo./I love you. I adore you.
Come with me. Signed, El Aguila Negra/The Black Eagle." Then I
slipped it into her handbag while she sipped café con leche with my
mother in the kitchen.

A few days later I was playing with Randy Ott in the backyard when
I heard the Avon Lady call out my name. I turned around to see her
in a glowing smile just as she scooped me up into her arms, looked
warmly into my eyes and then she kissed my cheek. It was the kiss of
a fairy tale come true and in that moment of ecstasy and humming bird
rushes, we melted into a city aglow with fireflies and thunder, oh what
a perfect moment that was!

From that day on I was no longer sad because in my heart of hearts I
knew that the Avon Lady loved me. We were very happy with her little
winks and my secret little sighs of adoration.
A few months later Ramonita kissed me one last time before moving

back to Puerto Rico with her husband Teodoro from the church. She said "Thank you Corazon my love. Next lifetime we will run away to our magic castle and live happily ever after." Then she held me tight and left.

That evening while sitting and brooding on the back porch, I spotted an empty jar of Avon Night Time Face Cream in the garbage can. So I washed it out and it's been with me ever since.
And I know that somewhere on the island, under moon, sea, and sand, Ramonita the Avon Lady is walking barefooted on the beach reading the first poem I ever wrote and the only one she ever received: "Te amo. Te adoro. Vente conmigo./I love you. I adore you. Come with me. Signed, El Aguila Negra/The Black Eagle."

TONY HOAGLAND

Warning for Shoppers

You can get wasp spray that smells like fresh citrus.
You can get intelligent Velcro shoelaces
that know when to hold on and when to let go.

You can get birth control for cats.
You can get toilet paper printed with dead presidents.
You can get a car that subsonically enhances
                              the jealousy of others.

If that does not improve your mood,
you can get a capsule that eliminates
ambivalence

You can get above-the-knees preview
and backstage afterwards.
You can get sanctioned flirtations

and professionalized commitments of friendship.
You can get group cremation
for your entire volleyball team

and have the ashes scattered from a hot air balloon
painted to look like a big volleyball.
You can get many things,

but you can't keep the hope and disappointment
of being human
from rising up and rolling

off you in waves.
You surge forward.
You're dangerous, too.

TONY HOAGLAND

Wrong Question

Are you all right? she asks, wrinkling her brow,
and I think how unfair that question is,

how it rises up and hangs there in the air
like a Welcome sign shining in the dark;

Are you all right? is all she has to say
with that faint line between her eyebrows
                              that signifies concern,

and her soft, moral-looking mouth,
and I feel as if I have fallen off my bike

and she wants to take care of my skinned knee
back at her apartment.

Are you all right? she says,

and all the belts begin to move inside my factory
and all the little citizens of me

lay down their tasks, stand up and start to sing
their eight-hour version of The Messiah of my Unhappiness.

Am I all right?

I thought I was all right before she asked,

but now I find that I have never been all right.
There is something soft and childish at my core

I have not been able to eliminate.
And yet — it is the question I keep answering.

J. ALLYN ROSSER

ABC of the Human Condition

The HC remembers the Alamo but forgets what it starts with; is the
Bee in its own bonnet; is all about
Codification of other C's in relation to its own;
Distinguishes itself from any other, and depends on that distinction for
    delight and despair. The HC is the
Extenuation of every circumstance, doesn't take seriously enough the phrase
For all we know, nor for that matter
Go figure. The HC
Honestly thinks it should be funded just for being H, and has decided
    figuratively, and literally in English, to capitalize only one of
Its pronouns. The HC is a perfectly proportioned and conditioned
Jockey who fears horses; shoulders the silent *k* in
Knife like a rifle in a parade for peace;
Likes to learn new things if they're familiar; is the
Mother of beauty but does not have much of a maternal instinct;
Never says *never* convincingly, nevertheless remaining
Open to others' correct opinions; is much greater than a
Powerbook and smaller than a period's erasure; would like in the future to be
Quoted responsibly. The HC is what can't be
Redeemed by anything but what is outside itself; is completely
Sequestered inside itself, and aspires to the serenity of
Trees it will chop down for timber or the fun of chopping; claims it's
    famished for the
Ultimate while nibbling on the droppings in hand; makes a
Volcano from a vacuum; continually tallies
What it wants on paper pulped from what it wanted. The HC is the
X-acto knife applied to its deepest beliefs. It is a
Yearning, a yearning
Zooming in on its lens.

J. ALLYN ROSSER

Weekend at Trish's

It didn't matter that I'd never used a needle for anything but sewing, or that none of my husbands had used his hands to draw blood or stop my breathing. Isabel said Trish was her friend and I was her friend and that by Sunday Trish would be able to see why. Plus it helped that I had no religion, which Isabel knew would give me more exotic pathos in Trish's eyes than any amount of flood-damaged stolen merchandise or failed rehab on her side could generate for me. Isabel herself was at a halfway point between us, feeling cynically optimistic right after her divorce and before the new boyfriend would jam her credit and father a child with her neighbor — that was still several months ahead — and she said as long as we stayed away from the track (Trish might borrow on her food stamps) and a certain bar and the Asbury Park boardwalk we should be fine. And we were, though I noticed Trish sneaking looks at Isabel when I wasn't, and there was my gin-influenced mention of a year spent in Rome, which I think preceded her tirade on the Jews lousing up her neighborhood and her joke with the punch line "mobile homos"; then there was my reference to Nietzsche, out of my mouth before we'd had coffee — some pre-ground brand that could choke a cowboy. All this made Isabel so tense she couldn't sleep and spent half the night scanning the Net for a program Trish wanted to tape but didn't know what channel, hoping this would mollify Trish for my not recognizing Bob Marley's face on an ugly painting she had on the wall, and for accidentally throwing away a roach, and for things I still don't know I did wrong. Deep in the night while we slept she surfed and sighed, slumping at last on the desk with Google pop-ups twitching over her head like bad dreams. You have to know about Isabel that she hates being the klutz or ignoramus, hates when the ketchup packet finally opens by spurting up the length of her nose, or when she walks into a pole because her head was turned, or not understanding when someone says "That is so froody" or "Nice ink," so you'll understand how the whole weekend was saved when Trish told her it was a TV evangelist program called *Lakewood Church* she should have been searching for, when we were all (not just Isabel) spilling our awful coffee, tearful from laughing, not *Liquid Church*, which is what was streaming almost equally down our cheeks at that moment.

MARY QUADE

Cage
Nonfiction

I discover them a few stalls down from the white ducks huddled in a spot of shade behind a tarp, past the speckled eels circling a blue plastic tub in a few inches of water — the sparse amenities of the doomed. The market runs along one side of a street in the Old Quarter of Hanoi, several blocks of vendors under tin roofs. Across the street stand more permanent buildings: a narrow café open to the sidewalk, where men sit on foot-high red plastic chairs reading the newspaper; a temple flanked by two shops selling coffins and funeral wreaths. On the market side, nestled next to an aquaria merchant with tropical fish swimming in jars and luminous artificial plants displayed on a plank like a festive centerpiece, the cages teeter in towers, tremulous wire and bamboo. Some hang from the corrugated tin roof, skeletal bells with swing clappers — the birds inside ringing. Some catch the morning light on their thin bars, scattering sun.

A cage keeps a living thing in, but doesn't keep the world out. The breeze, the rain, the noise, the cold and heat, the darkness and bright, the reach of man, the insects, the poisonous air — all these pass through the bars to the thing inside. The word *cage* comes from the Latin for cage, *cavea*, which makes me think there have always been cages. No one knows where the word *cagey* comes from.

My husband and I have been in Hanoi for a day. Before that, we were on planes for twenty-four hours. And before that, I was home, in the United States, in North America, the continent where I'd lived my whole life and never left. I was sitting on my front porch, watching morning traffic pass by and reading the paper in the sun while cicadas rattled the sycamores.

At the bird stall, some of the cages are hidden by red fabric covers. Some of the cages possess ornately carved bases. One has a perch decorated with dragon heads. The finer bamboo cages have tiny white and blue ceramic dishes for seed and water; the wire cages, plastic feeders. The wire cages rustle with feathers and beaks. One, the size of a milk crate, holds a dozen yellow-green parakeets. In each bamboo cage, a single bird, every kind unfamiliar to me, yet distinct. A bird with a black crest, red cheeks, a white belly. A green bird with a blue throat, red mark on its head. A small grayish-green bird with curved beak, white spot around its eye. I've never seen birds like these in cages, or anywhere.

In a wire cage resting on the ground, a pair of bantam chickens, a cock and a hen. Next to the chickens, also in a wire cage, lies a thin white kitten, listless. The kitten's cage is a bird cage, with a dish of water and a wooden dowel for a perch.

A bird is fragile; it's hard to find someone to care for them properly, someone to notice their needs. For fifteen years, we've had birds. First a duck, then a quail, then more ducks, then chickens, more quail. I've never left my continent before because of our birds. When I look at the bantams in the cage at my feet, I imagine my own little rooster back home, his call much like the rooster outside our hotel window on Yên Thái.

Above the bantams sit several large wire cages full of dull brown birds. Unlike the birds in the bamboo cages, whistling tunefully, these birds cheep. Their feathers frazzle, dotted with droppings. They ricochet around, grasping the wires with their feet, then letting go. They look familiar. Unlike the other birds, which have seed, the only food these birds have is a pile of cooked rice on the bottom of their cage.

I'm certain I should be outraged by these birds at the bird stall — their conditions, their probable poaching, their expendability. As I stand there, a man scoops a pile of the dead up off the ground with a shovel. The temperature is one hundred degrees and rising. And yet, somehow, I'm elated by the birds — their precise beauty, their delicate homes, their graceful dishes of seed. When the din from the motorbikes in the street dies down, I can hear them singing.

It takes me a few minutes to figure out what the dull birds are. Sparrows. For cooking and eating. Now I understand the crowded cages, the rice. I only wonder about all the little bones.

Sparrow is the name of an air-interceptor missile used by American forces. Originally designed for targets Beyond Visual Range, Cold War threats hurtling towards the homeland, it was fired from planes and guided by radar to take down enemy aircraft. In the Vietnam War — or the American War, as it's called in Vietnam — it wasn't really used this way because of concerns about Identification Friend or Foe protocol. Instead, pilots had to see who they were shooting before firing. In the end, its "kill probability" during the war was considered disappointing. This language surrounding the Sparrow feels resistant, an obstacle I can't quite cross. I've never seen a Sparrow missile in real life, but in the labeled pictures, the Sparrow is a long tube, with a cone on one end, four wings in the middle, and four fins at the end. The difference between wings and fins appears imperceptible. To me, they all look like wings.

Depending on who's telling the story, the names change. Sometimes it's a story about South Vietnam versus North Vietnam and the Vietcong. Sometimes it's a story about the People's Army of Việt Nam and the National Front for the Liberation of South Việt Nam versus the American-supported puppet regime. Sometimes it's a story about the Army Republic of Việt Nam versus the Việt Cộng and the communist North. These names are all variants of *us* and *them*.

At the bird stall taking pictures, I'm a tourist; this is what I do — record it so I can process it later. I want to research these birds, find out what they are, put a name to something mysterious. Surely there's a book out there somewhere with these birds in it, neatly marked with a list of facts. I move from cage to cage, the camera finding the focus. Only after the woman running the stall grabs my wrist, shaking her head angrily at my camera, do I remember that this is someone's life I'm standing in. If I could speak the language, I could tell her I just enjoy the birds and want to keep a memory of them with me. Instead, I must seem nosy and judgmental, or simply in the way. I feel ashamed or sad, and can't decide which, a confusion that grows later after I look at my photos and notice in them something I'd missed: a small Vietnamese boy, crouched down, taking pictures of the kitten.

In a neighborhood south of the market lies Hỏa Lò prison, built by the French in the 1880s to house Vietnamese prisoners and known to American prisoners of war by the nickname Hanoi Hilton. There are stories of torture and inhumane conditions and executions from when the French ran the prison, and there are stories of torture and inhumane conditions and executions from when the Vietnamese ran the prison. One of its more famous prisoners was United States senator and 2008 presidential candidate John McCain, who was captured after his plane crashed into a lake in Hanoi. Another prisoner was Joseph Kittinger, the man who holds the record for the highest, fastest skydive. Today, much of the prison is gone, destroyed to make way for new construction; what's left is now a museum, which I don't visit. It isn't something I feel I need to see, just like the preserved body of Hồ Chí Minh at the mausoleum complex, which I also skip. Both of these are on my guidebook map, along with the Temple of Literature, which I do visit, and something simply labeled "Paddleboats," which I don't.

Back home, when we'd lose one of our birds to predators, we'd devise new ways of keeping them safe. For nearly eight years, we carried a much-loved pet duck inside each night to sleep in a tub in our basement. She died while we were on a trip away, when the boy watching her failed to get her in before dark. Something chewed her head completely off, leaving no trace, though her body was perfectly intact. We once built what we thought was a secure cage for a few dozen quail we were raising to release. One night, a raccoon reached in and killed six or seven, pulling parts of their bodies through the chicken wire. We lost chickens to hawks that flew into the yard and hen house. I came home once to find a bantam hen being eaten alive, the hawk pulling off breast meat as she still breathed. I always thought maybe if I had done this or that, it wouldn't have happened.

There are also stories of torture by the South Vietnamese, using methods taught to them by American forces, overseen by American soldiers. One story that's difficult to deny is of the Côn Sơn Island "tiger cages" off the coast of Vietnam. Here men and women — suspected communists, people who protested against the government and war — were kept in five-foot by nine-foot cells with bars on the ceiling, three to five prisoners to a cell. Before the cages were discovered and revealed to the world by two visiting United States congressmen, the Chief American Advisor on Vietnamese law enforcement and prison techniques, a former Deputy Chief of the Los Angeles Police Department, had compared Côn Sơn to a "Boy Scout recreational camp." After their revelation, he said, "You aren't supposed to go poking your nose into doors that aren't your business." Prisoners of the cages tell stories of drinking their own urine, of having lime dumped on their bodies, of eating rice mixed with sand. Photographs published in *LIFE* magazine in July 1970 taken by the aide of the visiting congressmen show both of the politicians standing over openings in the floor and emaciated prisoners staring up through the bars. The bars are bright stripes, out of focus in the foreground.

The Vietnamese language is tonal, each word carrying six potential meanings depending on the pitch — mid-level, low falling, low rising, high rising, low broken, and high broken. When I first heard Vietnamese in a film many years ago, I thought it sounded very like birdsong, lilting and musical compared to the clacking string of consonants in English words. I tried to learn some Vietnamese before traveling, listening to hours of lessons on my commute to work, speaking aloud the words in my car, chatting with the scripted recorded voice. Each lesson began with a conversation, which first I was just supposed to listen to, an incoherent exchange between two parties. Then the lesson took apart the conversation so I could learn the pieces, begin to recognize them in context. The lessons would present scenarios: "Now suppose you are an older man, speaking with an older woman, how would you say hello to her?" And I'd try to imagine myself an older man in a place I'd never been and say aloud, "Chào bà."

My father, an American veteran of the war, suspects that many Vietnamese people *disappeared* after the end of the war. This is the word he uses, disappeared, a term sometimes paired with passive construction "were disappeared," which really means "were executed." No one I meet in Vietnam speaks of this; I don't expect them to. And I would never ask. I think of the United States, a nation with the world's highest documented incarceration rate, nearly one percent of its own population. A country that actually has more people in prison than any other in the world; a country that has executed 1,200 of its citizen criminals since 1976.

When you put something in a cage, you know it's your responsibility. The burden of being caged is on the caged. The burden of the cage is on you.

On March 1, 1972, flying an F-4D Phantom over the mountains of Laos, Joseph Kittinger shot down a MiG fighter plane in air combat using Sparrow missiles. Two months later, he was shot down by the People's Army of Việt Nam and held prisoner for eleven months in Hỏa Lò. Before this, in the late sixties, when my father was stationed in Germany, he met Joe Kittinger, whom he described as a quiet, unassuming guy. At first, my father told me, the young special forces officers in Bad Tölz didn't know who Kittinger was, and they razzed the older man a little, thinking he was a "leg," which is, as my father would put it, "a soldier who doesn't jump out of perfectly good airplanes." Then someone found his name in the record books, longest parachute free fall — four and a half minutes. Skydiving, he'd approached the speed of sound. In one jump, my father thinks, Kittinger had probably fallen longer than most of those officers had spent falling in their careers.

The recorded voice says, "Ask the older woman, 'Do you speak English?'" Then silence as it waits for my question: "Bà có nói tiếng Anh không?"

The deaths of my birds troubled me, but also strangely eased my worries. Eventually the quail all disappeared or died. The ducks now fly around, living a semi-wild existence, refusing, for the most part, to be protected by my measures. I can only keep so much at bay. The chickens live in a wire-enclosed fortress, have a house with latches and locks. When they occasionally escape, they linger around the outside edge looking confused and can easily be corralled back.

When John McCain ran for president in 2008, a group of veterans named Vietnam Veterans Against John McCain claimed he cooperated with the enemy in Hỏa Lò. They called him "Songbird." Though I find no reason to believe this, I'm never sure what to believe, except that the whole story isn't ever told. Or if it is, no one listens. Or if someone listens, they misunderstand. When I watch the 1967 film made by a French journalist of McCain as a wounded prisoner in a Hanoi hospital, I see this: a man lying in bed, head propped on a pillow, smoking a cigarette. His voice on the film is sometimes obscured by the voice of the interpreter, speaking French. When the interviewer asks about the food, McCain jokes that the food isn't like the food in Paris, but that he still eats it. He has the look of a man remembering something, a man about to cry.

The phrase "một ít," pronounced with a low broken tone, means "a little." The older woman on the recording tells me she speaks English a little.

My father learned some Vietnamese when he was in the military, during his second tour as an officer, through the Army Special Warfare School in the late 1960s, first at Fort Bragg and then at Fort Bliss. He tells me stories of practicing his pronunciation while wearing headphones, of a Vietnamese female instructor who spoke only Vietnamese in class. While he was in language school, he was also in Army Special Warfare training to prepare to be part of the Phoenix Program, an operation overseen by the CIA which aimed to destroy the infrastructure of the Vietcong. When I ask him what he did in those classes, he says, "It's kind of hard to explain. I don't know whether I can explain it." He sighs and says, "You know, frankly, a lot of that period draws a blank for me."

On my return from Vietnam, I watch a recording of a Vietnamese film shown to tourists at Hỏa Lò prison museum about the treatment of prisoners. At first it seems clumsy, like a parody of a propaganda film. A clip of prisoners sweeping the grounds with whisk brushes contains the caption, "The American pilots [sic] prisoners were taught to do things that every single Vietnamese child knows well how to do." It describes the prisoners as now having "the time and opportunity to learn more about 'their enemy,' whom they did not know very well before." The film shows a prisoner playing pool, a prisoner adding a whole pineapple to a full tray of food, a prisoner enjoying a water pipe. Then the film turns, oddly, to a series of shots of prisoners smoking cigarettes cut with shots of bombed out Hanoi, of Vietnamese bearing a coffin, of an injured woman being carried on a stretcher. In this segment, there are no captions.

My father isn't sure why he was chosen for language school. He'd never learned a language. He'd begun taking classes in German while stationed in Germany, but he was an athletic guy in his twenties, and the classes were at night, and it was ski season, so he went skiing instead. He passed the Army language aptitude test by one point.

The older woman now asks me, an older man, "Ông có nói tiếng Việt không?" Do you speak Vietnamese? I'm instructed to pay attention to the tones and reply, "Một ít tiếng Việt." A little Vietnamese. I'm comfortable with the phrase "một ít." It's easy. Unlike the word "ba," which has a tone I can't quite master. I may be saying "you" to an older woman. But I also might be saying, "three" or "any" or "waste" or "poisoned food."

What we don't see in the film of John McCain is a Vietnamese prison commander watching the scene. We don't see McCain's broken arm, which a doctor has been trying unsuccessfully to set without anesthesia right before the interview. We don't see anything below his shoulders. What we know is only what he tells the interviewer — that he's "treated well here," which isn't much, and may or may not be true.

My father explains the Phoenix Program like this: the goal was to identify the covert Vietcong government, to determine who these people were and "neutralize them." "Ideally," he tells me, "you didn't want to kill them." This is how my father tells some stories about the war, encircling them with language that only partially obscures. He tells me about priorities. The first priority was to recruit them, then send them back to gather information on the VC. "That," he tells me, "was pretty tricky," and didn't work out very often. The second priority was to capture them and convince them to defect. These people, he says, were put in a camp to protect them, but also to make sure they really would defect. The third priority was to capture them and hand them over to the South Vietnamese. The fourth priority was to ambush or assassinate them. The articles I read about the Phoenix Program either praise its effectiveness or, more often, condemn its reliance on the third and fourth priority. My father's stories fall somewhere in between. He tells about the infrastructure the military repaired that had been ruined by war, about the civil engineering projects he supervised; he tells me the Vietnamese are "good people."

I love birds but am a second-rate birder. I forget markings as soon as the bird disappears back into branches or sky. I know only a handful of songs or calls of the most ordinary birds. They pass through my brain, and I can't hold them.

In a 1973 *U.S. News and World Report* account of the Hỏa Lò filming, McCain describes the commander, the broken arm. He doesn't share much more about the moment, except that the French journalist was a communist. In the same article, he writes, "As far as this business of solitary confinement goes — the most important thing for survival is communication with someone, even if it's only a wave or wink, a tap on the wall, or to have a guy put his thumb up. It makes all the difference." He also uses the word "gook" often and writes that "a lot" of the guards were homosexual; I try not to let this get in the way of my understanding, or maybe I am trying to understand this.

I come to Vietnam really only knowing how to say one thing very well, which is "Tôi nói tiếng Việt, không khá lắm" — I don't speak Vietnamese very well. Or literally, I speak Vietnamese, not very well. In Vietnam, I practice this phrase on various tour guides, who repeat it back to me, kindly correcting my pronunciation.

If you put something in a cage, it transforms into your other, and you into its other. The cage comes in between, though on unequal terms.

I ask my father what happened to the prisoners handed over to the South Vietnamese. He tells me he'd observed South Vietnamese interrogations. When I ask what they were like, he's unable to describe them. He says, "They weren't very nice." I take this to mean the prisoners were treated in ways unimaginable. He says he made complaints, because he felt if the prisoners weren't Vietcong before the interrogations, they probably would be afterward. From our conversation, I sense he wants to believe that this cruelty is unique to a particular culture; I want to believe that he doesn't truly believe this.

My phrase book has the Vietnamese for *bird* — "con chim." The word "con" can mean son or daughter, it can be a classifier used for the names of animals or of people pejoratively. Vietnamese for song is "bài hát." The phrasebook doesn't contain the word for cage.

Although I feel certain the mysterious birds in the bamboo cages are exotic, whatever that means exactly, they aren't. They're common birds in Southeast Asia — the red-whiskered bulbul, the gold-fronted leafbird, the Japanese white-eye. The leafbird is a mimic. As it turns out, the white-eye, introduced to Oahu in 1929, is one of the most common birds on the Hawaiian Islands, and a small population of bulbuls lives in Florida.

I ask my father if he used his Vietnamese much during his time with the Phoenix Program. He says not really, that he felt more comfortable using an interpreter because there was "less chance of misunderstanding." But he also says it was good to have enough Vietnamese to know if the interpreter had skewed what he'd said.

I imagine myself as a younger man speaking to a younger woman. *Hello*. Chào chị. *Do you understand?* Chị có hiểu không? The younger woman is the wife of a Vietcong guerilla leader, who isn't at home when I visit her in the village. We're having tea. Tôi nói tiếng Việt, không khá lắm, so I use my interpreter. We're discussing her husband, how we might be able to get him to defect. Through the interpreter, she tells me it's unlikely, because even when he's in the house, he's never alone, there's always someone watching him. Another day, I'm in the village and she runs out to my jeep. Her baby is very sick, and she needs someone to get her into the hospital. Tôi hiểu. I understand. I have a baby daughter back home. So they climb in my jeep, and I take them to the hospital, make sure the baby gets care. I imagine myself as a younger man, a man who tells this story, a man who is my father. Afterward, my father explains, he wondered what would happen if he went to her house and her husband were there. What would the man do to the American who saved his baby? He never found out. One day, after an ambush, my father was the one who identified the man's body.

In Southeast Asia, some Buddhists practice the ritual release of birds. Birds can be purchased to then let go in a symbolic act of compassion. The popularity of the practice has led to problems. Birds are captured in large numbers and kept in small cages, transported far from their homes. Sometimes, when released, they are too weak to fly. There are stories of temple grounds dotted with dead birds.

One description of Hỏa Lò prison in 1914 tells of letters, presumably tossed over by Vietnamese prisoners, littering the pavement outside the wall.

When my father was in Vietnam, he sent my mother cassette tapes he'd made, and she'd send tapes back to him. I remember seeing the tapes when I was little. I never listened to them, nor have I ever asked what was on them.

In the lessons, I learn to say "I'm not Vietnamese." This isn't a phrase I ever need to use, and I quickly forget it. If anything is perfectly clear to anyone here, it's that I'm not Vietnamese.

Maybe I appreciate the bird stall because it has nothing to do with me. I can't buy the birds, so no one tries to sell me any — unlike the branches of spiky red rambutans, the long baguettes, the hats with the red stars, the rides on motorbikes I'm constantly being offered. The birds have nothing to do with America, with obligation, with perspective, with translation. The cage-birds are about the people of Hanoi, their pleasures. Through the birds, I can see a world without me, and by seeing that world, I can perhaps better understand it.

From Hanoi, we take a tour to Halong Bay, where we'll spend two nights on a boat. The tour van stops en route at a place the tour guide calls a "tour stop." It's a center for disabled people, who learn skills like sewing and embroidery. In a large workshop, fifty or sixty children lean over panels of fabric, embroidering elaborate scenes they copy from cards. Big fans move the air around the room. Most of the children have their shoes off and their feet resting on little stools. The children look like they're in their early teens, maybe, or younger. Next to one girl's workspace is a little paper fan decorated with pink princesses. Signs around the room tell us no photography is allowed. The children work on one side of the room, while on the other, tourists sit at tables eating snacks from the snack bar. It's hard to tell how these kids are disabled. One child wears a leg brace, but the others seem fine, stitching quietly away with their needles and skeins of bright thread.

Then a woman, one of the tourists, comes over to the workspace. She begins to shape the air with her hands — sign language — and dozens of the children look up, watch her, surprised. Then all of their hands are moving at once as they sign back, responding to the woman — a silent cacophony. They're smiling, and I wish I knew how to say something, anything, to them, like the woman reaching effortlessly across this barrier. On my way out, I buy some postcards and stamps, and a man who looks my father's age adds up the bill using a pen strapped to his upper left arm, which ends in a scarred stub. His right arm is missing entirely.

A bird in a cage is a common sight here, like the child-sized plastic stools everyone sits on on the sidewalk or the wall-mounted fans in restaurants and shops. Cages dangle under awnings outside businesses, on the balconies of apartments, from trellises in the park. I see few lanterns, but many cages. For the most part, the birds are songbirds. Their songs are hopelessly cheerful, as though they can only say nice things. In places around Hanoi, I notice clusters of hanging cages, the birds inside brought together to sing to one another, which they do. What passes through the bars — a few shared notes, a gesture, a bit of seed — makes all the difference.

ACHY OBEJAS

Trial Run   *Fiction*

for m (madrid-barz-paris)

Do you see the Capitol Building? It's an excellent example of neoclassical architecture. It has a central dome that rises above a rotunda with two wings, one for each chamber of Congress: the north wing is for the Senate and the south for the House.

It's exactly eighty-eight meters tall. At one time, building anything taller was prohibited, but the law was amended in 1910 to restrict the height of any structure to the width of the adjacent street plus 6.1 meters. An absurd formula, there's no question. As a result, the Capitol Building is actually the fifth tallest structure in Washington, DC.

Now, imagine it scaled down: that's the Capitol Building in Havana. If you visit someday, you'll see.

The Cubans will tell you it's bigger than the one in Washington but if you take a couple of photos and compare the buildings, especially if there are tourists posing on the stairs, then it takes on a certain human dimension. . . . The tourist in Washington, of course, will be Latino and short (as a result of having been raised in the Third World or in an American ghetto), and the one in Havana, big and American, of course, but none of that really matters. (Americans in Havana are usually recognized by their Che T-shirts. Cubans who wear one do so only for marches, or when they're in Europe, in order to comply with the laws of colonial expectations.) It's quite likely the American has never visited the Capitol Building in Washington.

One more detail about the Cuban Capitol Building, and this is purely tropical: There's a twenty-five karat diamond embedded in the floor of the main hall, which marks Ground Zero in Cuba. The original was said to belong to Czar Nicholas II of Russia and sold to the Cuban state by a Turkish merchant (now you can see there's a Russian connection but that Turkish merchant probably had very little about him that was Turkish, because in my Cuba very little is as it seems, and that merchant, who was perhaps Polish or German or Dutch by birth — who the fuck knows! — was no doubt a Jew). The diamond was stolen March 25, 1946, and was mysteriously returned to President Ramón Grau San Martín three months later. In 1973, it was replaced, as mysteriously as when it first disappeared, with the reproduction that you now see.

The Capitol Building in Havana is actually four meters taller than the American one, four little meters that push the dome toward the heavens, but that can't really be applauded as a Cuban achievement, although, usually, the islander who boasts about it — insolently and loudly — has no idea that the great national symbol was designed by a pair of native-born Cubans under the watchful eye of — surprise! — an American company.

And in spite of the obvious — the shamelessly obvious — similarity to the American capitol, the architect, Eugenio Raynieri, died insisting that his inspiration was never Washington — no sir! — but the cupola at the Pantheon in Paris.

Please note the aspiration to the spirits of Voltaire, Rousseau, Marat, Zola, and so many others. Imagine the level of delirium it takes to imagine that in spite of the evidence in sight — just look at the fucking photos! — it would be possible to impose like that on common sense.

But never mind. Let's stroll for a while. Just turn into that little street and you'll see how pretty it is. . . . Yes, undoubtedly La Rambla is just one of many little streets around here . . . that's why they call them Las Ramblas, or Les Rambles in Catalan. I think it comes from the Arabic and means something like "sandy bottom." If you go by the Plaza de Catalunya to the port, there's La Rambla de Canaletes, and the next one's called La Rambla dels Estudis, and so on: La Rambla de Sant Josep, La Rambla dels Caputxins, La Rambla de Santa Mónica, and La Rambla del Mar. Years ago, the sea walk ended right at the water, but now it's more or less at the Maremagnum — wait until you see that crazy thing, the result of savage capitalism, with its Lacoste and Oysho and Scapa Sports; not my favorite place in Barcelona by any means. García Lorca said La Rambla was the only street in the world he didn't want to end. As you can see, they didn't give a shit about Federico.

Oh well, it's a pretty walk anyway, right? I like to go shopping at the little stores and to watch the street performers, like those over there, or that fire-eater . . . it can get insufferable, especially during tourist season. Usually there are more tourists than locals, and this has changed what the stores have to offer, as well as the general character of the streets themselves. That's why it's become such a target for pickpockets. And the prices are through the roof.

But if you can imagine it in miniature, that's the Prado in Havana. If you go to Cuba with a tour group, you'll see it because it's on the list of favorite places for all the guides in Havana.

Our Prado only goes from Parque Central, near the Capitol, to the Malecón. It was built in the eighteenth century, but when it was remodeled in 1928, it benefited from the neocolonial style that includes the little marble benches, the lampposts, and the popular bronze lions, silent witnesses and protectors of those who like to stroll under the trees.

Of course, in a modern city, a place like the Prado is not going to be the oasis that it was originally conceived to be. Life on the Prado moves at different rhythms, depending on the hour. The kids who skateboard all day long are replaced at night by eager young women who will follow any blond man the length of the Prado to ask him what time it is. It's best to ignore them, as well as all the guys promoting little restaurants, or selling cigarettes, cigars, rum, mulatas, their sister or brother, their wife or husband, their mother or father or whatever relative they have on hand. On the weekends, artists sell paintings of revolutionary icons (but not of You-Know-Who) and picturesque scenes of an imaginary Havana.

People looking to negotiate for housing also gather here. Some are looking for smaller places, others for a better location. Any difference in price can be fixed by bartering or with cash. A short distance from the housing market, couples arrive in convertibles at an old Spanish casino with Moorish, Gothic, and Renaissance architectural elements. It's the Wedding Palace. Up to five couples can marry at the same time. Some talk the security guard into letting them go up on the roof, where you can see the entire Prado. The nearby rooftops offer their own vistas: couples in flagrante, a drag fashion show, a suicide about to happen. If you wait a bit, you'll surely hear the woman who screams out every night: "Matches! Alcohol! Fuck you, motherfucker! Give me the matches!"

But as I was saying . . . what I like best about Chicago is South Lake Shore Drive. It was part of the 1909 Burnham Plan, which had broad streets and boulevards, parks, and other green spaces. Since the death in 1912 of Daniel Burnham, the city's designer and architect, much of his vision has become reality. The results of his model are most clearly seen along the lake and in the adjacent parks.

It's along here where you can see some of Chicago's finest cultural institutions. There's the famous museum campus: the Field Museum of Natural History, John Shedd Aquarium, and Adler Planetarium. Soldier Field, where the Bears play, and McCormick Place, a convention center that attracts more than four million people a year, are also in Burnham Park. Just to the south is the Museum of Science and Industry.

Jackson Park has many marvelous attractions, including ponds, ports, walking paths, and the only eighteen-hole public golf course in all of Chicago. The Paul H. Douglas Sanctuary, located on an island jungle, is also a popular place. It contains more than three hundred different species of birds. The Jackson Park field house has an interactive fountain which simulates the movement of a merry-go-round with lights, music, and swirling arcs of water that leap up to three meters in the air.

Now imagine it without a hint of green, without ponds or beaches, without museums or a golf course, without a convention center, without an interactive fountain or any kind of bird. Imagine it as a stretch of concrete seven kilometers long with a seawall that hides the coral reefs, the offerings, the lovers, the contraband; imagine it bordered on one side by buildings wasted by sea salt and indifference, or in the process of restoration (soon to be turned into hotels or some kind of condos for foreigners and Cubans with connections abroad), and on the other side by picturesque fishermen with rods on inner tubes (yes, on inner tubes — don't ask), with loving or angry couples, hustlers of all colors and sizes offering all sorts of interactive activities, with dealers who will just as soon offer you a complete silver tea service, a Rolex, a first edition of Richard Wright's *Native Son* (for only $2.50 USD), a Che doll (with "Homeland or Death" printed on its T-shirt), or a photograph of a semi-nude Benicio del Toro vomiting on the tire of a '56 Chevy (at least that's what the seller says, and it sure looks like him . . .), and with Olympic masturbators who can shoot longer than three meters. This is the Havana Malecón! (Of course you'll experience it — it's impossible to avoid, especially late at night on the way home after a party, when there's nothing like a little sea breeze to get over such drunkenness.)

Did you know they say there are still monkeys in the trees around here? Yes, yes, monkeys, like in Tarzan. I think it was in '56 that forty-five monkeys escaped from Tierpark Hagenbeck and got lost in Hamburg. The police were only able to catch twenty-four of them, and in the meantime the others snuck in windows and stole toothpaste and soap and whatever they could find along the way. Maybe it's just legend that there are still descendants from those monkeys hanging around, right? It's hard to imagine the German police wouldn't have been efficient enough to capture them all. Or that the monkeys of their own volition didn't return to Teagarden Hagenbeck, given that there are few zoos that compare: it's known as the first zoo to use open spaces surrounded by moats instead of cages. It's a kind of paradise — if it's possible to find paradise when you're displaced. Of course I'm referring to the monkeys, the displaced monkeys. Anyway, I like the story . . . I like the idea that in Hamburg there might be monkeys in the trees.

At the Havana Zoo nothing like that has ever happened. The animals do not run away. They multiply. They live happily. In fact, the administrators are preparing to transfer animals to Venezuela next month. I'm not making this up — it's true.

In the same way that Cuba sends doctors to Venezuela in exchange for 92,000 barrels of oil a day, Venezuela will now provide medical equipment to Cuba in exchange for the animals. The list of animals is still being prepared, but among those already confirmed are a lion, a miniature hippopotamus, two hyenas, an antelope, and an African ankoli cow. It's possible they'll send a white rhino later. There's also a giraffe named Evo, after the Bolivian president. This Evo eats bananas, potatoes, squash, milk and hard-boiled eggs — the truth is he eats better than my neighbors, but, well, it's a giraffe and that has to be accounted for. It's not the same as a child or an elderly person.

I remember a few years back (during the Special Period, my dear, and that takes more explanation than I've got time for now, so just try to imagine an endless black hole, yes, just like that, and think about this story in that context) an artist friend of mine wanted to do a thing with meat and she decided to go to the zoo to see if she could borrow some. The idea was to use the meat they fed the lions in her art project and then return it, and that way everybody won, her and the lions. I swear to God, I'm not lying. She wanted to upholster a box with meat. It was a performance, OK? The thing is that when she talks to the guy at the zoo about it, the poor man almost dies laughing. "What the fuck meat are you talking about? The Havana zoo has the only vegetarian lions in the world. They eat carrots, mountains of carrots!"

What's incredible is that the Havana zoo has still managed to develop one of the best collections of African animals in the world. More than four hundred zebras (descendants from one that was ground into sirloin during the Special Period, and which was enjoyed by the entire neighborhood) have been born in captivity in its eight hundred forty acres, as have three hundred lions, and many have been sent to zoos in other countries. Of course, no one talks about the lions' vegetarian past. It would be like saying they're sending metrosexual lions, faggot lions, and though homosexuality may be in vogue in Havana, that won't get far in, say, Caracas.

Some of the lions can be traced back to the ones that the Tanzanian president, Julius Nyerere, gave You-Know-Who in the seventies. Everybody remembers Nyerere, always more African than socialist, but a socialist to the end, a socialist until his death. But few recall the moment when Nyerere realized the Tanzanian economy hadn't prospered under his economic system and, before retiring from the presidency in 1985, in an act of singular honesty during his farewell address, declared: "I failed. I have to admit it."

Well, that *here* . . . just imagine!

Translated from the original Spanish by the author.

RICHARD JONES

My Samovar!

Whatever happened to my samovar!?
It *couldn't* have just disappeared —
ornate, ostentatious,
it commanded attention
and fetched compliments for its beauty.
Purchased by my wife at a flea market
and presented to me on my birthday
with wishes that I should live forever,
it wouldn't have simply vanished.
Tall, round, vase-shaped,
a copper and brass work of art in the dining room,
entire chapters of life were written
at its table, brewing and pouring
black tea from the jeweled and gilded teapot
that sat atop the inscribed kettle
like a little god,
medicinal and therapeutic,
guiding us through each day, each season,
insisting we slow down, live slowly,
and invite not only the body
but the soul to partake —
mint, jasmine, orange peel,
rose, linden flowers, lemon,
tea with champagne,
tea with blueberries and currants,
honey tea, peach tea, tea with apples.
I drank from a tulip-shaped tea-glass,
my wife from a white porcelain cup.
Our ceremonies
were quiet, serene,
characteristically Japanese,
or ritualistic and proper
in the English manner;
but sometimes
like Turks or Russians
we were unrestrained and expansive,
everybody talking as music played
and the children ran around

eating cookies and cakes.
I must admit
it is strange to lose a samovar.
If I could lose *it*,
what else at this moment
might be slipping away?
Without my seeing or knowing,
what else like my beloved samovar
has gone missing
and now is lost, never to return?

JEFF KNORR

Taking Leave

At the train station in Sacramento,
the young veteran is on his way home
for leave after a long stay in Iraq,
and this valley seems so distant now
from his reality, he goes straight to telling
me of patrols, of tracer fire, of one bright
afternoon in Mosul when his Humvee rocked
with concussion like the sky had imploded.
They had just entered the plaza on a Wednesday
near 11, late morning, people making their market runs
and in the center of this roundabout was a fountain
and on the sidewalks he noticed a young woman
with her small boy and she was kneeling,
wiping something from his chin and he could see
her mouth moving saying something sweetly
to him, not yelling or reprimanding, and it had reminded him
of shopping with his own mother; and then he
noticed an old woman haggling at a stand
selling papers and books and she was shaking
her head and fingers at the old man.
Across the plaza, a young man driving
the small Opel entered the roundabout,
and he passed the young woman wiping her
boy's chin, then he sent a prayer out like a thousand birds
screaming until the plaza and the roundabout became
chaos of smoke and glass, of bodies and car parts.
The Humvee on its side, the soldier crawls out
and begins looking for his platoon members,
and then the woman with the boy, and they are gone.
He cannot find her or the small boy, and there is
glass everywhere, glass like jewels scattered among feet.

And now, I'm thinking of you, and how I felt
in the bright Saturday sun looking at photos —
one of me holding the dog we shared, another
of you jumping in my arms in my brother's yard,
and the shrapnel of divorce tears through me,
the phantom limb of you, the field amputation,

holding a piece of your body because I might
find you belong to it. And then I think about this
young man's world exploding and you must have
felt this way the day I broke your heart,
like I had walked with a suicide belt of C-4
into our living room, your limbs going cold,
the lights extinguished; only tears and darkness survived.

What is war but counting bodies?
This is about casualties and making our way back.
There is no returning to the same home on leave.
The ceiling fan is batting overhead
like chopper blades and the land has changed.
Everything familiar here has taken on a new shape
and this evening fades to the flat gun-metal gray of memories.
This young soldier and I sit on our bench awaiting the train.
We are looking for the color of a new country,
for the curve of hills and valleys, for blue rivers'
peace running easy like our hearts.

THEODOSIA HENNEY

Pit Ponies

A Shetland pony can pull several times
its body weight, which is why
they were put into the mines.
Draft horses pull less pound-for-pound,
though they may weigh up to a ton,
and would not have fit
down the shafts.

Before elevators
ponies were lowered in slings,
a miner standing on their backs
to mind the hook and say, "It's all right.
It's going to be all right,"
as ground ate the sun.

Law decreed they be four years
of age to enter the pit — they lived
in stables built into the rock, doors
and feed bins made from railway ties,
shaft supports. Some had electric lights.

The ponies might surface
once a year, for the colliery's holiday,
or a long strike. Some died
when turned loose after months
below ground; bucked and galloped
until their hearts gave.

1913 in Britain
and 70,000 ponies lived underground,
hauling thirty tons of coal in eight-hour shifts
(silver in the States) until
they were twenty or dead.

The ones brought back up
wore blindfolds, seven or eight layers,
one to be removed each day
so they would not go blind in the light.

BAYO OJIKUTU

The Last Days of Dick and Hank   *Fiction*

My final task on Tuesday mornings is taking the president his peanut butter on rye and dried plum lunch. Madame Richard has placed him on a high fiber, meat-substitute nutritional plan: "The Virgin Oil Regimen," I believe it is called by the American ex-pats. All vegetable oils, protein spreads, grainy breads, and, on Fridays, beans. The First Lady was only able to persuade the Chief to submit to the diet after four years of cajoling — at least as long as I've been with him. Her efforts were buoyed by the announcement that the doctor who treats the head of the Commonwealth Fund has found cancer all about that banker's prostate.

The president still refuses to call these five wrinkled balls rolling about aside his grainy sandwich spread what they are — "prunes", as the package shipped across the Pond properly labeled the black fruit. This is his last bit of resistance, a chief executive's prerogative, as he says. "Bring my noon sandy on your way in, Henry," Clement Richard's morning e-mail confirmations remind. "Don't forget the dried plums. Madame would have a tizzy if I didn't get me midday shrivel."

Portraits of the leaders who preceded President Richard line both walls along the path to his office's oak door. The Governor-Generals and Admiralty take the lead, those caretakers of the last of the three empires to rule the old colony — each festooned with chest-high regalia earned on behalf of kings and nobles. Gray-bearded knights of lordship orders who commanded our small pool within the Pond, such that they might deliver minerals, sugar cane, and the sweet fruit taken from this earth to all the four corners. Men, each of them, with light, wide eyes lidded by bearskin hats — or by the shakos topping the last few of them.

These images are succeeded by glossy portraits of the six Heads of State who have served since Independence Day, 1969. Newly-gilded frames hold the renderings of these five men and the one woman in their varying shades of slave, master, and indigen. Their gallery begins just before the hallway's bend with the first — Jean Rubadoux — whom my own father served as chief of staff. Rubadoux the Shepherd of the Nation, a leader I recall as the gentleman who gifted me my first wicket as a lad, and with whose sons I attended boarding school in the Old City. In a nod to the metropolitan legacy, Rubadoux the Shepherd wears the traditional bearskin in his near regal capture.

Just before Clement Richard is the country's sole woman commander-in-chief, his banished predecessor, Lady Charlotte. She whom the Americans love so, whose whole name no longer bears utterance within the chamber. "All the pale carpet totters from the North have purchased their pet sable sapphist a villa far off in Brussels, somewhere where they send their spooks and initialed snakes to slither around the veranda with that spider, plotting her return to the island. Why mourn what will surely crawl again? They have invested in their web what they have stolen from my people." President Richard spoke of his predecessor's circumstances as such after I'd made the early mistake of interrogating his thoughts on the prior administration. The "sapphist" bit was a quote directly from one of the Old City's brilliant scribes.

I avert eyes from Clement Richard's unfinished portrait before the plate in my left hand to enter the presidential chamber.

"What of the mines, Henry?"

The president pushes his lunch to the far end of the desk — his gaze does not leave the map of seas just left of his daily appointment calendar. His latest intelligence chief stands at attention in the office's corner, over Richard's right shoulder. The president is splendidly pressed in the silver-gray threads of the island's officialdom — a color of sufficient gravity to convey authority, with fabric threaded to stave off our most ferocious of suns. His gold wire rims slide along the narrow path of his nose as he surveys latitudes and longitudes. Stubby fingers push the spectacles back to his face before they reach flaring nostrils. The same hand yanks his dotted Windsor knot tie then sweeps across the center of his luxurious forehead.

"Which, sir?"

"Sulfur," says the Chief, and he looks up for a moment, over his shoulder at the brass-shone intelligence man. "For what does Treasury pay you, Henry, you and that Cambridge mind of yours, to bring me meatless sandwiches on pumpernickel bread?"

The brass man chortles behind his closed lips. The President peers at the map again, and his thumb presses the island into his desktop.

"Rye, Mr. President."

The upper-crust Noire of the isle have reveled quietly in these post-'69 positions, if only to place melanin-less men in servile station. This is the reversal of fortune which very nearly all of my father's mates feared upon the grant of independence, why the balance of them escaped sure comeuppance, leaving the island to its dark seeds and the remaining aborigines rather than suffer the toll of a century turned on its head. Wasn't that the point of the peoples' late 1968 uprising? Come Independence Day, the cabal of French landowners,

Anglo industrialists, and Roman friars alike piled upon carnival liners bound for the Old World — treasure chests, whelps, and mistresses in tow. They left behind the mines and their fields and palaces, freedom, and their debts, too. They relinquished former subjects to their own will, to divine fate, and to themselves. Were not the vestiges of colony recompense enough — why must the rightly born serve? — they asked while waving goodbye from starboard side.

"The mining union will not stand down from this call for pay increases. The most recent reports indicate they are ratcheting up the pension angle. Increased state pay-in and the like. Their strike continues strong."

"Unions . . . NAFTA!" The President says both words as if they are epithets, even as he peers my way with eyes unblinking and shining wet. "The mines are to produce. The workers want to be middle-class, some sort of Bushman bourgeoisie? Do they hear me when I speak of national deficit? A middle-class produces, middlemen deliver goods. These scamps should be grateful they are no longer making their way picking seeds from stems like their pappies. They watch too much of the telly, Henry, beamed over from the States. They think themselves a movement — we can't have workers leaping ahead of the tide. Would Rubadoux have bent to such whimsy?"

I sit in the low-backed chair before his desk and cross my left leg over right, as I recall my father posing in a photo with the Shepherd on our living room mantle. I tell the President what he wants to hear this noontime. "I suspect that we wouldn't be here if he had, Mr. President."

Richard nods his approval and glances at the brass man again. "Intelligence informs me that the strike can be broken. They are loosely organized and predominately unarmed, according to the reports. Young ragamuffins. It may take combining police and our reserves from the parishes, as there are nigh close to a thousand in the streets of the Westmoorland shanty. But I am told we could end this in less than an afternoon."

My legs uncross. "My information indicates their youth and nonviolence is reason to stave off extreme reaction." The brass man sneers slightly even as he gazes near the palm trees below us in the palace's garden. "Caution is warranted."

"Perhaps there are criminals sequestered among the miners, Henry, plotting to stir trouble." The Chief unfolds his map's last flap while staring straight across the desk. "Who is to say? Maybe there are saboteurs. When does the nation barter with terrorists?"

"The tide has long turned, Mr. President. Sagacity is found in caution during these times."

"What does that mean, 'caution'? Those mines are to deliver minerals to our partners. Hasn't it always been your way to remind me the exigencies of the marketplace, fulfilling contracts — talk to me of Global Mining and the Commonwealth Fund, your forefathers — what else is the purpose of our enterprise? I thought that was the chief consigliere's job. Aren't you still my Kissinger, Henry? Tell me of the subtle implications of this ruling business when I might be congenitally distracted by sound and fury."

"Give this pause, Clement." I lean forward upon the seat cushion. "I am doing the job of chief of staff as I know it. The world is watching. Eyewitnesses keep lasting record in 2011 — your adviser is telling you to take caution when wielding the power of your position against the people."

"My position. My people —" the Chief needlessly reminds.

"Our country." There is an extended moment of silence in the chamber, and the brass man stands at attention once more. Whatever caught his gaze outside has flown off, bound for the shore. The President looks back to his map, without touching the paper island. I continue, "You call them middling ragamuffins, these strikers. Turn on the telly now and again perhaps, Mr. President. All chaos requires is one bushman with a Facebook log-in or iPhone."

"Jehovah warned us in the beginning of biting the apple, didn't He?" For the first time, the intelligence man speaks, uttering "amen" in the muddy patois of his inland clan. The Chief pushes himself from the desk and crosses his own legs in repose. "Madame Richard still attends Sunday services at Santa Dominica. Pays convicted mind to that bishop over there."

"Father Mark still heading the bishopric?" I ask.

"Josephat. New pastor sent from Guyana, a Creole. Madame loves him in some impassioned way. She spends every Monday, Tuesday, Wednesday, quoting bits from his last homily. Going upstairs to the middle of a sermon this evening. She'll follow that up Thursday-to-Saturday, cajoling me into doing what I can to persuade the diocese to turn this priest into an archbishop. Endow the church with state funds, build a new pitch for the orphans. No one hears me speaking of deficits. Does she think that I have the Pope's ear, Henry . . . ? The Lady suggests that I give them one more week before acting."

"The strikers?"

"One week for them to come about the blessed reason of Jehovah."

"Makes fine sense, Mr. President," I counsel, equally without need. The brass man allows a grunt to slip through.

"Ah," President Richard smiles, "the Church is good for women."

"Indeed." The raise of the brass lid and the crooked furrow passing over the Chief's brow suggest I should have offered an "amen" instead. "For we men, there is very little left in this life of action, Mr. President. Particularly scant for men of proper position and responsibility. Those days have passed on. These are our lives, not our fathers'."

The intelligence man steps from his corner, ready to escort me to the portrait gallery.

"We've traded living majesty for theatrical sensitivity, Henry," the President says as I am turned toward oak. "We are lost. Ruling is all show for the hordes."

When I accepted this post in 2007, just before the hedge fund collapsed beneath the weight of the sovereign wealth debacle, the American spooks still drove about the coastline in their black SUVs. Gleaming and cruising invisibly in vehicles built to lurk — specially outfitted with right-side steering wheels to conform to our Commonwealth way. Just post-independence, the agents of the Empire to the North (as the dissidents of my father's day referred to the States), tooled about in Lincoln-Mercurys. Town-cars and Continentals floated quietly in the sea breeze. Young mendicants along the Row were known to pause before scampering to the American machinery with hands outstretched, awestruck amidst their hunger.

These days, the States' appointed sorts drive the beach in electric cars, which still reflect our sun's rays and swelter in metallic blackness — but the grills and hoods are bereft of manufacturers' emblems. Our only outlets with sufficient power to charge these autos are housed at the airport and on the U.S. Army-built base in the upper cape, so we receive the benefit of full warning when these Yankees are bound for the Row.

The Americans stop me in the gangway between the Mandarin noodle restaurant, the Kentucky Fried Chicken front, and the Sephardic dry-goods merchant at the Row's west end. I have taken steps toward the sedan's rear doors before the front window sputters open midway for a driver more pallid than I to offer invitation. He speaks in the pleasant tenor of the Stateside Plains.

I know this woman in the car's rear seat, encountered her at a palace gathering — here or over there, perhaps. Or I have seen her on the telly, clarifying talking points on behalf of the U.S. State Department above plasma screen block letters and streaming non sequiturs. She is what we called a mulatto when I was a lad; what the township folks labeled "zambaggoa." She sits upright against the electric car upholstery, hair pressed to the nape of her neck, terse eyes scanning about the screen of an Android cellular device held between the lapels of her linen pantsuit jacket. I recall this comportment of hers from the televised exchanges: clipped and crooked-lipped, monotonous yet curt, as if reading from an exasperated script. She seems an excessively severe woman, particularly for an American of her apparent thirty-something age. As if the jaundice in her bearing intends to dissuade those who might take her for a tragedy.

"Welcome to the Island," I crow and sit behind the driver's seat. Her chauffeur closes the rear door after thanking me for cooperation.

"Henry Lycan," she looks up from the phone screen, and the crook in her mouth partially straightens as if for a smile. Then, without introducing herself, "How are things in the President's office?"

"There are challenges, as you know —" She wears no badge, and the attaché case on the seat between us reveals no monogram. I recall only her last name and her position from the telly — Piedmont, State Department Liaison — and I am not absolutely sure of either, so I refrain from address. "The strikers rage on inland. Sugar cane and tourism remain hampered from Hurricane Will. But I presume you read CANA this morning —"

"Indeed, Mr. Lycan. Your *Economist* as well," the screen on the Droid phone darkens, and she tucks the device into the inner pocket of her suit. "Does your chief plan on taking action against the Westmoorland miners?"

"Negotiations are ongoing. Global Mining is directly involved."

"What of the military? And the security service? Etat Gendermarie?" She uses the term for Rubadoux's old palace forces, and her words sing a Nice lilt — neither praising nor seeking to impress, but as if she is of their legion herself.

"The President plans to afford a full week for assessment. We are watching the situation on the ground, staying the course with all options on the table." I glance at the Breitling face. "Four more days, President Richard has allotted for our review. Tuesday next week, we determine our plan of action with finality."

"What will happen in four days, Mr. Lycan," her hands cross upon her lap as she stares eastbound through the electric car windshield, "that has not transpired in over six months?"

"The President's hope is that we will reach a mutually beneficial resolution, for the people, for the government: our assessment of circumstances on the ground, the legitimacy of the strikers' demands, safeguarding Westmoorland and the entire island is a complicated process, Ms. Piedmont."

I believe that I have guessed her name correctly, although her crook remains unmoved. "Richard is planning concessions?"

"If needed," I say before straightening the palm tree print tie pinching at my throat, "where warranted."

Piedmont inhales. The driver's blue eyes peek over the rim of his Hollywood spy shades, up through the rear view's rectangle. "What else could change the conditions for those miners, Mr. Lycan? Is Jesus climbing down from his messianic cloud throne to bless the caves, such that there will be no avalanches to bury them and their children in blackness? Is He rubbing their bellies at night such that they will believe themselves fed well, even after dust has left the men unable to breathe poison-less breaths, much less pound subsistence from the bowels? Is the Good Lord going to pull open their eyelids so that these wretches see the world Clement Richard sees? So that they share the boon of his larceny and his splendor, or appreciate the depth of their own obeisance? So many interests to consider here —"

For all of their ardor, Piedmont recites her words, as if the escort or I hold a network microphone to the lapel where her droid lurks. "— before taking action," I agree.

"Those interested question whether there is action to take —" she says, "is there some legitimate course within Richard's sight line? Anything aside obvious brutality?"

"The President's priority is the stability of the nation, and the safety of its people."

"Not governance? Nor its maintenance?"

"Elections are almost two years off. This President's fixations are not political, Ms. Piedmont, nor electoral. Go back and tell your supervisors in Washington. Clement Richard's concern is his people."

"That's our hope, Mr. Lycan." Piedmont looks at me finally, dull brown eyes scanning the worn creases and the tan-resistant craters dug by my fifty years. She assesses the allegiances to be revealed by my visage, just as she assessed the telephone touchscreen.

Yet she betrays no conclusions. We idle near the low-rise stone flats just off the Row. "*Your* supervisor must keep it straight. For him, there is governing his people, there is governing the government, and there is governing in the wake of those who foster the nation-state. We can't have violence in the interchange of the three — he has many neighbors, allies, and those to whom the nation will be indebted long after we are all gone."

"The President knows his stakes."

"Were he to confuse the task of governing for his benefactors with governing the people, that would be a problem for him. Once there is bloodshed, we will all have problems. We don't want any confusion. Yours is an emerging nation, or it can be. That is why you have stayed here, no doubt, with all of your background? Your heritage and the like."

"Heritage?"

For the first time, I notice the liaison's blink. "You could have gone anywhere on this earth, at your own volition."

"This is my home," I remind, and I do intend to say so with pride welling. "I was raised to embrace the ethic of state service, giving back."

"Hence, 'your heritage,'" she quips. "How does Richard explain goons in uniforms savaging workers? They're peaceful, their demands are within reason, their rhetoric is hardly revolutionary. What is the justification when blood spills?"

"*If*, Ms. Piedmont . . . the state will take no action for four days more."

"Granted. Next Tuesday then, what will Richard's office say?"

The Americans' electric car has returned to the Row, sputtering west in the capital's midday gridlock. We inch behind an uncovered pickup truck carting chickens that peck at their wire coops, bound for market. Feathers blow unto Piedmont's windshield view to stick, before silver blades swipe them into the roadside. "The nation's debt accrues. The largesse of the past — such as it was — is just that. Bygone. And yet our private creditors still drive about the seaside in Humvee trucks. Even a developing nation such as this prioritizes its friendly obligations."

"Debt and deficit are the priority then, and not the people's welfare? Truth is sovereign all around when governing the affairs of government, Mr. Lycan. Thank you for letting go the bit about prioritizing the people in the run-up to next Tuesday. If I may, I found that canard just a tad insulting. Professionally speaking."

"You think I take kindly to referencing our security forces as if they are subhuman? 'Goons'? Calling into question the office's intentions, offhanded allusions regarding my heritage, you say —"

"I'm not here to engage you in tit for tat, sir. Accept my apologies." Piedmont not only turns to me, but she removes her attaché case from the seat divider, sliding leather beneath her thick-heeled shoes. "All those interested hope to see Richard's current term come to a peaceful conclusion as per your constitution, in 2013."

"And then what?" Unless one of the Chief's paranoid bouts has taken hold of my senses, I swear that I catch Charlotte Durant's specter (we are far enough from the palace to even think the ex-president's full name), dancing in this liaison's pupils. "Regime change?"

Piedmont's chin drops into the hollow of her throat. "Peaceful transition," she says, "either to another term for Richard, or to a democratically elected successor."

"American style?"

The liaison laughs and removes the Android from her inner pocket. "Turn up the air conditioner, Joseph." The driver nods, and the ventilated air immediately drops five degrees centigrade. "The Cold War ended when I was on the debate team at Mater Dei. There is no more empire. America reaches from the Yukon to the tip of Chile, and includes this splendid island of yours. Can we close that history? As I understand it — very literally — all of us are Americans."

"Peace, democracy, and transparency."

"And the first of these is peace."

Five quarter-clothed children run to the car, escaping the curbside cauldron, as we stop meters from a blinking streetlight. They knock on the empty front passenger window, and Joseph cuts out of traffic, accelerating through a gangway that borders the residential quarter. The fade of Piedmont's laughter is replaced by both of her thumbs pounding virtual keys. I cannot tell whether she takes notes on our exchange for the State Department record, or whether she is scripting her next message for delivery in these seas. I am not certain, but I suspect the latter.

"You know, Mr. Lycan, considering your background, the commitment to public service and such, there will be a permanent place for you in this country's governmental ranks. A tenable position, no doubt. We all wish there were more of your sort. Believe me . . . would you rather we return you to the State Building, or shall we drop you in the street where we located you?"

I pause to consider her options, as if she cares about my response. "To the State Building." I tighten the floral knot to pinch. "It is a bit muggy for my afternoon constitutional."

Tear-gas stings my eyelids kilometers from the mines. Westmoorland's constabulary office is sealed; the windows show few cracks, and encased air blows about from oscillating fans and one chain-operated device with wicker blades that dangles from a low ceiling. But I wipe pools of tears and sweat from the skin beneath my eyes, and the streaks slice my face. Both eyes blink, battling the wisps of remaining gas from Wednesday's debacle. When I force my lids closed, the pupils swell.

Since midweek, the Chief has made the right column of all the news sites hosted between the Old City and Hollywood. "Richard's Troops Pummel Miners" on the *Times*; "100 Dead, More Injured, As Strike Spreads Island," the *Herald*; "Deadly Island Action Leads to 72 Hour Clash," the *Daily News*; "Black Smoke Rises Over Fruit Marchers," the *Post*.

The miners never came to Madame Richard's Good News. Quite to the contrary, their own resistance hymns have spread to the south and east. We are fortunate that the Bushmen have not started Twittering to their kin beyond Westmoorland; otherwise the World Service would have declared the Carib Spring by this Friday, as the capital surely burned to embers.

I press the remote power button for this flat screen stretching opposite the sheriff's command center. Richard speaks on a makeshift stage assembled on the grounds of Global Mining's rural facility, twenty-five kilometers from the sheriff's office and the blood-soaked parish streets. KITS-TV broadcasts his comments across the telly from the outset.

After the old Rasta spread warning down from their hills that they could see Americans, the Commonwealth, and Territorials mobilizing to restore constitutional order if mayhem persisted or Richard's marshal law lasted beyond thirty days, the President suggested it best I stay at some remove from his first post-riot speech. It is a smart call, given the impressions taken by the masses during such turmoil — and so I hole-up alone in the Westmoorland parish constabulary. The balance of the capital citizenry, the AP office on the Row, and all the shoreline resorts carry the state's network on the cable lines, after all. "Particularly in the murkiest of times," my father used to say, "subtle shadings and heightened awareness of appearances are the means of our preservation."

Richard wears a khaki hat of the American baseball style, pulled midway between his brow and hairline as he rises to the podium. His white short sleeve is unbuttoned to show a silver St. Augustine medallion at his chest. The camera zooms to fix on the Chief's upper body and avoid the Global Mining corporate insignia likely posted mid-podium. Richard and the brass intelligence chief over his shoulder are the only figures the lens captures.

"It is time for our country to take stock. Our faith in God, our collective honesty, the bounty of our seeds, has allowed us to survive no matter the rise of the tides all about us. But it is our embrace of the rule of law that creates opportunity for us to thrive within these shores. The sanctity of that law and its orderly processes are the grist for the turn of our mills, the irrigation of our fields in the most blazing days before the harvest. Law and order is the light that guides us through tunnels and caves, down to the unknown depths of our homeland. When the rule of that law wavers, our national franchise is interrupted, the best of what we are and the potential for what our country can be is rendered in shambles. It is the calling of the State to fortify law, quiet these tremors, most especially on the darkest days."

The audience for his speech is made up of the congregations from the capital and the townships, bused in by the state police. They cheer when he wipes his brow, sing amidst his pauses. When their volume is insufficient, officers raise the sound on hidden stereo speakers to bolster air with celebration recorded at football club matches. This is a tactic of my own initiative, learned while taking my A-levels.

"Those who threaten the rule of law and seek to replace rightful order with their own vapid moral relativism, we recognize their acts. The mob's vile behaviors: false countrymen showing indifference to right and wrong, fellows with twisted moral code, those with a complete absence of self-restraint. Acting in the name of interrupting enterprise. These sorts have foregone their right to be called 'countrymen.' They say that they are strikers? They are interlopers, doing the bidding of forces far beyond our shores. They come from all directions to disturb our comity. They carry guns and liquor in their marches as well. They break our laws, stirring their chaos pot to bring about the shedding of blood. They come to our island just to misguide our children. It is the calling of this State, as long as I am its head, to rebuke these stealth invaders."

For all of his courtly manner and schooled grace, the president whom my father served was a man of the people. They called Jean Rubadoux "Shepherd" because he was known to brush goat's hair with carefully manicured hands while crouched in sharecroppers' stables, and then nibble Ox-tail at thatch-tables, surrounded by subsistence farming Bushmen and their cousins. In those winsome days, Rubadoux pulled at the sparse meat's gristle with teeth ivory, square, and straight. He sopped the sud of Irish brews with publicans, gray beggars, and traders alike at the ale houses along the Row, their drunken soca psalms led heartily by the Shepherd's noble baritone. Even the Rasta-worshipers-turned-guerillas spoke of their respect for Rubadoux as his forces permanently chased them into the hinterland hills. Rubadoux was a duke and a professor, a deacon and messenger, roles for which he was born, according to my father's tales. This was why those who owned the land and avowed the Commonwealth chose him to save our island from revolutionary perdition.

Now Clement Richard's hands flail about above the podium mantle as he speaks, until the left brushes the microphone, and reverberation echoes through the broadcast. He drops the palms to wood.

The generations in Rubadoux's wake — all of us — have sought a man like the Shepherd from the ranks of this nation for thirty years. The crux of our failure in this post-Age is that our search was in vain from the beginning.

"Let those who mean us no good from outside understand that they will not author our destiny. This tale will be told instead by natives who speak the language of the hills, fish the salt water of our beaches, those who tend the beaches and worship in the splendid cathedrals along Capital Row, the young trained in the goodness of our land in our schools. These rightful countrymen who adhere to our law and order and endorse the certainty of our morals will thrive in this day —

"— those who would disturb the daily function of national life should understand that we are all little dots on a map drawn by the hand of the one God, our Creator who has blessed us with paradise groves. The chicanery of the wicked will no longer connive us into forgoing this native right."

These closing lines are new to my ears. Either they are the president's improvisation in the moments of delivery, or Madame Richard whispered them into his ear as he slept upon goose-feather sometime last night. The two versions of the speech that I previewed noontime yesterday ended with a) "morals" and b) "God." As my own reading suggests, these are the most convincing English language terms to use with the Chief's constituency — particularly after we have struck the bells of dark and murky hours.

"If your seeing eye can't tell, the question you need to first ask is whether you're shooting backgammon or craps," says the German wireless caller.

"Ah, does the game go by bocce or bowling?" the Sicilian interprets.

"I figure what you're getting at now, mon frere," lassos the Texan. "Swinging at a twelve-inch here or a size sixteen?"

"Chekhov or Tolstoy?"

A voice of indiscernible accent laughs longer than it should. "Are you telling me this is a mission to be completed doggie-style, so to speak, rather than as a matter of sheer anal intercourse?" The connection is quiet suddenly but for the jet planes roaring above one of their heads. The X-national remembers himself, and his laugh fades. "Forgive me, Ms. Piedmont."

The State Department liaison has patched me into her midday Wednesday conference call, phoning as I approached the gangway noodle shop where her electric car impeded two weeks ago. Westmoorland has spent itself of ash by now, and the sugar cane workers never showed up to pick the fields this Monday past.

"Not to worry. But I think your comparison is a tad off, Konstantin," Piedmont says. "Before Bong-hwa went literary and mixed the metaphor, I'd say that the situation on the island should give pause over the question of tactics, not so much of strategy. Konstantin brings to mind chess/checkers, where a more apt analogue might be serving and volleying with tennis rackets versus chasing a shuttlecock over the badminton net."

188 • Fifth Wednesday Journal

"Aluminum or wood?" proffers the Texan, clarifying the matter for himself now more so than for his fellow callers. "Same game, but do you want it to make a 'ping' noise, or you looking to 'whack' that thing?"

"Are you following, Mr. Lycan?" The tone of Piedmont's question is of genuine concern.

"Clement Richard must go. Him and his entire fucking family," the Teuton spits. "Madame Richard, all of the children —"

"Those proper from the First Lady, living in the palace, and the others from his dalliances in the bushes, too. They all must go."

Bong-hwa clears his throat. "Peace is the objective. Speaking tactically and strategically."

"Sounds like Dostoyevsky to me," I say. The Korean laughs.

"Glad to hear you are on board, Mr. Lycan. Finally. These last ten days have taken their toll."

"But I don't believe the president will agree to depart the island. I don't intend to speak for him now, but I can surely counsel as to what I think rests in the best interests of the country, of his own well-being, and that of his family. But I cannot promise that my perspective will compel the president, given his take on ground circumstance."

Steps slow as my stomach grumbles, noon-time fish-and-chips fried in virgin oil digested. I approach the residential quarter, so I cross through the Row's traffic jam toward the opposite path. My off hand covers my lips as I dodge automobile bumpers.

"What warrant does he require?" Konstantin asks. "You tell us. Will it take more bloodshed? Due time has elapsed."

"There ain't no big stuffed envelopes getting sent down there, Hank. Not for you, not for him. I know the market hurt you — better believe it hurt a lot of us, in a lot of places. Even popped the tech sector here in Houston upside our heads. We take what the market can bear now, and that ain't much. Payday long passed us by —"

"Peace and stability for the island is what we offer, Mr. Lycan, and the way thereto."

"That's right. We ain't looking to send any drones down there. Not in our backyard. Our man Konstantin'll be the first to confirm there's ramifications to those kinds of strikes. Widespread consequences, ain't that right, K?"

"We might as well have never stopped hiring snipers and planting bombs in the undercarriage," Konstantin agrees. His accent shifts, and he speaks as a Frenchman might: "This is a secure line, isn't it, Ms. Piedmont?"

"Whether it's the howling jackal or the stealth wolf, the dog tracks bloody paw prints all about the grounds as he departs his prey," the Italian hums.

"Or hers," I say.

"Are you on the peace team, Mr. Lycan?"

I near the Row's dry goods shop — an old man whom I had not noticed while walking east stands just beside this storefront, holding a sign high above his deeply receded hairline. He smiles toward the street, showing rotted teeth and gums. The sign reads, in red marker scrawling: "The Future is Nigh, Am I?"

"You will not find a more staunch ally for the cause of peace within this government's service. If that means we are on the same team, Ms. Piedmont, then I say 'amen' to your message. But as a practical matter, from the position of Chief of Staff, I remind you the pragmatics. Even if I were to counsel him of the best interests at hand, Clement's patriotism and sense of honor will advise against retreat. That patriotic honor won't have to make a particularly convincing case to have its way. On a secure line, I myself might agree with those who consider Madame Durant a more efficacious potential leader for the future. Meanwhile, President Richard fancies himself a Rubadoux for this century. All the stories he's heard teach that the Shepherd of the Nation would have happily accepted his own death rather than submit to some kind of exile from this island."

"I knew Old Johnny well," the Texan recalls. "Would rightly call him a 'friend of ours.' Your boss is likely right on this one. In his day, Rubadoux woulda took two bullets to the gut before he let somebody cart him off that there Row alive, or from them pretty beaches. Back in 1981? Yes siree, took em without nary a blink, much less a tear. One score and ten passed by since his days in that palace you people built, though. We act according to the moments in which we live, not by what we remember. Memory is like a nursery rhyme, Hank. I suspect, were my friend Johnny Rubadoux alive and a leader in 2011, he'd be more than smart enough to swim with the tidewaters."

"Don't use words like 'exile' and 'retreat' with him, Mr. Lycan. Refer to it as we used to in the Volkspolizei, as a 'Beurlauben.' I believe your word is 'furlough', or 'vacation' —"

"With most emphasis on 'vacate.'"

"It is in the interests of all stakeholders were President and First Lady Richard to pack their rightful belongings some time after midnight — and before sunrise — this Sunday morning, round up the family, and evacuate the palace for Chancellery Airport." Bong-hwa explains this. "A Boeing BBJ will await their arrival, fully fueled to transport the Richards to a choice destination."

"Where do you envision the man agreeing to go? Zurich? Milan?"

"Cyprus is beautiful, if he remains given to sea climes."

"What of Fiji?"

"There will be no ease in this. I am all aboard for peace on the island, trust me. But it is a difficult thing of which you call upon me to advise this president."

"Don't underestimate your abilities, Mr. Lycan," Piedmont's words soothe, no matter their pointed delivery across wireless waves. "We surely have not. Give it some thought, and get back to me before the end of business Thursday. That's tomorrow, GMT minus five."

I cross the old man's path. His right hand drops from the sign to pat my shoulder with surprising vigor, twice. He speaks without showing his teeth. "I hear of Westmoorland," he says. "Pray the calamity stays far from us. Give the president fine tidings from a fellow native son." He pats a third time before his index finger points to the scrawling held crookedly now by one fist.

"Wait, wait," I spew into the cellular device. "We flew into one of your stateside cities during the previous administration. Madame Richard liked it very much, I think: Miami, Florida. Allow me to confirm before making the arrangements. If not there, then someplace similarly hot, multicolored, and nearby. Ensure that they have a veranda . . ."

I use my good hip to push open the oak doors, as I require both hands to carry the full lunch-plate. I am mostly inside the chamber, heavy wood slid away from my side, before I note that I have again forgotten to check progress on Richard's hallway portrait.

Clean rays light the walls of the chamber, as new red-trimmed drapes hang narrowly parted. The sounds of parrots yammering nonsense as they flit amidst the palm trees seeps through windows with our sunlight. I check the arrayed food before carefully sliding the presidential dishware onto the center of the desk. There is no map of the sea before him. I wait for the Chief's invitation to be seated.

"What of me mines, Mista Lycan?" the brass man posted in the president's chair asks in his Bushman patois. He ponders dried dates straddling bacon this noontime. Before tasting, he adds in clearest King's diction, "Does the sulfur still flow?"

JAMES HARMS

Other, America

I thought I was home or near
as I drove through Other, America,
which seemed to carry its dream
close to the ground like a dropped
handkerchief all dusted with mist.
It reminded me of Hundred
in Wetzel County, West Virginia,
named for Henry Church,
who sat rocking on his porch
across from the station
as the trains rolled in, so regular
a presence the passengers began
relying on him. They'd
cry out, "Thank God —
there's old Hundred,"
an ancient man whose name
they never knew, who
lived to be 109 (his wife
died at 106). Still,
337 of 344 residents
of Hundred, West Virginia
are white, and Other, America
is mostly black and brown
though just as poor. I hit
the gas when I recognized
my mistake, who waved
from the side of the road
too proud to ask me to stop,
her gingham dress so thin
with washing it seemed a veil
of cellophane on her fat body.
Old Hundred fought for the British
in the Revolutionary War.
The town is named for him.
And Other, America is named
for my mistake. I watched her
grow tiny and disappear
in the rearview mirror.

JAMES HARMS

This poem is called "The Devil's Eye," which is a movie by Ingmar Bergman, though the poem isn't about a movie that was made in 1960, the year I was born. I was thinking instead of "The Devil's Eye" by The Go-Betweens, circa 1988, off the album *16 Lovers Lane,* though it isn't about a song either, obviously.

Yesterday the goose
well not a goose but from a distance
even pigeons have a certain
joie de vivre, a strut that up close
becomes a pout, but it seemed
like a goose with her gaggle,
a waddling line of dryer sheets
following some goosey thing
down the bike path,
but I'd lost my grip I mean my contact lenses,
the way a stranger glances sideways
and seems to know you,
that devil's eye sort of thing
that spins a person twice: once
to see what the heck is he looking at
and twice to be certain and sure enough
no one's there: no goose or fedora
floating in the middle distance,
which is scary, and what's your name
anyway? why do you keep talking as though
I wish I really wish I'd been right
about the goose, the evidence
is mounting as they say, something
is about to happen, something important,
as if I were going to graduate
from a gaggle and become my own
good goose, make my own decisions
about north and south, well that's it
isn't it? that goose was a symbol
and I'm OK with it; I've got my compass
in my pocket and, Wait, it's ringing
and I'm going to answer it: Hello?
I think it's for you.

MIKE PETRIK

Weathering *Fiction*

Every decade, another inch of sand is drawn off Louisa Island's south shore and carried by the deep currents to the north, building back to the mainland. In 1985, the same year that Oliver Lucas was born across the sound in Narragansett, Rhode Island, so much land had been drawn from Louisa's south side that the South Lighthouse leaned out over the bluffs. The islanders lifted the South Light a foot off the ground and hauled it back twenty yards, enough for another few centuries. It took Oliver all of his twenty-four years to make a home on Louisa, to fashion himself an islander, to fall in love with the place and his new wife. Now, he was banished back to the sea.

Oliver spent all morning sobering up from the previous night and battening down his temporary home, a diesel lobster boat called the *Tara*, for the coming storm. It took time to make himself presentable for the trip to shore. The wireless buzzed with news of the storm while he shaved and brushed his teeth with the cold salt water. By all the estimates from weathermen, disc jockeys, and Long Island broadcast personalities, the hurricane would hit sometime just before sunset. Everyone thought the season was over, but this early October warm spell was feeding the storm on its way up the center of the Atlantic; it was far enough off the coast that it wasn't losing any steam, and the men and women on the radio spoke breathlessly about how it had barreled past Bermuda in three hours and left six dead. The scariest thing was its lack of a name. On the radio they were calling it "the hurricane." It didn't seem right for something so near to be nameless.

Oliver rowed his little skiff to shore from the *Tara*. He looked back at the boat that was both wrecking his two-week-old marriage and berthing him since his wife had kicked him out of their new home. He had been thrown out over the wedding gift he gave her — the boat — named for her. "Well, not really the boat," thought Oliver as he pulled on the oars. Really, the *Tara* just made his Tara a bit cold and angry and unpredictable. What had really done it was telling her he planned to sign on to join her older brother Daniel aboard one of the long-liners that fished out of Point Judith on the Rhode Island mainland. He thought it was a good way to put them back in the black before the next summer, give them options. He thought it would get her to stop raging about spending their money on a boat, be it a gift, without her say. He knew she'd let the boat go, eventually. She wanted to troll the coast, pull up crabs, and cruise across to the mainland every so often just as much as he did. But when he told her about the job, she had stopped shouting. He had watched her jaw let loose and her green eyes soften.

"Leave this house," she'd said quietly. "Leave and take that boat and your job. Leave this island if you like."

That was the last she'd said to him until the morning of the hurricane. For hours he'd tried different tactics with her, explaining and apologizing and cursing and pleading and joking halfheartedly. He even went to her brothers for help. They both winced and advised him to steer clear of her for a time. With that he'd given up. He'd driven to the Louisa Island Grocery, then to the liquor store, then parked his truck by the boat launch and rowed out to the *Tara*. Once there, he drank, hoping to make sense of things and find a solution or fall asleep to the sound of the wireless. When he woke, he cooked and ate until he was stuffed, then started off drinking again. That went on until he woke to news of the hurricane bearing down on Louisa.

At least the *Tara* looked comfortable in its mooring. He had used the heaviest anchor he owned and a well-tested half-inch chain that gave her plenty of lead to play out in any wind the storm could muster. And the False Harbor was as good a harbor as there was from New Jersey to Bar Harbor, despite its name. In truth, it was just the island's Salt Pond, but in the early 1800s the island families had petitioned to have a dredger cross the Sound and tear a permanent channel from the sea to the pond. It was about half full with boats. That was a lot for this time of year, well past the tourist season, but most of the craft that normally docked in the True Harbor or Spirano's Marina had fled around Beacon Point and away from the island's east side, where the hurricane was likely to make landfall.

The skiff slid across the slack water. Oliver was thin and not tall, but he put his back and legs into every row and kept the skiff in constant motion while his eyes surveyed the harbor's other inhabitants. Some of them weren't ready for the storm, particularly a few of the weekender tuna boats. He didn't like what their fiberglass hulls could do to the *Tara* above the water line if they slipped their moorings in the storm, let alone what their twin engines would do below. He contented himself with the fact that none were in the radius of the *Tara*'s chain. He dipped his hand in the water and used it to brush his sandy, straight hair back from his eyes. Twin hills stood sentinel over the far side of the harbor: Scotch Hill to the left and Honey Hill to the right. Men buzzed over the hills' scattered houses with hammers, saws, drills, and plywood — covering any visible glass.

Oliver jumped out, barefoot, when he reached the public boat ramp, and turned to haul the skiff from the water. When he turned, his new house was in plain sight. A square two-story home with the same gray-shingle siding as most of the buildings on the island, it sat on a spit of rocky hill some thirty-feet high, jutting between the road and False Harbor. During Oliver's childhood summers on the island, the house had been a kite-shop, but the owner died, and her son had no interest in staying on Louisa for longer than a week each summer.

Oliver's wife came around from the front of the house, dropped a hammer in the grass beside their outdoor shower, and made her way toward him. Her black hair hung down just below her bare, pale shoulders. She wore a green dress and a pair of his boat shoes. Oliver laughed and bent to tug on a ragged pair of sneakers. He didn't take his eyes from her.

He picked up the front end of the skiff and waited for her to come around and lift the back. They lugged it up the hill toward their house.

"Good morning, Tara. You look nice. What's the occasion?" he asked.

"We always dress for a hurricane," she said.

"And 'we' must mean all you black-haired-witch-women," he said. "How about the shoes? Another tradition passed down to you from Long Kate Kattern?"

"They're for the nails," she said, "and don't be a smart ass."

They flipped the skiff in a fluid motion and set it in their concrete ground-floor garage. Oliver walked back into the front yard and surveyed the house. All the windows were boarded over, save two square feet in the corner of one looking into the living room.

"I would have boarded them up for you," he said.

She rolled her eyes and pursed a corner of her mouth.

"Want me to finish off that last spot?" he asked.

"You leave it be," she said. "That's for me to watch through. If you need something to do, you can fill the lanterns with kerosene. Then be on your way. I don't want you lurking around, in my way all day.

She walked to the well in the corner of the yard, flipped a switch that took it off the sure-to-be-lost electric system, and engaged its hand pump. Oliver looked up at the sky and raised his arms resignedly. It was the most they'd spoken since their honeymoon. They had been back for two weeks and already she moved with an intimate knowledge of the house. He hadn't slept there once.

He trudged into the garage and filled the six lanterns set beside the full kerosene jug. Even this task was mere pity on her part, and he knew it. But he took his time, because he didn't know where else to go. This was Tara's island. She was the local, born to a father's name and a mother's face and hair and skin that carried Louisa's legends and history. Oliver loved Louisa Island; he had spent every summer there in his grandmother's summer cottage. But Tara was his connection now.

Without her he wasn't likely to stick out the winter — his first. Oliver carried the last of the lanterns up to the back porch and returned for the kerosene jug. He wanted it close at hand for her.

When Oliver stepped out of the garage, he looked up at the still-blue sky. Nothing, not the smell of the air or the direction of the breeze or the sweep of the few clouds in the sky, looked like what he had seen before other storms. And yet this unnamed and already accomplished killer was hurtling toward them. While he looked up and watched the clouds, a rusted out Bronco pulled into the drive.

"Plenty of time yet. Still hours before we'll even catch a whiff of her if they are right," said Tara's father, Bryan Horn, from the driver's seat. He slapped a thick hand against the side of the Bronco. "Hop in. I figured that girl would have put you out of work by now. We are going to go and get the church ready."

Oliver climbed into the back where Bryan Jr. and Daniel, his new wife's brothers, greeted him warmly. Daniel, the middle Horn child, was half the reason he was in this mess. Tara's grandfather, also a Bryan Horn, turned around from the passenger side and clapped Oliver on the shoulder with a paw that matched his son's.

"We all know she's tossed you out," he said, "She told her mother, and so we all know. Not just the family, either. So don't worry about feeling bad around any of the boys or me. We won't have it from you."

"If I wasn't blood, she'd have cut me loose as well, long ago," Daniel said. "As it is, I can't get a smile out of her after all this long-lining business. So it's not all set on you. That's something." He shrugged.

Bryan Jr. leaned over his brother and whispered loud enough for everyone to hear, "Do what you can to put even more blame on Dan. It's worked on our mom for years, so why shouldn't it work on Tara?"

The Horn men laughed, and Oliver smiled. He never worried Daniel would take his sister's side; they'd been friends too long. Still, it was good to be welcomed by the other men.

A few other cars and trucks had just arrived at the church parking lot when they pulled up. Oliver recognized all of the men. He had worked for three teenage summers at The Twisted Apple Bait Shop and Motel, which may as well have been working at town hall. This was the island's old guard. Men with island family names and faces, like the Horns with their slight frames and thick arms and hands, the Littles with their longshoreman's muscled legs and a fur of red curly hair over their heads and bodies, or the Fieldings with their dark eyes and Spanish noses. With all the mixing of blood over generations, the degree to which features followed name was astounding. A few years back, when Oliver was working at the bait shop, an ethnographer hired by an elder Fielding had tried to make sense of those island families, but everyone agreed that the result was a failure. Also present were the transplants — the few men who had come to the island and made themselves a part of it just as Oliver had hoped to.

The oldest generation set up lawn chairs and drew beers from the half dozen coolers dragged out of the cars. They barked orders to their sons, who ignored them and stood and laughed and shook hands in a small cluster standing around one of the coolers. The youngest men moved doggedly toward a set of stairs leading under the two-story, white-shingle-sided Catholic church. Oliver followed and joined the fire line they formed up the stairs and onto the grass. He stood beside Daniel Horn. They passed heavy black storm shutters up the line and stacked them in the grass. Daniel spoke to Oliver as they worked.

"The old men know what they are doing. We don't get many hurricanes, but we get enough for every generation to dread having to haul and hoist and fasten these bastards over the stained glass windows. They act like they're here to supervise. But me, I know the truth." He winked at Oliver. "They come here to get out from under foot of their wives," he said. "Every one of them comes and blusters about the storms they've seen and orders us around, because the truth is they are scared white by their own wives."

"And what about you?" asked Oliver, smiling. "No wife for you. So, are you just here because your old man said so, or is it the good of your church that compels you?"

Daniel laughed.

"I said wives Oliver, but what I meant was wives and mothers. It's wives and mothers that compel us." He crossed himself and glanced up. "Sorry, Lord, for my blaspheming."

They laughed with the men around them.

The men worked in teams of four raising the shutters and another hammering home the pins that held them in place. The sky filled with gray cumulus clouds, and the wind blew just enough to make their work difficult and to scatter a few drops of rain. As his group worked on the particularly heavy shutters that would protect the stained glass above the church door, one of the old men, Edgar Grace, yelled up to Oliver, who held one end of the shutter from the top of a ladder.

"They tell me you are two weeks married and already kicked out," Grace said. "If you don't mind my asking, how in hell did you screw it up so quick?"

The oldest and middle generation, who had taken to sitting in the grass and drinking, stopped their conversations and turned to watch Oliver.

"I bought her a boat," Oliver shouted down from the ladder.

Edgar shrugged and turned to the crowd. "He bought her a boat."

"And was that all you did?" He shouted, now again to Oliver, who had the shutter in place and was nailing in the pin.

"That and I mentioned signing on with a long-liner for the winter. Those two, and I was out," he said.

Some men cringed, some laughed, and some guffawed.

"Not very smart," said Edgar Grace tapping a long finger to his temple. "A man takes his life in his hands when he talks with a Kattern woman about taking to sea."

"It's true," said Tara's father, "married thirty blissful years to a Kattern woman, and all because I took over her pop's farm with never a word of long-lining or trawling or any such nonsense."

"Don't listen to the softy, Oliver," said Tara's grandfather. "Mine had a bit of Kattern blood, too, and she took me back after my first season on the boat."

"Yeah, but Grandpa, you hate Grandma!" Daniel shouted from his ladder opposite Oliver.

The crowd laughed, but the Horn patriarch pointed a finger sharply at his grandson until they were silent.

"That I do, Daniel, that I do," he said somberly. "Oliver, sorry to say, you're good and fucked."

The crowd laughed again, and rain began to fall from the sky with meaning. Oliver descended the ladder while the other men drove home the last pins, bolted the doors shut, and made ready to return to their homes.

"A real helpful bunch," he said to Daniel as they leaned a ladder against the side of the church.

Daniel held his palm against his heart and struck a dignified pose.

"We Louisa men speak only the truth, brother Oliver, as hard a truth as that may be."

Oliver frowned and looked up into the rain. "Then fucked is what I am," he said.

"It's this island," said Daniel. "If our women had their way, they'd uproot the whole thing and plant it smack in the middle of some continent. But truth is, they hate the ocean too much to let it out of sight."

When the Horns pulled into Oliver's drive to let him off, the wind had begun to pull and churn the Salt Pond like a dark green sheet stretched and shaken out. The rain kept up in a steady drum on the water. He walked around to the driver's side to speak to Tara's father.

"Don't worry, boy, she'll let you in before the real storm hits," he said. "She's an island woman. She's like her mother and her grandmother and every other woman with that hair and skin and those eyes they get from old Long Kate Kattern. Every one of them carries that hate for the sea, even if they don't fear it and can't leave it."

Oliver looked to the long, white clouds of the storm front moving up from the Southeast.

"Get home safe," Oliver said, and rapped his knuckles on the hood of the car as he walked to the house.

He went around to the relative shelter of the back porch and knocked to let Tara know he was home. She didn't answer. She wouldn't yet. In the false harbor, the *Tara* swung on her chain and settled with her nose to the wind. A few boats had already slipped anchor and run aground in the mud shore. It was not a good sign for the storm to come. Oliver settled to a seat on their deck and watched with pride how the *Tara* handled the changes in the wind.

Sunset and the true hurricane winds and rain were almost upon them, and Oliver was soaked through, by the time she opened the back door for him.

"Not a word of apology or begging or sweet-talking or you are back out," Tara said.

He raised his hands in open-palmed compliance. Her hair was damp from whatever last touches she'd put on securing the house after the rain started, and it clung to her face and neck. The green of her eyes was set off by the green of her dress and matched the green of the boiling Salt Pond. She padded barefoot back to her station in the living room by her spot of open window. The first floor of the house was full of unpacked boxes. She had not put a thing away in the three weeks at their new house.

"Help yourself to food in the refrigerator while the power is on and we have it," she said.

He hadn't realized how hungry he was. He hadn't eaten all day. In the kitchen he found bread, mustard, and salami, and he made himself two sandwiches. While he ate the first, he listened to the wireless she had beside her on the couch. It was much of the same: wind speeds, estimated land-falls for Long Island and Montauk Point and the Rhode Island mainland, wave-surge heights, and the Bermuda death toll. It was now up to eleven. There was still no name. The radio weatherman said that they had decided it wasn't fair to shoulder a name with deaths that had already been tallied. He said it looked as if the hurricane would remain nameless. The electricity in the house was working, but Oliver knew that would not last. The entire island grid went with every thunderstorm; there was no hope for it against this unnamed hurricane.

He looked into the living room. Tara sat on the beige couch they had bought on the mainland before their wedding. Her feet were tucked under her body and one lantern burned beside her. Out the front window the dune grass and the few trees were bent double. The wind buffeted the house with gusts that thumped like thrown fists against the shingles. Through the porthole of window, the sky looked sickly yellow. He doubted it was the sunset carrying through the clouds; more likely it was the storm proper. Over the wireless radio a voice from the Point Judith weather station said "the hurricane" would make landfall on the mainland in an hour. That gave the residents of Louisa thirty minutes.

He walked back through the still foreign halls to the back door, unfastened the dead bolt, and stepped out into the rain and wind to see to the *Tara* once more. She was not where she should have been. Two of the sleek fiberglass pleasure boats had gotten tangled and slipped down onto the *Tara*, dragging her off her mooring with them. All three lay abreast of the pilings of the low pier that jutted out into the foam whipped Salt Pond. The fiberglass boats let out a crack with every wave that washed them against the pilings, but the wood and aluminum of the *Tara* caterwauled as every wave ground it against the pier. Oliver looked back into the house.

"Tara, I'll be right back. Stay inside." He shouted over the wind. Slipping on his sneakers, he took off at a run toward the pier. Its planks were at least a foot under the rising water. Tara ran out onto the porch behind him.

"Leave it alone!" she yelled. "It doesn't matter, damn it, leave it be. Oliver, come back, now."

But it was her boat, and the way the metal on wood shrieked every time it clashed to the pier was too much. Oliver rushed out through the knee-deep water over the pier, moving quickly across the open space and using the pilings for support. Tara's shouts ordering him to stop continued, but Oliver slipped and stumbled over the pier's edge and onto the deck of the *Tara*. He took a knife from the still protected cabin and cut her loose from the anchor lines of the other ships. For once, the diesel motor spluttered to life on the first try. Two of the front windows had already lost the planks he had secured over them that morning and were broken out. Oliver ran to the front of the boat and hauled on the half-inch chain. It was still intact and fastened to its anchor.

The rain was coming in horizontal, and the terrible yellow-gray sky was upon the island. He turned the wheel with one hand and set the nose into the wind — with the other he took up the heavy chain foot by foot as the *Tara* made slow headway in the teeth of the storm. Tara watched from the porch-rail of their home, silent. Once over the anchor, he climbed to the bow, set his feet against the gunwale, and hauled back with all his weight. The anchor came up from the mud and he drew it quickly up and over the rail. The wind had turned the boat and drove it back — too close to the pilings — while he dealt with the anchor. It took him the better part of five minutes to track into the spitting rain and storm surge and out into the open water. The diesel motor sputtered and coughed with the wet effort. Half the boats had slipped their moorings and run aground, so it was easy to find enough space to safely re-moor the *Tara*. Oliver again climbed over the wet side to the bow. He took up the anchor. It took all the strength he had just to shove it over the side. He waited a long minute with his stomach on the planks and his hands gripping the deck cleats as the *Tara* spun and flew back toward shore, but the chain finally went tight, the anchor took hold, and the *Tara* turned her nose steadfastly to the storm.

To get back, Oliver would need to chance a swim. He took a life vest from the hold and hopped over the *Tara*'s side into the water. He floated along with the broken branches, shingles, and boards that coursed toward the shore he'd set out from. The stirred-up water was warm from all the rain. It had surged high enough that he escaped the rocks of the shore and washed straight out onto the soft grass. Tara met him, set her shoulders underneath his arm, and raised them both to their feet. He began to shake as soon as he was out of the water. The strength was all gone out of him. She guided him back to the house. It was all he could do to propel his weight forward.

"You are a damned fool, Oliver," she said softly.

Once inside the house, she bolted the door behind them and dropped a plank behind it to keep it from blowing open. The island had lost power while they were out in the storm. She sat him on the couch, covered him with a blanket, and lit the other lanterns. The one station still broadcasting over the wireless delivered news of the wind speeds across the Northeast, but Tara shut it off as the weatherman went on about the track of "the hurricane's" eye. Oliver tried to take off his soaked sneakers, but his white-knuckled hands shook too much and were cramped from the exertion aboard the *Tara*.

"Let me," said Tara. She stooped and tugged on the sneakers until they came loose with a sucking noise. She carried them into the hallway. Oliver watched as she drew back the door to the washer and dryer. He had forgotten that was where they were housed. She opened the dryer hatch, drew out a mound of still-wet bed sheets and pillow cases, closed the sneakers inside, and turned the dial to heavy dry.

"That way they'll be the first thing to get dried when the power comes on," she said.

Oliver nodded and tried to stop his trembling. Out the gap of planked off windows in the darkening night, he watched the phosphorescent storm-surge speed over the dunes across the road. They were safe from it on their little hill, though the concrete garage would flood. Tara drew open one side of the blanket and sat beside him. They were both soaking wet, but warm under the blanket. Tara set the fingers of her left hand on the back of his neck. She nestled against him, and he hunkered under the blanket.

Across the island, families gathered in their living rooms around their oil lanterns. Some of the houses were so battened down that no light escaped them, but many glowed with an eye of yellow light from a small square of window. Men and women and children gathered beside these portholes and watched, as Tara and Oliver did, as the ocean washed over their island. They waited to see the calm of the unnamed hurricane's eye, and waited for it to pass and the storm to fall upon them again.

BECKIAN FRITZ GOLDBERG

Refrain

Tonight is for the nostalgia of lilacs and summers spent
nowhere but in your own head. Scent
surprised you by being so familiar. At last
you could name the bush outside the farmhouse
window of your childhood. It had stayed
where memory left it and now it blooms back to you
because of a blue fragrance, and you are so
unsure of the time. This is where a ghost
gets serious: Here's something you never meant
to remember. Not far from there was a willow
you couldn't see from inside. Now they come, fresh
hallucinations. The petals darkening like clouds.
Memories bomb your house. What can you do
but get used to it? For decades a silence called the present
made your touch audible like a spark. But these visitations
are transparent, you can stick your hand through them
and not burn up. When you look out this window at the desert
you can imagine it gone — We think there's nothing
we can keep but from time to time we find we've kept it
all, down to the molecule. Mother is planting lilacs in a row
along the path from the road to the house, down
one side, then the other, like a refrain, and you're the girl
watching. You stoop to smell one bloom. Then you stand up
in your 57th year, stunned, curious, translucent. Perfumed.

BECKIAN FRITZ GOLDBERG

Bees on Cocaine

We live in the wake of bullshit.
But what's left of the evening is pink
electrified along the naked line of the horizon
the desert's three trees darkening against it,
veil, cluster, shadowy pompadour. Some things
we understand. A clock speeding through
outer space will run slow. There are countries
that want to kill other countries. This is why any
field is sad. Net, taper, black lace. Nobody
says please anymore. Nobody minds.
The sun goes down like a fever. And sonofabitch
there's the moon. If there weren't, we'd
fly off the earth and take the oceans with us. Maybe
we will. Ironwood, mesquite.
Inkbleed. For two years mother talked
to the ashes in the closet, Why did you leave me
in such a mess? A truck goes down the road,
hauling a boat, and the aftershush pulls away
until your mind comes back. Dark matter
rushes through us at every moment. O Cosmos tonight
I am going to the grocery store where the sparrow
flies o'er the apples. The cashier says
the bird's been in the store for two months and
she doesn't know why they don't call someone.
Who do we call. Ice, cigarettes, coffee. All summer
Scorpio hangs around the house. The voice
from a passing car radio carries until the black
bushes along the arroyo sing *you been gone*
and one long subsiding vowel. What you hear is not
what you get. Not at all. We live in the wake
of the spill, the swindle, the big explosion. Abandon
earth. The human being talks to himself in his head
at the rate of three hundred to a thousand words
a minute. The government funds a study of bees.
I pour the strong black coffee over ice, sit out on the step
with the voice. Speaker, listener, the wailing ephemera.
I wish, I wish, amen amen amen amen amen amen

amen amen. Mother says these days Stepfather
often can't remember where he is but they're OK.
We don't say soon he won't know her. Sometimes
she hears him argue in the living room with someone
who's not there. No other bird. But he's happy, she sings.
Hypothesis. Experiment. Constellation. In the study
they applied a drop of liquefied cocaine
to the back of each bee, then watched as the blow
sank into their nervous system and they rose
without knowing that they were bees, that they were
each a particular bee and that a bee was a cluster of
molecules as every living thing bewildered
by an ecstasy sudden, magnifuckingfying bee
and being as if joy were all along some higher
form of confusion. Oh, they did what bees did, they
walked into the flower. They danced if they found
food. But the bees on coke danced more
for less, even if the larkspur held only a taste.
Amen. The night sky is clear and I've been looking
for constellations. I have found Antares rowing
in place like the light of a boat. I sit with the house
and all my books and things in it strapped to my back
like a sack, cup in my hand as if I'm going somewhere
far in the black heat, the exhaust of August
while the sparrow in produce floats over
the wild apple forests of Kazakhstan and on
to a pyramid of canned corn. Here, the light of a plane
is crossing the shape of a teapot I've traced in the sky.
Closer, I hear the hum, I feel its slow arc pull
the top of my head. At night we are bodies who think
we are not bodies. At night we look up
into nothing and speak. Sometimes all we are
is a lonely conversation between the one who loves
and the one who dies which soon enough
will be the same, floating in the darkness, the brief
vibrations of an even briefer form, unlistened to,
unheld, unhelpable and eventually insane among
the quarks and muons more fit to be

than being is. Finally Mother gave the ashes
to the sky in the eye of the lake. Why did you
leave me. Another car falls, & another
on the skirt of the last, drifting away where the road
shrinks to point and the landscape ends. All right,
I'm going in. Miserable listener,
I leave you the hostage sparrow who scats
on the shores of lettuce. We are the wake
of stars, our true deaths of long ago, and there are
planets that want to kill other planets, there are
messes left. Some things we know. Give freebase
to bees and you get stoned bees. This is why
every government is sad. No one gets off the phone
anymore. I hear what I hear. No wind.
Desert beetles tick against the lit window, fall
back into the fallen light on the ground. I'm not willing
to forget this. But we will forget this, switching
off the light for mercy and touching our way down
the dark hallway of the house to the breath
of someone we love and who has forgotten us
in their deep sleep. What can we do but undress
ourselves before them as always in their last
bloom for our last touch, our one drop left, and dance
more for less.

MARK HALLIDAY

Ducks Not in Row

I thought our understanding was that you would meet me
at a certain Brazilian beach resort. Gina? Jennifer? Michelle?
Did we somehow not get our ducks in a row? Were we not quite
on the same page as regards the certain Brazilian beach resort?
There we were to sip tall yellow drinks in the softening air;
the breeze would be almost comically gentle;
we would stroll on the white sand watching a lithe sloop
as it crosses the bay with slim buoyant confidence
and then we'd be back on the terrace with further drinks —
I love the word *terrace* and it goes splendidly with *drinks* —

and soon our sex would be so all-encompassing
and so easy and wet and unambivalent
the world would become a sphere of sheer affirmation.
The sheets would be green and yellow. Your freckles
would resemble those of Sharon who played cowboys with me
in 1957. As I recall, this was the gist of our understanding.
Jennifer? Or Gina? Michelle, is your receiver even charged?
Somewhere along the line a ball was dropped, because
we definitely have not met at a certain Brazilian beach resort!
We are not on the access road to such, and in fact
around the word *Brazil* there is starting to form a penumbra
of what some adult might call mild-old-joke-tinged-with-pathos.

MARK HALLIDAY

Ferguson High

Those boys who go to Ferguson High — they must know things
I don't have a chance to know. Their lives have hard edges.
The intersections on both sides of Ferguson High are complicated
with different rules for different times of day, and a cop,
and they have numbered stickers for parking
and their football uniform is purple and black — that's amazing.
Ours is just red and white. My life is so obvious.
My life is like, Monday Tuesday Wednesday.
It's like "Yeah, of course"
and there's nothing in it that somebody would call experience
if the somebody was Donna Prout or Michelle Boudreaux.
The car my parents let me drive is just a blob on wheels,
silver gray like some old lady's hair, it smells like a dog
even though we don't have a dog
and the back seat is full of my dad's old golf bag.
Imagine going to pick up Donna Prout with this car.
Or Michelle Boudreaux. It can't be imagined.
So it makes sense if they both go out with guys from Ferguson
according to what I heard today in study hall. Because

Michelle and Donna naturally want *experience*
which is what I for some reason can never have
because wherever I am life just automatically becomes
exactly what you would have expected while you were dozing off
in study hall. I don't see why I deserve this —
did I choose to be a decent dull dweeb
who has to drive a silver-gray blob past the Ferguson High
    neighborhood
to the mall to get a replacement lint-filter screen
for the dryer in the basement of my totally obvious house?
I don't remember choosing that.

Ferguson High — their uniforms are purple and black like a mean secret.
And somewhere there's a girl shaped like Michelle only taller
with swirly black hair and a purple flower between her teeth oh hell
oh *hell* oh hell.

DONALD REVELL

Air and Angels

What if they knew.
We shall unearth them,
Drink the alcohol from their matted hair.
Unclosing their eyes, we shall perhaps
Find that final retinal flare
Of the angel or eruption
Into new life of a birthing star.

Breathless is the word.
Comes a time there is no other sound
But intake, but inspiration
That tilts my head into an empty cloud.
The animal finds a way to the window.
The soul, in one last fling of desolation,
Dives underground where it must not go.

DONALD REVELL

Debris

Antiquity shivers in the unbuilt tree.
She laments (antiquity is a widow, braided
Into the rained-upon color of desert trees
After a windstorm) her perfected dead.
The sound is keen, as though it were somehow calling
The windstorm back into its own debris.
Just so, it reaches me this Sunday morning,
Second of May, a day with no future but driving
Farther into the desert, into no mind
For anything but driving to the end
Of present days. The future is all fences,
Stray cats, and heroes walking backwards.
Antiquity shivers at the sight of me.

JEFF GUNDY

Meditation with Wallet, Eyeglasses, and Little Riley Creek

"The weak force of God settles down below in the hidden interstices of being, insinuated into the obscure crevices . . ."
— *John D. Caputo,* The Weakness of God

Which card is it that will open the steel door?

I know that one card will take me anywhere, or almost, and another will reassure the authorities that I might be allowed to board an airplane.

The kingdom of God, says Caputo, is like a beautiful old poem whose author is completely unknown.

My glasses have tiny rainbow sparkles on the front of each lens, spreading as I scrape at them. The anti-scratch coating is separating, the office worker says sweetly, sometimes that happens, sorry they are not under warranty, well it's been two years and I will have to ask the doctor, what if something has changed?

The idea of one true religion, Caputo says, makes no more sense than the idea of one true poem.

For the fourth day in a row the brown roar of the creek bears tons of topsoil and effluvia toward the ocean.

Is there one true creek?

God is a *weak* force, says Caputo, a call, an event, a voice. All the rest is rouged and painted theology, the invention of men wishing to be strong.

If I scrape the anti-scratch coating entirely away, will I see something new?

If God is great but not strong . . . I take a deep breath, let it out.

A wren in the pine tree, pecking at the new cones, visible only when it moves.

It leaves a branch quaking as it disappears.

BETSY SHOLL

Atlantic City, Mid Morning

and a woman still dressed in the sequins
of a green evening gown sits transfixed, eyes
on the dealer's hand for one card to turn up.

In morning's harsher light she looks pale, spent,
as if all night she'd been chasing, reaching
too far, grabbing for any stone or shell

or salted glass the tide tumbles in
like coins from a country that no longer exists.
Now, without lifting her eyes, she pushes

more chips onto the felt, while outside
Atlantic City's glittering windowless rooms,
the waves rise to a curl, then calmly subside.

But what if the ocean got tired
of being no more than a nightclub logo,
a peeling billboard on stilts, got tired

of people gazing through glazed fixations?
What if those green fathoms gathered themselves
into one enormous swell?

It could rage through this town,
or if it wanted, just rough up one woman
already shedding sequins along a split seam.

The rubble line's all about loss, loss rolling
through waves that toss their load of shattered dice,
loss seeping up the hem of the green gown,

as if that's what she wanted all along —
loss like the turned-out silk of a pocket
when luck goes cold, and there's nothing left

but noon light gleaming on boardwalk slats,
glinting across the simmer of waves, light
erasing all but its own brilliant self.

DAVE SCHULTZ

Colt 45   *Fiction*

"Colt? That's a black man's drink."

I snapped a tenner straight so he could see it clearly, and laid it on the counter, "What's your point?"

He shrugged, like the joke was on me. "That's what I've been saying all along." He turned his head and hollered, "Yoshi, two forties ah-Colt."

I balanced the paper guitar case, eased back on the counter, and took a look around. I'd seen a plywood sign outside, it said; "Melvin's Liquor and Lotto." There was a sign inside, too. It was cardboard. It said, "No Tabs, No Credit Cards, No Checks!" Beneath that was a list of other no's, not as prominently lettered on the brown rectangle. "No Colors, No Representing, No Smoking, No Soliciting, No Toilets, No —" I quit reading there. The cardboard was hanging on a floor-to-ceiling chainlink fence that divided the customers from the merchandise.

Yoshi appeared on the other side of the fence. He was middle-aged, Asian, with a sleepy eye and a gut. He looked at me suspiciously.

I turned back around. The clerk was putting the bottles in bags. I doubted if he lived close by. He was the clean-cut type, trim, with coffee-colored skin, and nice clothes. He looked at me like he had figured something out. "Man, you trolling for a sister, you best be fishing with more than a couple of forties."

I snared his eye in mine and let out the cold. "Maybe I'm looking for a brother."

His brow knotted, and he gave up a huffy laugh. "You in the wrong place all together." He turned away from me. "You hear that shit, Yosh?"

That's all I listened to. I took my malt liquor, my little guitar and walked out the door.

It was 10:30 a.m., Thursday. I was heading south from 300 North Pulaski. This was the middle of Shitsville, home for the alkies and schizos who were pushed west as the inner city became gentrified. It was no place to raise kids, but if you were a drinker you could find a fifteen-dollar-a-night room, and fifty percent of the stores featured reinforced adult beverages: Night Train, T-bird, Richard's, and Colt. A regular Garden of Eden, at least from a drunk's point of view. Up a block I cut into a gangway. There in the shadows was a door invisible from the street. I pounded, waited, then pounded again.

"What?" A sleepy weak voice squeaked from the other side.

"Timmy, it's Diamond."

Silence.

I waited ten Mississippies then pounded again. "Tim! Open up."

Another second slipped by, then finally a soft thud. The door spread. A gush of cool musty air poured out. "What the fuck?" Timmy Drake stood there all skinny in a white wife beater, and money green boxers.

I pushed passed. "You said early."

"Early afternoon."

The door was closed, the lock turned back. It was dark and cool inside. Mold was growing somewhere. A digital clock glowed. I let my eyes adjust. This was one of those old Chicago buildings diced up into smaller apartments. Tim's place was a two-room with a stool and a shower plugged into what had to be the original pantry. I heard him cough. Then a lighter flicked, and tiny blue-gold flame illuminated his face. He pulled on a Kool.

"Here!" I held out one of the forties in the flame's glow.

A switch turned. Subtle lamplight lit the room. There wasn't much to see: scarred beige walls, a dirty green sofa, a tiny TV on a stand, a coffee table, two chairs, the kitchen variety. Tim had planted himself on the sofa where I guessed he was sleeping. He pulled the bag off his bottle, coughing again. "Look at you, come a-knocking at seven A-fucking-M." He held up the Colt. "This supposed to put a full grown man on the good foot?"

I held my hand, palm up, and hooked it to me. "It's closer to eleven, and if you don't want it, give it back."

He laughed. "You would be an Indian giving motherfucker, wouldn't cha?" He pulled a paper towel from the roll and coughed into it. He had a spell, hacking until something came up. He rested, then coughed again less violently, like he was finally clear.

"You all right?"

"Yeah." He crumpled the towel and tossed it into a cream-colored bucket, pulled a moist towelette from a medical-looking dispenser, and wiped his hands and mouth. That wound up in the bucket too.

"You sure?"

We sat while he caught his breath. "I'm all right." He jerked forward and plucked a bottle of Canadian Mist from the table. "And getting righter." He twisted the cap and took a good pull, coughed again, then held the bottle out to me. "Wanna hit it?"

I bobbed my head. "You're a funny guy."

The corners of his mouth turned up slightly.

I smiled, too, and tipped my drink. "How did the gig go?"

"Last night?"

"Yeah."

He gave a little laugh. "Dead."

"Anybody out?"

"Cece was there."

"Really? How's she doing?"

Weariness shaped his words. "She ain't looking too good. Meth, I think. She had all the symptoms." He cleared his throat. "I didn't get into it."

A picture of Cece came to mind. I let the image linger. She had been a wild one, pretty and wicked when we were kids, and we both fell in and out of love with her depending on the moon, but that was two decades ago. I turned a shiver into a shrug. "That's how it rolls. The sporting life's never been gentle."

Tim thumbed at the Colt's label. "And the bitches get the worst of it."

We sat together, and let the sting of that wear off.

"See anybody else?"

"Some youngsters turned out, boys in earrings and engineer's caps, skinny girls in Oshkosh bibs. They've been coming 'round lately, but nobody from the old days." He shook his head. "Hell of a way to end it, huh?"

"Did you get paid?"

"The tab got covered."

"Wednesday nights," I hissed, "man, why waste your time?"

"Wednesday's can be all right. Smith Ringwheel sold out Walter's Black and Blue's last night."

"Walter's is a tourist spot. It's always full."

"Man, I'd do Walter's, but they won't do me."

"Don't start bellyaching."

"I'm not. I'm just saying they won't book me." Tim had his tone.

"I ain't getting into all that, not with you, not now."

"Ain't nothing to get into. It just doesn't make no sense."

"It's show business. Sense ain't got all that much to do with it."

"Pfffffffff, yeah right!" He blew me off.

"Don't be pfffffing me. Ringwheel delivers."

"Ringwheel's a hack."

I held my hands out as if that in itself explained something. "This is Chicago, home of the electric blues, remember?"

That was answered by a well-rehearsed look that expressed perfect nothingness.

It was pointless. I quit lecturing. "Do me a favor, man, get a Strat, find a rhythm section, and shut the fuck up."

Tim chuckled. "And slaughter poor Robert? Please. If I hear the Blues Brother's version of 'Sweet Home' one more time, I'm killing somebody."

"It ain't like you ain't been told." Then I met him up eye to eye. "It's bad enough you're a folkie, but yodeling? A yodeling black man? It just ain't natural."

His face went plastic, and he held up his middle finger.

"Just 'cause you got TB don't mean you're Jimmie fucking Rodgers."

"And just 'cause I'm black don't mean I'm Otis fucking Rush."

"I've heard you play, man, nobody thinks you're Otis."

"Ha, ha, ha, now you funny, too." Timmy fished a cigarette from the white and green pack, and lit it with the short one burning in the orange plastic ashtray.

"How many cigarettes you gonna smoke?"

"As many as I want." He French inhaled, and a slithery serpent of blue smoke went up his nose. He exhaled out the side of his mouth. "So you wanna do this deal or not?" He leaned way over and pulled a case from the opposite side of the couch. With a quick flip he undid three draw bolt snaps, and let the top fold back.

We both sat there looking at it. It was beat and scratched, but there were no cracks. That counts. As far as we knew, the little flat top had always been a player's guitar. If I was going to buy it for resale that was a point of consideration. Players like guitars that have been played. Collectors like guitars that are "out of the box" perfect. Collectors tend to have money. Players do not. I had to keep my guard up. My player side was strong. The guitar had a dark tobacco burst with a raised tortoise pick guard, and an inlaid logo on the headstock. A circa 1928 Gibson Nick Lucas might net up to twelve grand, if you have patience. Not everybody can drop that kind of cake on a couple-a pounds of wood. On the flip side, not everybody can be patient.

Tim coughed. "I strung it up before the gig." He looked at it in the case. "Play it if you want."

I'd played it before. I changed the subject. "Here, check this out." I opened the paper case I brought in.

"What's this?" Tim said, an uneasiness in his tone.

"Remember that kid I've been telling you about, the kid who's building acoustics? He's getting pretty good." I snatched the little blond parlor from the case. "Listen to it." I played a chunky progression three times through, then let the last chord ring. "Sweet, huh?" Then I played some single string licks. "Bright and loud, it's a nice little fella."

Tim's eyebrows were up. "So it's a boy guitar, huh?"

"Yeah."

"Tell your boy his ass end's a little tinny."

"It's a parlor, no tinnier than that Lucas."

Tim waved me off.

"A-B it. The Lucas is right there, pull it out, let's hear it." Tim hesitated.

"Come on, man, let's hear it."

Tim pulled the Lucas from the case. He thumbed the bass E.

I pushed a pick at him.

He did it again. The Lucas did have a slightly richer tone on the bass end. "See what I'm saying," he said.

I hated it when he was right. "I can't tell," I lied and fished a slide from my pocket and noodled around. "Let's hear them together, I think they'd blend pretty well."

Tim shook his head no. "I ain't doing this, man." He sat there, the cigarette between his lips, the guitar on his lap.

"Ain't doing what? Let's just hear them together."

"I'm done with it. I'm selling it. I'm getting out."

"Out? Out of what?"

His eyes went low and flat, and he coughed, "Ju —" He held up his hand to wait, then fell into a hacking jag, same as before. He waited till he caught his breath. "Just out," he said finally. "Out of the bottle, maybe. Out from under this fucking guitar for sure." He let the Lucas slip around to its back. It lay like that: in his lap, on it's back, him still holding it by its neck. His lips curled, and he flicked ashes into its sound hole. "I hate this fucking thing."

We sat quiet for a minute, pulling on our drinks. I remembered all the gigs we did. Over the years Tim had had a hundred guitars, but the Lucas was always his bottom bitch. "You got it from your aunt, right?"

He turned toward me. "Aunty Leeta, Leeta Mae. She was my great aunt." He sat up out of his slouch. "I've told you all this."

I sniffed, "Tell me again."

He took a second — to get it straight, I suppose. "She was a singer, did a solo with a guitar." He propped up the Lucas. "With this guitar. She was a regular on the Chitlin Circuit from the thirties to the fifties."

"Was she any good?"

"Don't know, never heard her. I only met her once. She died of syphilis before I turned twelve."

"Syph? Tuberculosis? Does everybody in your family have to be so dramatic? Can't you die regular, heart attacks, diabetes, normal shit?"

His eyes brightened slowly. He turned and looked at me. I hadn't seen that look since we were kids, like everything was beautiful.

"What do you think it was like, the Chitlin Circuit?" His smile was fresh and clean. He was pain free right then, and not sick at all. "Can you imagine us doing the Chitlin Circuit in the day?"

I smiled, too, for my friend. "Smokey and dark, spittoons and card tables, cocaine and whiskey."

"Midnight trains and Mexican weed," he added.

"Straight razor women, dealing stud, all pistols on the tables."

"Rough cut and low down." Timmy was beaming now. "We would have rocked that shit." The Lucas started to ring. Timmy had his eyes closed. He slid in soft but with frayed edges.

"All around the water tank waiting for a train
A thousand miles away from home standing in the rain
My pocket book is empty, my heart is filled with pain
I'm a thousand miles away from home waiting for a train
Yode-lay-ee-o, A-lay-ee-o, A-lay-ee"

I followed him out of the Jimmie Rodgers song with the little parlor, padding the notes of the yodel.

The fresh light in Tim's face faded. He was sick again, and back in Chicago, back in the two rooms that didn't smell too good. We sat a second without saying anything. He sipped off his beer, sniffed, and said something to break the silence, "So you buying?"

I tilted my head, "I'm thinking on it."

We resumed our quiet, and he hit the Canadian Mist again. "You know what? All those places I been, all them tours, all them bars, it was nothing. It seems like I never went anywhere."

"I know. Me too."

"The Chitlin Circuit!" he snorted. "Was there even ever such a thing? Ain't one now. Beale Street's a joke, a tourist trap."

"New Orleans and Chicago, it's all bullshit."

"So why did we do it? Why did we waste all those years?"

"We didn't waste 'em, we spent 'em."

"Spent them on what? If I spent them I ought to have something to show, right?" He shrugged. "So where's my shit?"

"You want some shit, like what?"

"Like a boat. If I spent my years, I ought to have a boat."

"Like a big boat?"

"Yeah, a big fucking boat, a yacht, out on Lake Michigan."

"A yacht? You can't even swim."

"What does swimming got to do with a yacht?"

"It's a water thing. If you can't swim, you probably don't like the water, and if you don't like the water, what the fuck do you want a yacht for?"

"That doesn't make any sense. You never make sense."

I sat back.

Timmy hacked something up.

"Know what?" I said after a pause. "I think you're looking for a *It's a Wonderful Life* moment, angel wings and Donna Reed."

He smiled that tired sick smile and thought about what I said. "Who cares what you fucking think."

"Yeah, *It's A Wonderful Life*. Angel wings and Donna Reed."

"Angel wings?"

"And Donna Reed."

Another light slowly came up in his eyes. It was one I knew well, tainted and wicked. "I'd've taken a little piece of that Donna Reed in her day," he said, and we laughed.

"Jimmy Stewart would have kicked your ass."

"Donna looked like she could keep a secret," he nodded. "I betcha Donna had more than one service man coming up on her back door?"

We laughed again.

"So you buying?" he said after a new cigarette was smoking between his fingers.

"Yeah!"

"It's worth eleven or twelve."

"I'll give you nine."

Tim flared, "You fucking robber." He took a pull off his cigarette and looked at me. "You got nine grand?"

I shook my head no. "I'll pay you installments, fifteen hundred a month."

His expression started to get tight.

I went on. "Let me finish. I give you fifteen hundred a month, and you keep it. You hang onto it." I stopped and looked at him. "But don't play it out anymore." I smiled. "Since you're quitting it shouldn't be a big deal."

"Hey man, I still have to make a fucking living!" He was up into it.

I looked at him, at the traces of blood in the corners of his mouth. The doctors gave him six months. I wondered what he thought the fifteen hundred a month was for. "I'm leaving Blondie here for you."

He looked at the little blond, reached and pulled it from my hands.

"It's a loaner," I said.

"OK, so I hang on to the Lucas, and the blond. For how long?"

I did not want to do this part. I looked away from him. "Till you don't need it anymore."

"I see." He turned it over in his mind. He took a pull off the Canadian Mist and balanced the pack of Kools on its end, pushed it over and did it again. "And I suppose you want me to sign something too?"

I stopped cold. "I don't know, I didn't think about that."

He laughed at me to himself. "Yeah, you're a real business man. Maybe we should just shake on it." He coughed in his hand then held it out, laughing.

"Cute!" I said, then brought it back to business. "So is this a done deal?"

Timmy nodded his head, "Yeah, sure, absolutely."

I dug out the first installment from my hip pocket. It was seventy-five twenties in a roll with a rubber band around it. I flipped it to him. "Done deal, partner." I stood. "I gotta get moving."

Timmy stood and followed me to the door. "Are you sure you don't want to write something up?"

The door opened. "Like what?"

"I don't know. Something legal, something that says you get the guitars when I die?"

"Like a will?"

"Yeah. A will."

A sad sourness rose in me. "I can't write your will. You have to do that and sign it, too."

"I'm not writing a will." There was just a splash of beer at the bottom of the bottle. He drained it. "I won't. A will's just —"

"Eerie?"

"Creepy!"

The gangway was gray, that shade of gray that made every other color seem alive. I stepped out the door. "See ya."

"A bill of sale," he said.

"What?" I asked.

"A bill of sale's what we need."

"For what?"

"It's business. You never know what's going to happen. You could go before me. You might walk out there and get shot." His eyes went wide. "We might even go together, some freaky accident. If something like that happened, how's your people going to get your shit?"

I thought about it and shrugged. "I ain't got no people, man, just you." We stood there a minute. "You thinking of willing that thing to somebody else?"

He looked past me at the gray. "No, I ain't got nobody either. My sister's somewhere, but I haven't seen her in twenty years."

"So what's the point?" There was a streak of sunshine out in the street. I wanted to be in it.

"I guess there isn't one." He looked at me then, eye to eye. "But that's OK, I mean there doesn't have to be a point, right?"

I started walking. "I guess that's what I'm saying."

RAVENNA PRESS
Lea Graham

Book Review

THE RANGE OF YOUR AMAZING NOTHING
By **Lina ramona Vitkauskas**
123 pp. Ravenna Press, 2010
Paper. $14.95

Lina ramona Vitkauskas's *The Range of Your Amazing Nothing* reads like a dream. These poems recall dreams set in unknown places with unknown people with whom we are familiar. The speaker dialogues with epic and pop cultural characters, leads us to strange linguistic juxtapositions, guides us through the land of intuitive knowledge, the land of non sequitur. The poetic language that does "not follow" allows for humor and surprise even as it reminds us of the removed state where language lives, and the "mysterious theater" of human experience (123). We go from lines like "carnivorous sister in a hothouse" (102) to "Jacque Derrida and Superman, / Janet Leigh in the morning" (15) to "Let the lice freeze" (104). These poems stack, leap, and impel us from one allusion to another, from metaphor to further abstraction, from scientific language to art, popular culture, and other found materials. They replicate the pastiche of thought and the speed of our culture so that we never end up where we think we will. As the Surrealist painter Giorgio de Chirico once inscribed on a self-portrait, *Et quid amabo nisi quod aenigma est?* ("What shall I love if not the enigma?"), the guiding energy of these poems is in its enigmatic turns (Hughes, 160). Yet, this is never just strange for strangeness's sake as we learn that the myriad materials gathered here create the loss and humor and quirky celebration that make up its organizational prowess.

In the opening poem, "Round One Elimination Criterion," "the Sartre cowboy rides in from the East," bringing a landscape where "words divide, uneaten fruitcake / halves at a neighbor's Christmas luncheon" (9). Thus begins the dialogue between the intellectual and the domestic, the jocular and the serious, the abstract and concrete. Then, mid-stanza, it transforms itself figuratively, turning the synecdoche of "writhing" into a simile:

> here in our tombs,
> the involuntary, the voluntary,
> the sudden quips and quirks,
> 1950s architecture, writhing

>   in stiff cotton, wrinkled
>   and undone as mouths,
>   a Q & A on clumsiness,
>   later, a speed-round of regret

The poem enacts its own writhing, twisting away from its early bravado into fun and brief remorse. No matter how strange and hairpin-curvy this terrain gets, these poems recall the unnamable ache of the human. We trust them for the way we have to stretch for and employ our intuition to meet the truths within them: "I've found retribution / in staring at things longer, hearing plunging blindness".

In "Please, Gene Hackman," the poem opens with turning the predictable meditative phrase, "It was a time of . . ." by quickly accumulating popular cultural allusions, "pre-Lex, Jimmy Doyle" and "pieces of Piaf / lost in a toy store," alongside scientific and metaphysical dictions: "A time for irrational men / to master the distinct biology / of watery fate" (82). But it's the final address where the speaker pleads with her subject in the words of The Smiths that surprises us out of the "raging parable of [Hackman's] hands" to "*let me, let me, let me get what I want / Lord knows it would be the first time.*" What seems at first to be a peripheral rendering of Hackman and the speaker's imagined interactions with him and his world becomes a poignant plea. Yet, it is the jolt of the oddly juxtaposed Hackman and The Smiths which leaves us connected to the speaker, which leaves us unsettled. Like a de Chirico painting, the poem gives us recognizable materials, but dislodges expectations in its collocation, its thoughtful disordering.

"Pataphysic Uvula" is a poem that begins with the announcement that "the unfamiliar [has] stopped" (13). Indeed, it is the intriguing, unfamiliar combination of the two-word title that is Vitkauskas's trademark in this collection. "Pataphysics" is a philosophy dedicated to the study of what lies beyond metaphysics or "the science of imaginary solutions," while "uvula" is the small flap of tissue that hangs in the back of the throat, an extension of the soft palate. Just as these two words separate the real solution with the imaginary, the visible cavity of the mouth from the invisible part of throat, the poem is arranged in distinct movements:

>   You, responsible for my snapdragon hips.
>
>   You, the actuary asking about a Jericho
>   malfunction, you a converse mercy.

> Just do it for Johnny.
> Do it for love.

There is a shift from the second person description to the command in which we are all addressed. Even if the command's reference to The Outsiders isn't immediately recognized, it echoes the familiar: a mother's statement, a lover's plea, a Nike advertisement, a greeting card, catching us — as a catch in the throat — in a common place, preparing us for inevitable loss.

>   where/
>   always/
>   some/ death
>   /in the earth

The Range of Your Amazing Nothing is a book that extends the imagination and what we believe to be possible within poems. It thinks and sings and sighs across the pages. It is not a book hinging on the epiphany or the expected volta. It is not a book that attempts to improve us; neither does it act like "a middle-aged mother trying to get her kids to eat too much cooked meat," as Frank O'Hara once wrote. Rather, it satisfies like that dream you've had in which there was a pipe organ and a red blouse and the smell of roasted corn from an apartment in a city you've never been to, but know by heart.

Lea Graham is the author of *Hough & Helix & Where & Here & You, You, You* (No Tell Books, 2011) and the chapbook *Calendar Girls* (above/ground press, 2006). Her poems, collaborations, reviews, and articles have been published in many journals and anthologies. Her translations are forthcoming in *The Alteration of Silence: Recent Chilean Poetry* (University of New Orleans Press). She is assistant professor of English at Marist College in Poughkeepsie, New York, and a native of Northwest Arkansas.

LA ALAMEDA PRESS
John Bradley

Book Review

SEEDING THE COSMOS: NEW & SELECTED HAIKU
By John Brandi
240 pp. La Alameda Press, 2011
Paper. $14.00

Don't let the word "haiku" in the subtitle scare you. Yes, there are many (yes, too many) haiku practitioners around the world, and many (yes, too many) of these poems could make one haiku-intolerant. But, please, don't take it out on John Brandi.

First of all, Brandi does not follow the traditional form. Here's how that form is defined at a website called "How to Write a Haiku Poem": Haiku is "composed of seventeen sound units divided into three parts — one with five units, one with seven units, and another with five units." The Japanese form usually contains a "seasonal reference," which has led many Westerners to see haiku as a nature poem. Brandi doesn't. Nor does he ever write in a pretentious tone, another tendency in Western haiku.

John Brandi's version of haiku, which he calls "twists," almost always fall into three lines. Some of his lines, though, may contain only one word:

> strained his back
> massaging
> hers
> (64)

As you can see, he centers his poems, uses no titles, and rarely employs punctuation. The "twist" occurs in the last line, as in this poem. That someone strains a back is not surprising, but doing it massaging is certainly unusual. And then there's that last word, "hers," someone the "he" may care about, someone he wishes to impress, that snaps his back out and snaps us to alertness.

His twists, the product of a sharp eye and a keen wit, are usually humorous.

> market day
> the prettiest woman
> wears the biggest knife
> (111)

The humor may be nervous laughter, as with the above poem, but it rings true to experience, and that adds to the punch:

> in the hair
> of the flower vendor
> a plastic rose
> (112)

But these aren't really haiku, some purists might argue. These are merely short short poems, written by someone who admires the classic Japanese haiku, like those by Basho and Issa. Real haiku must follow the actual requirements of the Japanese form.

I would argue that strictly following the format misses the true spirit of haiku. It's the vision of the momentary caught in precise and concise language that honors the art of haiku, regardless of syllable and line count. Here's one by Issa, in JB Bryan's introduction to *Seeding the Cosmos,* that could have been written by Brandi:

> frog and I,
> eyeball
> to eyeball
> (11)

That same informality, playfulness, economy of words, that same swiftness of thought can be found in a Brandi twist:

> sees his face
> tries to fix
> the mirror
> (30)

At this point you might be wondering how the word "haiku" would find its way into the subtitle of the book (as well as on the back cover). Perhaps John Brandi's publisher has a sly sense of humor? Or he wants the traditional haiku writers and readers to help pay the bills? Or this is another of Brandi's twists?

Whatever you choose to call the poems in *Seeding the Cosmos*, they will entice and delight and never bore you.

John Bradley's most recent book is *Trancelumination* (Lowbrow Press, 2010). He teaches at Northern Illinois University.

HAWTHORNE BOOKS
Adam Gallari

Book Review

AFTERMATH
By Scott Nadelson
286 pp. Hawthorne Books, 2011
Paper. $15.95

Aftermath, Scott Nadelson's aptly titled collection, is an exacting and incisive study on those moments that, without our realizing it, suddenly become the fulcrums on which the remainder of a life rests. Taking place primarily on the outskirts of Manhattan and in the suburbs of New Jersey, Nadelson's stories delve into the psyche of mostly Jewish young men in the wake of something irreversible. He writes with such an empathy and pathos that it is often easy to overlook the faults that have brought these characters to their present stalemates in life. They are often voluntary martyrs, but Nadelson's skilled nuance and his impeccable dialogue render these characters less as victims or symptoms of a situation than as case studies in loss and regret.

In the hands of a lesser writer, much of *Aftermath* would be pitiable at best, contemptible at worst. But with Nadelson these men are human, and it is because of this that they transcend the simple tragic and become that which, in literature, is the epitome of empathy: heartbreaking.

Silence is as much at the heart of *Aftermath* as anything, and the notion of communication, especially the failure of it, rings loud and true throughout the eight stories that comprise the collection. It seems that these characters are forever stalled, that they can articulate in thought but are incapable of verbalizing all that might be able to save them, because for Nadelson it seems that the idea of "saving" is a tragic myth. It can be believed in, and often it is, but it will never arrive no matter how much it is wished or hoped for. Life is how it is, and we must learn to accept that, regardless of how much or how often we may dream. While the focus of Jewish characters might seem, to some, myopic in choice, as the events scattered throughout *Aftermath* could befall anyone, it is this world and religious view that serves as a baseline to unite much of the collection and to explain motivations that otherwise might appear passive or skewed. In many ways, *Aftermath* recalls that age-old mantra of Job, "The Lord giveth and the lord taketh away."

Nadelson's work expounds on this in modern context, encapsulated very early on in "Dolph Schayes's Broken Arm," when we are told, "By the time I made it to my parents house, the noose around my guts had loosened the slightest bit, and I knew I no longer had hope for anything." Like many subsequent moments in *Aftermath*, Nadelson is simple and smoothly elegant in his taciturn withdrawal from the prospect that life will dovetail with the dreams we often assign to it.

On the whole, *Aftermath* is a solid book, though "Oslo" never seems to arrive at the intended point of revelation for Joel, the young protagonist seemingly trapped in Jerusalem with his grandparents. But perhaps the greatest oddity of the collection is also its greatest triumph. "West End," which stands as the final story in the book, is the one time Nadelson shifts his perspective from that of a young male voice to a female one. This first person account, a quasi-retrospective telling by a young woman named Amy of an ended relationship and a makeshift, transient life in Victory Park, a "slum" on the outskirts of Manhattan according to her overprotective and henpecking mother, is a classic coming of age story but defies all notion of cliché and convention. Taken alone, "West End" is a powerful novella, and could very well inhabit its own book. But placed at the end of *Aftermath*, it offers a telling coda to a book that, to this point, has taken tragedy and heartbreak in pieces but never treated the before, during, and after of a life's pitfalls and discoveries. "West End" is thrilling, profoundly sad, and worth the price of the book alone.

Nadelson has a gift. He is the rare writer who can discuss the precious and the loaded territory of nostalgia without his work becoming sentimental and trite, and it is because Nadelson is, more than anything else, honest in his depictions and descriptions of lives sans glory. Taken in a world where the denial of truth in favor of the easy and the simple is a norm, *Aftermath* stands out, and Nadelson shines. The literary world needs more authors like him, writers of serious prose who aren't afraid to tackle the metaphysical questions that constitute a life.

Adam Gallari is the author of *We Are Never As Beautiful As We Are Now*. His stories and essays appear widely both in print and online. He holds an MFA from the University of California, Riverside and is currently a PhD candidate at the University of Exeter in Southwest England.

CITY LIGHTS BOOKS
Dale Barrigar

Book Review

LOOK DOWN, THIS IS WHERE IT MUST HAVE HAPPENED
By Hal Niedzviecki
174 pp. City Lights Books, 2011
Paper. $15.95

Hal Niedzviecki is a writer filled with talent, and he has identified the enemy.

You can see it everywhere you look in his new short story collection. Flip to any page of his *Look Down, This Is Where It Must Have Happened*, described on the cover as "offbeat stories that confront society's intractable dilemmas." In the story "The Colorist," The Enemy is described well: "The cityscape," the author writes, "is dominated by the great color corporations, their massive downtown headquarters . . . and their teams . . ." At other points it's the SUV; the flat screen with surround sound; the shrimp buffet that's super cheap and super easy; the toxic printed names on all one's plastic medication bottles; the various plastics that create so many walls (and so much cancerous pollution). The Enemy is sometimes called Mass Culture, sometimes TV, sometimes "THE MEDIA," sometimes . . . other things.

This book is all about The Enemy. And that's exactly the problem. I agree that The Enemy *is* The Enemy (how could one not). Where we may differ is in the response.

This book is *all* about The Enemy. It focuses on The Enemy, hangs out with The Enemy, is disgusted by The Enemy, *can't get away from The Enemy*. Meanwhile, it seems like the author has had no time to look inside (himself or anyone else). There's a lurking tone that's become dishearteningly common in North American writing (often it can best be described as cynically glib [or self-satisfied smirking] and tenure-bound).

Personally speaking, my dog, a wise soul, doesn't use Facebook, isn't on e-mail, doesn't "tweet" his canine boy- and girlfriends, and would merely close his eyes if in the presence of *Dancing with the Stars*. He's a hundred-pound pit bull mix (i.e., mutt) who, as a pup, got pulled out of an alley along with eight of his brothers and sisters by some compassionate soul who saved them from oblivion (and took them to the shelter). When you're standing around the deathbed of a loved one, you tend to turn all the sell-machines off, too (these gadgets are not yet literally attached to our brains, though the screens continue to multiply like rain).

Truly human moments are everywhere, though, and there are entire undiscovered continents within us all to write about, at least until the moment of death (about after, we don't really know, which is also part of the point), even at this instant . . . at any instant, and in every era, and yes: there are still ways to live that don't involve intense identification with corporate gadgets, no matter how shiny and colorful they are.

There are other, better, longer dreams. And yes, there are still places deep inside where The Enemy can't reach. The Enemy *wants* us to focus on it, wants us to be obsessed with it, wants us, as Niedzviecki himself knows and points out, to be unable to get away from it.

For instance: the usual rap is that the next generations of Americans "won't do as well as their parents." And you could add: Maybe when the next millennium rolls around, there will be lots of people around who are poorer than us in *things* and artificial contact, and far richer in spiritual sustenance (less filled with selfish desire and thus more open to the universe, for starters; i.e., more *free*). Focusing so exclusively on the gadgets (Mass Culture Sell Show Mind Control) of the day is a recipe for landing in the dustbins of history (at best). The model is literature as art (think Mona Lisa or Sistine Chapel or Mozart at the outer reaches), not literature as career advancement scam (this is crucial both for critics *and* creative writers). It becomes as simple as "Don't Sell Out," "Don't Compromise Your Soul" (and then there are those among us who will forever be smirking).

I once heard a drunken fool at a party say (it was myself), "The literary universe has become little more than a shell game for middle managers" (right before passing out and being dragged into the alley). I want this new millennial literary universe to prove the drunken fool wrong. If Niedzviecki ever makes the human animal, and the human soul, his subject, I predict he'll leap from strong-talent (or "promising") writer (about passing surfaces) into Someone To Reckon With almost overnight.

Dale Barrigar is a fiction writer and a past assistant editor of fiction for *Fifth Wednesday Journal*. He teaches at the University of Illinois at Chicago.

BKMK PRESS
Breja Gunnison

Book Review

GEORGIC
By Mariko Nagai
163 pp. BkMk Press, 2010
Paper. $15.95

Mariko Nagai's *Georgic* is a collection of brutally direct short stories embedded in a rural Japanese landscape. Many of the stories are based on events in Japanese history and tales from Japanese folklore. Nagai gives them a reality all their own. Her characters, mostly farmers, depend on the unforgiving land, and are forced to make nearly impossible decisions when the well of fortune runs dry. Nagai's short, declarative sentences deliver her narratives with grave heaviness, and her vivid descriptions stick in the mind's eye, as if the reader has looked at the sun and now sees the bright circle everywhere.

The term "georgic," from the Greek word meaning "to farm," describes the agrarian livelihoods of several of the stories' characters, including the title piece. Nagai's stories pay homage to Virgil's *Georgics* by depicting humankind's struggle against a hostile natural world. The characters in her stories are subject to circumstance's chaotic pattern of fortune the way farmers rely on a delicate balance of weather patterns for their crops to thrive. When fortune eludes them, they must commit unthinkable acts. In "grafting," a daughter dumps her elderly mother on a mountain to die. In "autobiography," a mother sells her child for a one-way ticket back to her home. In "georgic," a villager eats rotting bodies from a stinking stream. After each story, the reader closes the book and means never to open it again. Twenty minutes go by. She opens the book, and begins another.

Nagai's triumph in these stories is that the reader comes away changed — less innocent, more aware of how vulnerable we are to chance and circumstance. Her characters yearn for better luck, as in "autobiography" when the narrator imagines, "If this were another time, and another land, if gods were kinder or heard your prayer" — but they must make do with cruel, deaf gods and move on with what is left in the empty echo of their prayers. Her last story, "drowning land," features a more hopeful message: a farm boy dreams of water during a period of drought, wakes up, and digs for it. The villagers need not starve through a harsh winter; he has influenced reality rather than be powerless against it.

Having studied history, Nagai also pays great attention to how historical figures remember and construct their accounts of events. In "fugue," six characters tell their version of the same story of hunger and desire as Nagai experiments with the musical notion of voices varying on a theme. In "confession," a mother loses her daughter in an air raid during World War II, so the question of whether or not she killed an American pilot is irrelevant to her. In "georgic," a starving woman tells herself, "This is not a man, but bean curd, a cake, jelly." The stories these characters tell themselves are influenced by the acuteness of their desperation, which inspires the reader's compassion all the more.

The more experimental of Nagai's stories — "georgic," "fugue," and "love story" — are the least effective in imposing a sense of movement. In "georgic," Nagai introduces the monstrous and inevitable event on the second page, which means that the next twelve pages are an aftermath and do not yield much surprise. "Love story" is really three love stories, united vaguely by their theme of the horrors of leprosy, and their climactic moments get lost as the reader tries to discern a stronger thread among the narratives.

But the rest of Nagai's stories progress gracefully, and the author makes them immediate to the reader, very real and deeply felt. Nagai has written an impressive collection of stories, grounded in social and political conflict and brought to life by the potency of her prose. The reader finishes the book more vulnerable, feeling as though she has made the choices the characters had to make when there was no water, no food, when their loved ones have been killed: live on, dig, forget, give in.

Breja Gunnison is a recipient of the Glenna Luschei *Prairie Schooner Award*, the Lois Mackey '45 Creative Writing Award, the White-Howells Prose Prize, and the David and Marion Stocking Prize for Nonfiction. Her short stories have appeared in *Prairie Schooner* and *Roanoke Review*. She is a graduate of Beloit College, where she majored in creative writing. This is her first book review.

CONTRIBUTORS

KIM ADDONIZIO's fifth poetry collection, *Lucifer at the Starlite*, was recently released in paperback. She is a founding member of Nonstop Beautiful Ladies, a word/music project. Find her online at www.kimaddonizio.com.

PHILIP APPLEMAN has published nine volumes of poetry, including *New and Selected Poems, 1956-1996* (University of Arkansas Press, 1996); three novels, including *Apes and Angels* (Putnam, 1989); and has edited half a dozen nonfiction books, including the widely used *Darwin* (Norton Critical Editions), and Thomas Malthus's *Essay on the Principle of Population* (Norton Critical Editions). His poetry and fiction have won many awards, including a National Endowment for the Arts Fellowship, the Castagnola Award from the Poetry Society of America, the Friend of Darwin Award from the National Center for Science Education, and the Humanist Arts Award of the American Humanist Association. His work has appeared in scores of publications, including *Harper's Magazine, The Nation, New Republic, New York Times, Paris Review, Partisan Review, Poetry, Sewanee Review,* and *Yale Review*.

ELEANOR LEONNE BENNETT is a sixteen-year-old internationally award-winning artist. Her photography has been published in the *Telegraph, The Guardian*, the BBC News website, and on the cover of books and magazines in the United States and Canada. Her art is also globally exhibited. She is published in the *Life Is a Bed of Roses* book for Macmillan Cancer and in the *CIWEM Environmental Photographer of the Year 2011* book.

FRANK BERGON is the author of four novels and the editor of the *Penguin Classics Journals of Lewis and Clark*. He has published journalism and photographs about the Zapatista revolution in Chiapas, Mexico. His most recent novel is *Jesse's Ghost*.

JAMES CARPENTER began writing fiction after retiring from the affiliated faculty of The Wharton School where he taught computer programming and system design. His stories have appeared in a number of journals, including *Fiction International, The Long Story*, and *Chautauqua Literary Journal*.

CAMILLE T. DUNGY is a 2011 American Book Award winner and the author of three books, including *Smith Blue* and *Suck on the Marrow*. She is the editor of anthologies including *Black Nature: Four Centuries of African American Nature Poetry* and *From the Fishouse: An Anthology of Poems that Sing, Rhyme, Resound, Syncopate, Alliterate, and Just Plain Sound Great*. Professor in the creative writing department at San Francisco State University, Dungy's honors include an NEA Fellowship, two NAACP Image Award nominations, and two Northern California Book Awards.

JIM ELLEDGE's most recent books are *H*, a collection of prose poems, and *Who's Yer Daddy? Gay Writers Celebrate Their Mentors and Forerunners*, coedited with David Groff. His *A History of My Tattoo* won the Lambda Literary Award in poetry. He directs the MA in professional writing program at Kennesaw State University and lives in Atlanta.

PETRA FORD grew up in Glen Ellyn, Illinois, and currently lives in Chicago with her son, photographing everything that passes in front of her camera lens. Days are usually spent shooting lifestyle, fashion, and beauty photography, but her true passion lies in finding and capturing life's un-posed, unseen moments. This is her fifth appearance in *Fifth Wednesday Journal*. Her work has also been published in *INK Magazine* and *Chicago Special Parent* and has been shown at Calmer House Gallery, MaNa Gallery, Gahlberg Gallery, and Wings Gallery. View more of her work at www.petraford.com.

MELISSA FRATERRIGO's short story collection *The Longest Pregnancy* was selected by Livingston Press for the Tartt First Fiction Award. Her fiction and nonfiction have appeared in a variety of literary journals and anthologies, including the *Massachusetts Review*, *Arts & Letters*, *Puerto del Sol*, and *Northwest Review*. Fraterrigo lives with her husband and daughters in West Lafayette, Indiana, and is currently working on a novel in stories.

JOHN GALLAHER is the author of four books of poems, most recently *Your Father on the Train of Ghosts*, coauthored with G.C. Waldrep (BOA, 2011). He lives in rural Missouri and coedits *The Laurel Review* and *The Akron Series in Contemporary Poetics*.

BECKIAN FRITZ GOLDBERG is the author of six books, most recently *Reliquary Fever: New and Selected Poems* (New Series,

2010). She teaches in the MFA program at Arizona State University and watches endless reruns of *NCIS*.

JEFF GUNDY has recent work in *The Sun, Cincinnati Review, Mid-American Review, Image,* and *Georgia Review*. His fifth book of poems, *Spoken Among the Trees* (Akron, 2007), won the Society of Midland Authors Poetry Award. He was a 2008 Fulbright lecturer in American studies and poet in residence at the University of Salzburg.

SUSAN HAHN is the author of nine books of poetry and two produced plays. Her first novel, *The Six Granddaughters of Cecil Slaughter*, will be published in fall 2012. Among her awards for writing are several Illinois Arts Council Literary Awards and Fellowships, the George Kent Award from *Poetry*, the Society of Midland Authors Award in poetry, a Jeff Recommendation, Pushcart Prizes, and a Guggenheim Fellowship.

MARK HALLIDAY teaches at Ohio University. His fifth book of poems, *Keep This Forever*, was published in 2008 by Tupelo Press.

JAMES HARMS is the author of eight books of poetry, including *What to Borrow, What to Steal* (Marick Press, 2011) and *Comet Scar* (Carnegie Mellon University Press, 2012). His awards include a National Endowment for the Arts Fellowship, the PEN/Revson Fellowship, and three Pushcart Prizes. He is professor of English at West Virginia University and director of the low-residency MFA program in poetry at New England College.

JANICE N. HARRINGTON's *Even the Hollow My Body Made Is Gone* won the A. Poulin Jr. Poetry Prize and the Kate Tufts Discovery Award. Her latest book is *The Hands of Strangers: Poems from the Nursing Home* (BOA, 2011).

THEODOSIA HENNEY can usually be found up a tree, inside a book, or both. Her work has appeared in the *Allegheny Review, Vestal Review, Ghost Ocean Magazine, Damselfly Press,* and *Ozone Park Journal*.

DAVID HERNANDEZ has published two books of poetry and numerous anthologies. He's received grants and recognition from the Illinois Arts Council and Chicago's Office of Fine Arts. In 1987 he was commissioned to write a poem commemorating Chicago's one hundred fiftieth birthday. He often performs his poetry to the accompaniment of his band Street Sounds.

BOB HICOK's latest book is *Words for Empty and Words for Full* (Pitt, 2010). In 2012, Luxbooks will release a German translation of his previous collection, *This Clumsy Living* (Pitt, 2007).

TONY HOAGLAND's latest collection, *Unincorporated Persons in the Late Honda Dynasty*, was published by Graywolf Press in 2010. His previous collection, *What Narcissism Means to Me*, was a finalist for the National Book Critics Award in poetry in 2004. *Donkey Gospel* received the James Laughlin Award. His recognitions include the Jackson Poetry Prize, the O.B. Hardison Award, and the Mark Twain Award for humor in American poetry. He currently teaches in the graduate writing program of the University of Houston and in the Warren Wilson MFA program.

B. J. HOLLARS is the author of *Thirteen Loops: Race, Violence and the Last Lynching in America*, and the editor of *You Must Be This Tall to Ride* (Writer's Digest Books, 2009), *Monsters: A Collection of Literary Sightings* (Pressgang, 2012), and *Blurring the Boundaries: Explorations to the Fringes of Nonfiction* (University of Nebraska Press, 2012).

RICHARD JONES is the author of several books of poems from *Copper Canyon Press*, including *Apropos of Nothing* and *The Correct Spelling and Exact Meaning*. The editor of *Poetry East*, he teaches at DePaul University in Chicago.

ALLISON JOSEPH lives and writes in Carbondale, Illinois, where she directs the MFA program in creative writing at Southern Illinois University. Her latest book is *My Father's Kites* (Steel Toe Books, 2010).

KATHLEEN KIRK is the author of *Selected Roles* (Moon Journal Press, 2006), *Broken Sonnets* (Finishing Line Press, 2009), *Living on the Earth* (Finishing Line Press, 2010), and *Nocturnes* (Hyacinth Girl Press, 2012). Her work has appeared previously in *Fifth Wednesday Journal*, where it was nominated for a Pushcart Prize, and in a variety of print and online journals, including *Blue Fifth Review*, *The Common Review*, *Poems & Plays*, and *Poetry East*.

JEFF KNORR is the author of the three books of poetry, *The Third Body* (Cherry Grove Collections, 2007), *Keeper* (Mammoth Books, 2004), and *Standing Up to the Day* (Pecan Grove Press, 1999). His other works include the coauthored *Mooring Against the Tide: Writing Poetry and Fiction* (Prentice Hall, 2005); the anthology *A Writer's Country* (Prentice Hall, 2000); and *The River Sings: An Introduction to Poetry* (Prentice Hall, 2003). His poetry and essays have appeared in *North American Review*, *Barrow Street*, *Connecticut Review*, *Red Rock Review*, *The Journal*, and *Like Thunder: Poets Respond to Violence in America* (University of Iowa).

CLINT McCOWN has published four collections of poetry and four novels since his teenage days as President Eisenhower's yard boy in Gettysburg, Pennsylvania. He has also worked as a screenwriter for Warner Brothers and as a creative consultant for HBO television, and has received an Associated Press award for his investigations of organized crime. He heads the MFA program at Virginia Commonwealth University and teaches in the Vermont College of Fine Arts low-residency MFA program.

JOE MENO is a fiction writer and playwright who lives in Chicago. A winner of the Nelson Algren Literary Award, a Pushcart Prize, and a finalist for the Story Prize, he is the bestselling author of five novels and two short story collections, including *The Great Perhaps*, *The Boy Detective Fails*, and *Hairstyles of the Damned*. He is a professor in the fiction writing department at Columbia College Chicago. His forthcoming novel, *Office Girl*, will be released in July 2012.

ROGER MITCHELL's newest book is *The One Good Bite in the Saw-Grass Plant: A Poet in the Everglades*. He edits poetry for the e-zine *Hamilton Stone Review*, and lives at the back of a field of inveterate grasses.

ACHY OBEJAS is the author of the critically acclaimed novels *Ruins* (Akashic Books, 2009), and *Days of Awe* (Random House, 2001). Her poetry chapbook *This Is What Happened in Our Other Life* (A Midsummer Night's Press, 2007) was both a critical favorite and a bestseller. She edited and translated into English *Havana Noir* (Akashic Books, 2007), a collection of crime stories by Cuban writers on and off the island. Her translation into Spanish of Junot Díaz's *The Brief Wondrous Life of Oscar Wao* (Riverhead, 2009)/*La Breve y Maravillosa Vida de Óscar Wao* (Vintage/Mondadori) was a finalist for Spain's Esther Benítez Translation Prize. She is a member of the editorial board of *In These Times*, the editorial advisory board of the *Great Books Foundation*, and a blogger for WBEZ.org.

BAYO OJIKUTU is the author of the novels *47th Street Black* and *Free Burning*. He has won the Great American Book Award and the Washington Prize for Fiction. His short work has earned a Pushcart Prize nomination and appeared in various journals, anthologies, and media forums, including *ACM*, *Other Voices*, *Chicago Magazine*, *The Reader*, the Akashic Press *Chicago Noir* collection, and the forthcoming (2012) short fiction collection *Shadow Show*, a tribute to the legacy of Ray Bradbury. Ojikutu has taught creative writing with various institutions. The author, his wife, and son currently live in Chicago.

PETER ORNER was born in Chicago and is the author of three widely praised books: *Esther Stories* (Houghton Mifflin, 2001), *The Second Coming of Mavala Shikongo* (Little, Brown, 2006), and *Love and Shame and Love* (Little, Brown, 2011). Orner is also the editor of two books of nonfiction, *Underground America* and *Hope Deferred: Narratives of Zimbabwean Lives* (McSweeney's). His work has appeared in *Paris Review*, *Atlantic Monthly*, *Granta*, and *Best American Stories*, and has been awarded two Pushcart Prizes. A 2006 Guggenheim recipient, Orner has also been awarded a Lannan Literary Foundation Fellowship and the Rome Prize from the American Academy of Arts and Letters. Orner is a faculty member at San Francisco State University.

MIKE PETRIK studied English and biology at St. Lawrence University and creative writing at the University of Memphis. He is now writing, teaching, and studying in Columbia, Missouri, where he lives with his wife, poet and writer Bethany Petrik.

MARY QUADE is author of the poetry collection *Guide to Native Beasts* (Cleveland State University Poetry Center). Her essays also appear this year in *West Branch*, *Grist*, and *Flyway: Journal of Writing and Environment*. She teaches creative writing at Hiram College in Ohio.

KEITH RATZLAFF's books of poetry are *Then, a Thousand Crows*; *Dubious Angels: Poems After Paul Klee*; *Man Under a Pear Tree*; and *Across the Known World*. His poems and reviews have appeared in *The Cincinnati Review*, *The Georgia Review*, *The Journal*, *New*

England Review, The Threepenny Review, Arts and Letters, Colorado Review, and The North American Review. His awards include the Anhinga Prize for Poetry, the Theodore Roethke Award, a Pushcart Prize, and inclusion in Best American Poetry 2009. He teaches writing and literature at Central College in Pella, Iowa.

DONALD REVELL is the author of eleven collections of poetry, most recently of The Bitter Withy (2009) and A Thief of Strings (2007), both from Alice James Books. He is a professor of English and creative writing at the University of Nevada, Las Vegas.

NATANIA ROSENFELD teaches modern English literature and creative nonfiction at Knox College in Galesburg, Illinois, where she lives with her husband, two cats, and a dog. She is the author of a critical book, Outsiders Together: Virginia and Leonard Woolf, and has published her poems, stories, and essays in many journals. Her prose poem "Bodies" received an Illinois Arts Council Literary Award in 2007. Her hobbies are reading, sleeping, eating, and reading.

J. ALLYN ROSSER's most recent collection of poems is Foiled Again. In 2010-11 she was awarded a Guggenheim Fellowship. She currently teaches in the creative writing program at Ohio University, where she edits New Ohio Review.

DAVE SCHULTZ, songwriter, singer, musician, and writer, grew up on the North Side of Chicago and in a small coal mining town in rural Illinois. A graduate of Southern Illinois University, he lives near Chicago with his wife and daughter. He performs regularly, and his day gig is with Hanson/Lakland Musical Instruments, a guitar and bass manufacturer, where he is the shop manager for their pickup division. For music and additional information, visit www.purplehank.com.

BETSY SHOLL's most recent book is Rough Cradle (Alice James, 2009). She teaches in the MFA program of Vermont College of Fine Arts and was Poet Laureate of Maine from 2006 to 2011.

MARC KELLY SMITH is creator/founder of the international Poetry Slam movement. As stated in the PBS television series The United States of Poetry, a "strand of new poetry began at Chicago's Green Mill Tavern in 1987 when Marc Smith found a home for the Poetry Slam." Since then, performance poetry has spread throughout the world, exported to over a thousand cities large and small. Smith continues to host and perform every Sunday night at the Green Mill in Chicago to standing-room-only crowds. He currently directs Chicago's Speak'Easy Ensemble, an innovative performance poetry troupe. He counseled and collaborated with Mark Eleveld to create *Spoken Word Revolution Volume One* and *Spoken Word Revolution Redux*, and coauthored with Joe Kraynak *Take the Mic and Stage a Poetry Slam* (Sourcebooks). His collection of poems *Crowdpleaser* and his CDs *It's About Time, Quarters in the Juke Box*, and *Love and Politics* are available through his website www.slampapi.com.

CHRISTINE SNEED has a creative writing MFA from Indiana University, was a French major at Georgetown University, and has lived in Chicago and Evanston, Illinois, since 1998. She teaches creative writing courses for DePaul University, Northwestern University, and Roosevelt University. Her story collection, *Portraits of a Few of the People I've Made Cry*, won AWP's 2009 Grace Paley Prize in Short Fiction, was a finalist for the *Los Angeles Times* Book Prize, first fiction category, and has been chosen as the recipient of *Ploughshares'* 2011 first book prize, the John C. Zacharis Award. Her stories have appeared or are forthcoming in *Best American Short Stories 2008, The PEN/O. Henry Prize Stories 2012, Ploughshares, Southern Review, Massachusetts Review, New England Review, Notre Dame Review*, and a number of other journals.

ASHLEY STROSNIDER hails from Kentucky and Tennessee, where she worked at summer camps, libraries, and bookstores. She currently serves as editor of *Yemassee* at the University of South Carolina, where she is a James Dickey Fellow pursuing an MFA in poetry. Her poetry and fiction have recently appeared in *decomP, Word Riot, Unsplendid*, and *DOGZPLOT*, with nonfiction forthcoming in *dislocate*.

VICTORIA BARRAS TULACRO teaches English at Chaffey and Riverside Colleges. She was born and raised in the Wrightwood Mountains of Southern California, where she still resides with her lovely family. When she is not grading papers or writing short stories, she is feverishly working on her first novel.

DEAN YOUNG's newest collection is *Fall Higher* (Copper Canyon, 2011). His *Elegy on Toy Piano* was a finalist for the Pulitzer Prize. His work has received support from the National Endowment for the Arts, the John Simon Guggenheim Memorial Foundation, and the Academy of Arts and Letters. He's currently the William Livingston Chair of Poetry at the University of Texas at Austin.

BOOK REVIEWS AT FWJ

In keeping with our mission of bringing a sharp readership together with the best storytellers and poets working today, *Fifth Wednesday Journal* is pleased to publish a book review section in every issue.

Literary books in all styles will be considered; however, an emphasis will be placed on the types of writing we publish in the journal, including short fiction, poetry, essays, and nonfiction works. Books devoted to black-and-white photography, either by one artist or several, also will be considered.

Publishers interested in having manuscripts reviewed by *Fifth Wednesday Journal* should send inquiries, galleys, and books to:

> Andrea Witzke Slot
> P.O. Box 594
> Wilmette, IL 60091

FIFTH WEDNESDAY JOURNAL

FWJ IN THE CLASSROOM

Our mission is to the larger community of writers, artists, our readers, and our supporters. FWJ has undertaken an active program of outreach with FWJ in the Classroom, a program offering subscriptions at deeply discounted rates to students of creative writing at colleges and universities in the continental United States. Professors receive free desk copies under certain conditions. We also offer a visit in person or via electronic media (Skype, etc.) by one of our editors when possible. We expect to extend this offer to more than 350 academic programs and an additional 350 academic libraries by the end of this year.

Familiarity with literary magazines and their role in nurturing literature in this country is important to early success for writers of creative work. A writer's first taste of success is usually in a literary magazine such as FWJ. In the past four years we have published more than 340 writers and photographers, 31 of whom saw their first publications in our pages.

Our editors volunteer their services, but printing and distributing flyers, shipping the books, and related expenses will add up to more than $400 this year. We hope to expand the program during 2013 with total expenditures expected to reach $600 to $800. Support for the program is needed and very much appreciated.

Fifth Wednesday Journal is a nonprofit 501(c)(3) organization, and donations are tax deductible to the full extent of the law. Donations may be made by check to:

Fifth Wednesday Books, Inc.
P. O. Box 4033
Lisle, IL 60532-9033

or online with PayPal or a charge card.

For a complete program description, please visit www.fifthwednesdayjournal.org.

FIFTH WEDNESDAY
JOURNAL

Defining literature. In real context.

Subscribe or donate online at
www.fifthwednesdayjournal.org

ORDER

Subscription	**U.S.**	**International**	
☐ 1 year (2 issues)	$20	$32	
☐ 2 years (4 issues)	$37	$57	
☐ 3 years (6 issues + T-shirt)	$54	$80	Size: _____ (S–XL)

Single Issue
☐ Current issue	$11	$18	Qty: _____
☐ Back issue: _____	$10	$17	Qty: _____

T-Shirt
☐ Size: _____ (S–XL)	$14	$20	Qty: _____

DONATE

Amount: _____ **Premium:** _____
(see website for details)

☐ Please use my name as shown: _____
☐ List my donation in honor of: _____
☐ Keep my donation anonymous.

Name: _____

Address: _____

_____

E-mail: _____ ☐ Send me FWJ e-mail updates.

Please mail this completed form with your check to:

Fifth Wednesday Books
P.O. Box 4033
Lisle, IL 60532-9033

Fifth Wednesday Books is a nonprofit 501(c)(3) organization. Donations are tax deductible. Questions? E-mail editors@fifthwednesdayjournal.org.